FLORIDA

First Edition
1990

TABLE OF CONTENTS

Imprint **238**
List of Maps **8**

HISTORY AND CULTURE

Welcome to Florida **11**
History of Florida **17**
- by Janet & Gordon Groene
Florida's Spicy Cultural Mix **41**
- by Janet & Gordon Groene

TRAVELING IN FLORIDA

SOUTHERN FLORIDA

Miami **63**
- by Laurie Werner
Miami Beach **70**
- by Laurie Werner
Fort Lauderdale and Broward County **77**
- by Laurie Werner
Palm Beach **83**
- by Laurie Werner
Florida Keys **92**
- by Andrew & Ute Vladimir
Everglades **101**
- by Andrew & Ute Vladimir

WEST COAST

Tampa Bay Area **109**
- by Steve Cohen
Naples, Fort Myers, Sarasota **119**
- by Steve Cohen

CENTRAL FLORIDA

Orlando and Disney Land **129**
- by Janet & Gordon Groene
Cape Canaveral **147**
- by Dan & Carol Thalimer
Daytona **153**
- by Janet & Gordon Groene
Gainesville **157**
- by Janet & Gordon Groene

NORTHEAST FLORIDA

St. Augustine 163
Jacksonville 168
Suwannee Country 172
- All written by Janet & Gordon Groene

NORTHWEST FLORIDA

Tallahassee 179
- by Dan & Carol Thalimer
Pensacola Gulf Coast 184
- by Dan & Carol Thalimer
Northern Panhandle 188
- by Dan & Carol Thalimer
Miracle Strip 193
- by Dan & Carol Thalimer

SPECIAL INTERESTS

National Areas / Camping / Underwater Parks 203
- by Andrew & Ute Vladimir
Everglades Day Trips 208
- by Andrew & Ute Vladimir
Theme Parks 213
- by Edgar & Patricia Cheatham
Golf and Tennis Resorts 216
- by Edgar & Patricia Cheatham
Cruises 221
- by Edgar & Patricia Cheatham
Florida Spas 224
- by Steve Cohen

FEATURES

Hispanic Influence 230
Immigrants 231
Retirees 232
Drugs and Violence 233
Hurricanes 234
Insects 235
Growth and Development 236
- All written by Laurie Werner

GUIDELINES

Traveling in Florida 240
Authors / Photographers 251
Index 252

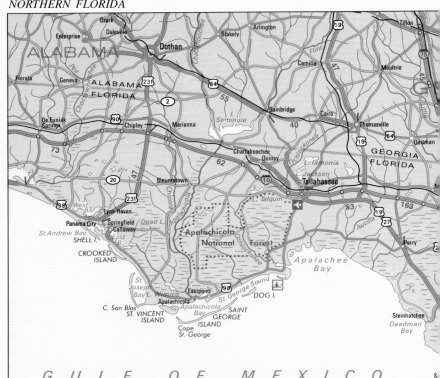

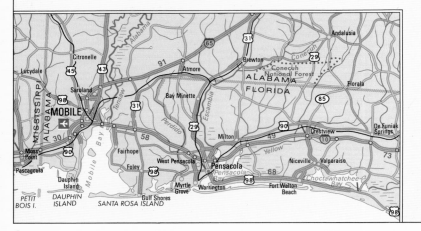

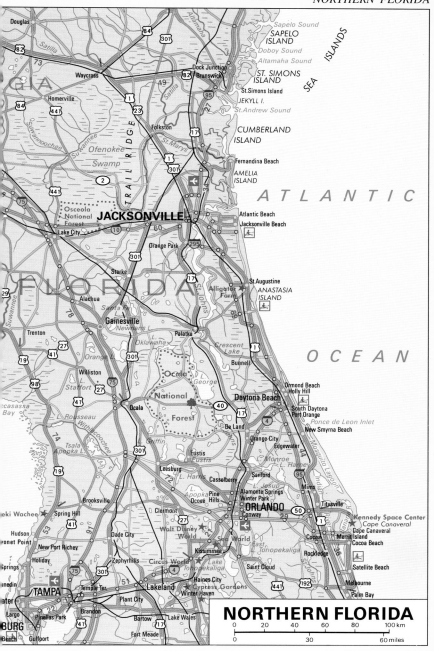

NORTHERN FLORIDA

0	20	40	60	80	100 km

0		30			60 miles

LIST OF MAPS

Northern Florida 6/7
Southern Florida 8/9
Miami - Miami Beach & Vicinity . . 65
Downtown Miami 69
Ft. Lauderdale & Vicinity 76
Palm Beach & Vicinity 84
The Keys 95
Everglades National Park 102
St. Petersburg -
Tampa & Vicinity 110/111
Downtown Tampa 112
Downtown St.Petersburg 115
Orlando & Vicinity 131
Disney World 136
Cape Canaveral 148
Daytona Beach & Vicinity 154
Jacksonville & Vicinity 169
Tallahassee 180
Gulf Coast - Miracle Strip 184
National & State Parks 202
Theme Parks 212
Golf 216
Spas 224

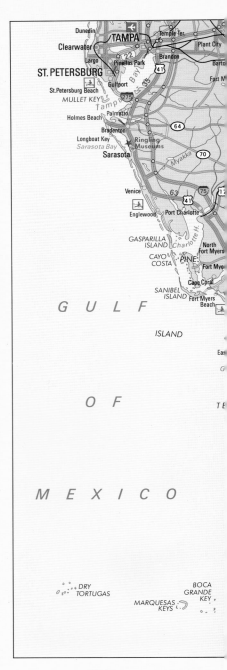

Please note: in some cases the spelling of the place names on the maps is not the same as in the text, because the spelling on the maps is according to UN guide-lines, whereas the usual English spelling is used in the text.

Haines City
Cypress Gardens
Haven
Singing Tower
Lake Wales

Lake
Kissimmee

Melbourne
Palm Bay

A T L A N T I C

Lake
Marian

Blue
Cypress L.

Gifford

Vero Beach

Avon Park

Sebring

Fort Pierce

Lake
Istokpoga

Okeechobee

Port St.Lucie

HUTCHINSON
ISLAND

L. Placid

Brighton
Seminole
Indian
Reservation

Stuart

St.Lucie Inlet

O C E A N

La Belle

Lake

Okeechobee

Clewiston

Pahokee

Belle Glade

Jupiter

North Palm Beach
Rivierea Beach

Settlement Pt.
West End
Settlement

F L O R I D A

Immokalee

West Palm Beach

Freeport

Greenacres
City

Lake Worth
Lantana
Boynton Beach

Big Cypress
Indian Reservation

Delray Beach

The

Tamiami Canal

Boca Raton
Deerfield Beach

Coral Sprs.

Margate
Sunrise

Pompano Beach

Big Cypress

Miccosukee
Indian
Reservation

Plantation

FORT LAUDERDALE

U N I T E D   S T A T E S

Everglades

Pembroke Pines
Miramar
Carol City

HOLLYWOOD

B A H A M A S

National

Hallandale
North Miami Beach

HIALEAH

North Miami

MIAMI BEACH

Reserve

Miccosukee
Indian Reservation

Kendall

MIAMI

Coral Gables

Alice Town

NORTH BIMINI
BIMINI
SOUTH BIMINI

Everglades

Cutler Ridge

Biscayne
Bay

NORTH CAT CAY

ISLANDS

Homestead

Biscayne
National Park

National

Whitewater
Bay

Park

KEY
LARGO

CAPE
SABLE

East Cape

Flamingo

Key Largo

SOUTH
RIDING ROCK

Florida

Florida Bay

ORANGE CAY

Marathon

Straits

K E Y S

of

Florida

F L O R I D A

of

SOUTHERN FLORIDA

0   20   40   60   80   100 km

0   30   60 miles

9

WELCOME TO FLORIDA

Florida welcomes everyone to its sunny shores – to the theme parks, resort hotels, restaurants and shopping malls that go to make this state a number one tourist destination.

In only 90 years the state of Florida has grown from a quiet backwater into a thriving, bustling land of opportunity. It has been a dizzying transformation and one that seems to be continuing as certainly as the sea laps the shores of the Sunshine State.

Florida is a warm home in the sun for millions seeking refuge from colder – or sometimes even hotter – climates. There is something for everyone in Florida, from rapidly changing fashions and landscapes to state of the art theme parks, from soaring Canaveral rockets to deep-sea diving. And yet traces of old-time Florida are still there to be found if you know where to look.

This text covers the history and culture of Florida. There are main travel sections on the regions and cities while the Guideposts provide details on accommodation, eating out, tourist offices, museums, festivals, activities and attractions. There are specialized itineraries that cover a single interest, such as theme parks, spas or cruises, plus comprehensive details on every aspect of travel in Florida to make life easy and convenient for the tourist. There's a lot happening year-round in Florida, so why not come and see for yourself.

– Steve Cohen –

HISTORY OF
FLORIDA

So you're going to Florida! Say hello to the Sunshine State, a brassy and brawling blend of Mickey Mouse and *Miami Vice*, of antebellum plantations, *Florida History* and vast wetlands, of timeless rivers and azure oceans, and of swelling legions of ever-higher skyscrapers edging a creamy surf line.

Whatever your interests, from Delius to Bach, from ancient Chinese porcelain to the world's largest collections of both Dali and CoBrA art, from prehistoric relics to the very latest from outer space, Florida has a long and absorbing history, as well as one of America's most vibrant, varied mixes of peoples of all ages, colors, and cultures.

The Size of It

Even with a map in hand, it's difficult to remember that Florida is as wide as it is long - about 450 miles from the Georgia border to Key West and the same distance from Jacksonville to Pensacola. In a long day's drive, you can range from the "Redneck Riviera" of the north to the end of U.S. 1 in Key West, which has often been described as "Fire Island with palm trees."

Florida has a land area of 58,560 square miles making the state larger than Hungary, Greece, or England and Wales. It's larger than New York, Massachusetts, and Rhode Island combined, yet no corner of the state is more than an hour's drive from the ocean.

Preceding pages: Docker at Port Canaveral. The ever-present pelican. Miami-Florida's metropolis. Neptune Beach near Jacksonville. Enjoying life at Key Largo. Left: In the Seminole reservation at Miccosukee.

At the turn of the century Florida was the site of the richest community in the nation, Key West, which then became the poorest after the Wall Street Crash of 1929. The state is dotted with 7712 lakes of ten acres or more, threaded with 34 rivers that are 10 to 273 miles long, and rimmed by almost 8500 miles of tidal shoreline. Its southern tip is 1700 miles from the Equator, closer than any other point in the continental United States.

Because it was the last area of the continental United States to rise from the ocean, Florida is America's youngest state. And, because the median age is 34.7 and higher than 50 in some counties, it's the nation's oldest state. In Sarasota, senior citizens make up 30% of the population; in Bradenton, 27%. Of all Americans over 60 who choose to move, 25% move to Florida. When the Silver Hair Legislature, or the Grey Panthers, or the American Association of Retired Persons speak, Florida politicians are all ears.

Be prepared for Florida's contrasts and contradictions. It is home to Walt Disney World, which is the most visited tourist attraction in the world, yet it has one of the nation's worst crime rates. Every 6.4 hours, someone is murdered; every 7.5 minutes a motor vehicle is stolen. The state hosts 56 species of cockroaches, has the nation's highest death rate from lightning, and 20 tornadoes a year. And 13.4 % of its people live below the poverty level.

Florida's Real Nature

To capture the essence of Florida is to travel from the frosty winters of Tallahassee to the steamy swamps of the Everglades; to sample the blaring hustle of Miami Beach; to walk barefoot along Miracle Strip beaches as white as salt; to stop at a shabby country church; to pump a glass of cold water from the well outside. Florida is a modern hub of state-of-the-art commerce, an American model in

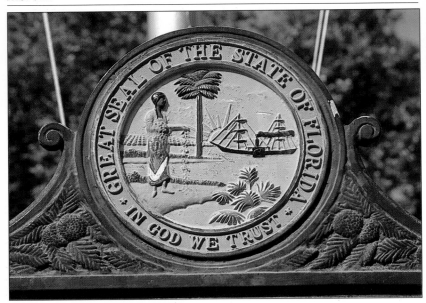

areas of tourism development and tourist services, not to mention international trade and banking which flourish here.

Then there is the countryside with endless acres of orange groves and field crops, rich ranches and hard-toiling farms. Scraggly Florida pine lands border "black gold" muck farms bristling with sugar cane, or dusty phosphate mines. Some Florida communities are strictly Dixie, with attitudes and accents of the old South. And the state has its share of solid, small town USA communities, not very different in temperament from small towns in Ohio or Nebraska. Scattered throughout are pocket communities sheltering relative newcomers from Cuba, Mexico, Nicaragua, Jamaica, Haiti, Greece or Southeast Asia. Arabs and wintering Canadians are attracted to Florida to build first or second homes.

Above: Even on park benches you see the coat of arms. Right: Still surrounded by a certain myth: natives call themselves Seminoles.

How it Began

About 150,000 years ago, a giant ground sloth slithered into a slime pit in what is now Daytona Beach, where its remains lay for millennia while the history of Florida took shape. Today you can see the sloth's massive skeleton, the most complete ever found in North America, at the Museum of Arts and Sciences in Daytona Beach.

A remarkably complete mastodon skeleton has recently been uncovered in the same area, another clue to the world of dark, primeval Florida pre-history. The scene must have been much the same near Tallahassee, where another mastodon disappeared at the same time, give or take an eon, into the misty blackness of Wakulla Springs. Its skeleton is now displayed in the Museum of Florida History. Partial skeletons of mastodons and saber tooth tigers are constantly turning up in the phosphate mines as well as in excavations made by developers. A turtle skeleton was found in an oil well 9000 feet

deep, where geologists have drilled as deep as 13,000 feet in some areas before eventually hitting impenetrable bedrock.

The scene now shifts to about 10,000-8000 BC, when ancient, unknown people spread through the state, living on rich harvests of shellfish, acorns, and small game. The massive shell mounds at Crystal River mark the oldest site to be continuously occupied in the present-day United States.

Two cultures, Weedon Island I and Weedon Island II, were unearthed and named in the 1920s in Pinellas County. Separated by distinct layers of dirt showing that there had been two periods of migration, the digs reveal a settlement that probably began with a group akin to the Muskogees or Muskohegean, who had brought with them objects typical of the Indian cultures of Georgia, probably acquired during their trek to Florida.

Another rich and interesting archaeological discovery was made on an island not far from Naples, where wooden Calusan artifacts were perfectly preserved in mangrove swamps. Other well-preserved relics are constantly being found in the state's deathless springs. In the 1980s, the oldest canoe ever found in the Western Hemisphere was fished out of De Leon Springs.

By the time the Spanish arrived, the Apalachee Indians were knowledgeable and talented gardeners. Their villages as far away as Tallahassee were recruited by the Spanish to supply food to St. Augustine. Tequesta Indians lived in the Palm Beach area, the Ais near Cape Canaveral. Timucuans, who had been in Florida since at least 300 A.D., occupied an area stretching from Tampa Bay to Jacksonville. The Jeaga Indians dwelled in the Keys, and the Mayaimi and Calusa in South Florida. So fierce were the Calusa, who were accomplished sailors and believed to be related to the man-eating Caribs, that the Spanish never did get a foothold in Southwest Florida.

Before the coming of the white man, the Indian population of the state was thought to be about 10,000. The various

tribes grew a long list of crops including corn, a food new to the Spanish. They had working systems of irrigation, which also included digging elaborate coastal canals. Pottery-making, scraping flint into arrowheads, hollowing hardwood logs by burning and shaping to form long-distance canoes, and basket-weaving were practiced.

Early explorers' accounts include reports of tattooed aborigines, self-mutilation and fingernails grown long and filed to sharp points. These early Florida residents wore deerskin clothing and antlers to help them sneak up on deer during a hunt. They used to adorn themselves with beads, rattles, and inflated fish bladders.

Springtime prayers were directed at a stag's head, mounted on a pole to catch the first rays of the sun. As a sacrifice to their sun god, in hopes of a better harvest, parents might club a firstborn child to death. There is little doubt that Florida's aboriginals were savages. Additional evidence has been found of prisoners being brutally tortured. However, they were not cannibals. As archaeologists unearthed many skeletons with missing or displaced bones, researchers jumped to the erroneous conclusion that the human flesh had been eaten. It is now thought that bodies may have been left exposed to the weather prior to burial.

An aboriginal widow cut her hair short to symbolize her grief. When it grew down to her shoulders, the mourning period was considered over and remarriage was permitted. As was common among pre-Columbian Indian cultures, inheritance and power were held by men, although passed on through the female line. A chief's death, for example, meant the succession of the son of the dead man's sister, not of the dead chief's son. Although women controlled their own spheres of power as producers of chiefs, they seldom ruled, although early Spanish and further studies have some evidence of female leadership in certain instances.

Elders met in tribal councils. Chiefs and priests built their lodges high atop square mounds. Evidence of the way these early Floridians lived can still be seen today, most notably in the Indian mounds at Crystal River and lodge excavations in and around Tallahassee.

European Settlement

Modern Florida history began at the close of the fifteenth century, when Spanish sailors first noted on their maps a land near the Bahamas blessed with "waters of eternal youth". The legend persists to this day, some saying that the Fountain of Youth is in St. Augustine; others pointing to De Leon Springs west of Daytona Beach.

Juan Ponce de Leon, who had been aboard Columbus' second voyage to the New World, brought his own expedition to Florida in 1513. The crew spent a few days exploring around the area that was to become St. Augustine. The first settlement, however, was made at Pensacola in 1559 only to be abandoned after two turbulent years marked by illness and Indian attacks.

St. Augustine was founded by the Spanish in 1565 and endured through fire, disease, flood, and battle to survive today as America's oldest city. The Castillo San Marcos, built by the Spanish, has walls 16 feet thick and a moat 40 feet wide. It was unconquerable in its day. Over the centuries the old fort changed hands many times for many reasons, but was never broached in battle.

French Huguenots led by Jean Ribault had settled nearby at Fort Caroline at the tail-end of the sixteenth century but, weakened by hunger and internal bickering, they were massacred by the Spanish. A bunch of vengeful French returned to St. Augustine years later and wiped out a garrison. In 1719, France briefly occupied Pensacola, but the French never really got another foothold in Florida.

St. Augustine remained Spanish until it was sacked by England's Sir Francis Drake in 1586. Still Spanish influence continued to spread with the building of forts and missions, strongholds against French and English ambitions. By the time Sir Walter Raleigh and his English settlers arrived in Virginia the Spanish had founded more than 200 permanent settlements.

Hernando De Soto was sent by Spain's King Charles V to explore and conquer the New World. He is said to have found a handful of pearls when he landed near Tampa Bay in 1539. His quest for exclusive riches would take him 4000 miles through territory that had never before been seen by white men.

Leading an expedition of more than 1000 men, De Soto spent his first winter at Tallahassee, which was already an advanced settlement of Apalachee Indians. The band then pushed into the Carolinas and Tennessee, then on to Alabama, where they were attacked by Mobile Indians. In a further search for gold, survivors crossed the Mississippi River, reaching as far as today's Arkansas River before returning to the Mississippi, where De Soto died.

The great Spanish explorer was buried somewhere along the Father of Waters. A stone monument five miles west of Bradenton marks the spot where De Soto landed, powerful and hopeful, four frustrating years before his death.

By 1622, gold-laden galleons were whizzing past Florida at a neck-snapping pace, ferrying treasures plundered from Central and South America back to Mother Spain. One ship, *Our Lady of Atocha*, sank off Key West and was not seen again for 350 years when Mel Fisher and his team of treasure divers began salvaging her rich cargo of jewels and precious metals. Some of the booty that made millions for Fisher and the state of Florida is displayed in Fisher's Museum in Key West.

An early and unwilling Florida tourist, Jonathan Dickinson, landed in the region

when he was shipwrecked off what is now Hobe Sound in 1696.

Dickinson's diary was published after he and his family survived starvation, Indian attacks, disease and near drowning. It detailed their early days of barefooted and nearly naked trekking, before eventually finding a way home to Pennsylvania. The adventurous book electrified the gentry of the time. The popular author Dickinson went on to become mayor of Philadelphia. Copies of his book, a riveting account of his escape, are still available, providing an intimate look at the Indians of that place and period, vivid descriptions of the problems faced by travelers in a land without roads, and a tribute to the courage and grit of an early American family.

As late as 1783, Florida was under Spanish control again, having been re-

Above: It was patience that brought gold worth millions to Mel Fisher. Right: Dozens of shipwrecks carrying gold are thought to be lying offshore.

turned by the British who had received the Florida territory as ransom for Havanna 20 years earlier. The Bahamas had fallen into Spanish hands. A swap was made. Spain received possession of Florida. In return Britain won possession of the Bahamas. Florida's Tories (British Loyalists), who had fled to Florida to escape the revolution in the colonies to the north, now set sail for the Bahamas or other British holdings in the West Indies, seeking yet another homeland where they could remain loyal to the crown.

Well into the twentieth century, remote corners of Florida such as Key West had closer cultural and economic ties with Nassau than with the fledgling United States. Some of Key West's finest homes were pre-fabricated in the Bahamas of woods cut in the once-great forests of Great Abaco. These houses, and subtle nuances in the accents of native born Key Westers, remain today as reminders of the days before the 1930s when the Keys were, like the nearby Bahamas, a string of sea-girt islands.

Florida's history is threaded with pirates and plunderers, duels and derring-do, and the swashbuckling of cocky opportunists whose wares have changed over the years but whose chutzpa endures with the centuries. Despite Florida's family attractions and placid retiree communities, the state is as much a magnet for adventurers as ever – immigrants, refugees, retirees, drugdealers, deadheats, single moms or dads, runaways, teen surf bums, time-share sales reps and developers – lots of developers – American dreamers all. All come to Florida and are welcome.

Miami had only 300 residents in 1900, so everyone is a newcomer. The result is a blend of blarney and dazzle that is sometimes beguiling, frequently befuddling or infuriating, but never dull.

Take 1812, for example, when a group of so-called Patriots got fed up with constant Spanish-British wrangling over Florida and proclaimed their own republic. The Patriots' flag was raised over Fernandina Beach, which became, for a time, an independent republic. A few years later, the fort was wrested away from a Scottish soldier of fortune, Gregor MacGregor, by Mexican Luis Aury who raised yet another flag over little Fernandina. American forces were in control again by 1817, just in time for the Seminole Wars to begin.

The Seminole Wars

By the late 1700s, most of the aborigines were gone. A Spanish visitor reported after a trek from St. Augustine to the Chattahoochee River in 1719, that he had not seen a single Indian. Many had been sold as slaves; thousands more died of European diseases against which they had no defense, such as measles, the pox, venereal disease, or the common cold. Scores of Timucuans died in an uprising against the Spanish in 1656. Another Indian attack was headed by Carolina governor James Moore in 1702. Probably a small number of Indians were assimilated into black or white families. A

colony of surviving Indians was taken to Cuba by the Spanish when they lost Florida to the British.

Stragglers who had escaped into the wild eventually united with northern Creeks who began migrating south from Georgia. The resulting groups became the Seminoles and Miccosukees, tribes which survive today on reservations in South Florida by selling cigarettes and running bingo parlors.

A series of bitter guerrilla attacks began in 1818 and went on for 40 years. Known as the Seminole Wars, the period is a fascinating footnote in American history. Curiously, the Seminoles have never surrendered. A truce was finally signed in 1934, followed by another treaty in 1937, thus ending the longest war in US history. The Seminole Wars included the massacre of Major Francis L. Dade and two

companies of US Army troops on a lonely plain near Bushnell. Some consider the ambush as shocking and tragic as Custer's Last Stand. Yet the Dade Massacre did not take a Custer-size place in American folklore because the nation was more fascinated by the wild west than by happenings in the muggy heat of the Florida territory.

Northern newspapers gave it little notice. The Seminoles were mainly a ragtag confederation of renegade Indians from many tribes. Joined by freed and escaped slaves, under a name meaning "wild runaways", Seminoles were fierce fighters who could melt into the swamps and savannahs, then survive for months until it was time to emerge and strike in a new surprise attack.

Against them fought the likes of future US presidents Zachary Taylor and Andrew Jackson, "Old Hickory", who also served briefly as governor of Florida before his time in the White House. In banishing eastern Indians to Oklahoma along what became known as the Trail of

Above: Invitation to the instructive Seminole Museum near Destin. Right: Pioneer days are commemorated at Orlando in a bigger-than- life fresco.

24

Tears, where many Indians died, Jackson presided over a shameful episode in American history. It was against this mass expulsion, and other land grabs by Washington, that the Seminoles fought almost to the last man.

Greatest of the Seminole heroes was Osceola, grandson of a Scot, stepson of a white trader, and son of a Red Stick Creek mother. Osceola's chief, Micanopy, caved-in to demands of the white man to sign over more territory. Osceola – who apparently hated whites because his wife, who had a trace of Negro blood, had been captured and charged as a runaway slave – slashed the treaties with his knife and went on the warpath. Osceola led his people on hit-and-run raids that were considered the start of the Second Seminole War. Eventually captured, he died in prison in South Carolina. Seminole ranks were murderously decimated when new leaders were persuaded to migrate to an Indian territory in Oklahoma. In 1842, about 3000 Seminoles were driven west.

Approximately 150 Seminoles resisted the transfer. Led by Billy Bowlegs, who would later start another Seminole war, they disappeared into the Everglades. Almost all Florida's Indians today trace their ancestry to Bowlegs and his band. The Seminole Wars surface time and again for the Florida tourist who seeks out historic sites. The ruins of sugar and indigo plantations burned by the Seminoles can be seen at Flagler Beach, New Smyrna, Port Orange, and Homosassa. The Dade Battlefield is a state historic site.

City names including Fort Lauderdale, Fort Pierce, Fort Walton, and Fort Myers remain long after the actual forts, built for defense against the Seminoles, have been forgotten. The war saw the building of dozens of forts and fortified posts, some of them now buried under great cities and others, such as Fort Ann, Fort Armstrong, Fort Casey, Fort Wacahoota and Fort Chokonikla forgotten sites in a forgotten war. Indian Key near Islamorada is being restored to the way it looked in 1840

25

when the tiny, 10-acre island was the county seat of Dade County. At the time, Key West had a monopoly on the lucrative wrecking business in the Keys. So rich were the cargoes and so hazardous the reefs, that an industry grew up around the salvaging of goods. Wrecker Jacob Housman was soon tired of jostling at the trough in Key West, which was then the center of the wrecking industry, so he bought Indian Key which was closer to the reefs. The key became a busy port with 50 or 60 inhabitants, shops, homes, warehouses and a thriving botanical experiment in which Dr. Henry Perrine grew tea, coffee, bananas and mangoes.

The prize was too tempting for the Seminoles to ignore. On one August morning in 1840, a force of 100 Indians attacked, killing at least seven people and burning the settlers' village. The actual

Above: The other side of heroism, a cemetery in Pensacola. Right: Heading for the new world, bone of the rebuilt Bounty. Far right: Marquis de Lafayette.

death total was never known because inventories in those days sometimes listed slaves as chattels rather than persons. Today, nothing remains but ghosts, foundations, fragments, and wild descendants of Dr. Perrine's botanical marvels. The island can be visited only by boat.

Altogether, American forces lost about 1500 men against the Seminoles. The last massacre occurred in the Everglades in 1855 when a group of surveyors was butchered by Seminole braves under their last war chief, Billy Bowlegs. It was the last straw. The government offered bounties on Indians who were hunted down like animals. Bowlegs and some of his men surrendered and were sent west. Remaining Seminoles, without a leader, retreated so deeply into the Everglades that the bounty hunters eventually gave up. From these few survivors descended today's Seminole community.

Unrelated to the Seminole Wars, but an interesting, sad incident in American Indian history, was the coming to Florida of the great Chiricahua Apache brave,

26

Geronimo. After his surrender in the west, he was sent to Fort Pickens in Pensacola and imprisoned there from 1886 to 1888. Although some reports say he was put on display and was an object of scorn and derision, others say he was a popular prisoner, known as His Medicineship. Three wives and his children joined him at the fort and one wife who died there is buried at Barrancas National Cemetery. Later transferred to Fort Sill in Oklahoma, Geronimo died there in 1909, at the age of 80.

Florida becomes American

Spain finally provided official title to Florida to the United States in 1819, in a deal in which the US gave up its claim to Texas, while Spain relinquished its claim to the Oregon Territory. By 1822, Florida had a governor and a legislative council and by 1824 the territory had a log cabin capitol near the present Capitol Building in Tallahassee. The old site lies miles from the beaches and today's population

centers. It was chosen because it was halfway between the state's two major settlements, Pensacola and St. Augustine.

The American Revolution had been won decades earlier, but it wasn't until 1825 that Congress got around to rewarding the Marquis de Lafayette, of France, who had sided with the Colonies. He was granted $200,000 and a parcel of land near Tallahassee. Although he never saw the area, he sent a colony of Norman peasants to plant grapes, olives, and mulberry trees. On the same site today, Lafayette Vineyards produce grapes for local wines that are gaining more and more international reviews.

The Civil War Era

Statehood was granted in 1845, at a time when Florida was populated by uncounted Indians, approximately 58,000 whites, 25,000 slaves working on approximately 300 plantations, most of them cotton farms in northern Florida, and 1000 free blacks.

27

Florida's first Congressman sent to Washington, DC, was David Yulee, a St. Thomas-born Portuguese Jew who served until secession. The ruins of his sugar plantation can be seen near Tampa. Near Crystal River, at the Gamble Plantation, which is open to the public, Confederate Secretary of State, Judah Benjamin, was hidden in canefields after the Confederacy collapsed. Florida played a dramatic role in America's Civil War, losing at least 5000 men between 1861 and 1865. When the war ended, $20 million in property lay in ruins.

Salt, produced at Cedar Key, was an important food preservative in pre-refrigeration days. Now a tiny community clinging to a little island at the end of a miles-long causeway, Cedar Key was once one of the state's busiest ports. When it was connected to Fernandina Beach by railroad, Cedar Key became a haven for blockade runners, and it was a

Above: Andrew Jackson. Right: Scene from the Civil War.

prime target for Union forces who captured it early in the war.

Although many white Floridians remained loyal to Washington, and many free blacks went north to fight for the Union, 15,000 Florida volunteers served on the side of the South. The state also produced beef, pork, naval stores, and other products for the Confederacy. Inland Florida remained fairly aloof from the war compared to other states deep in Dixie, but its well developed coastal fort system was targeted by both sides. Immediately after war was declared, the Florida militia took control of several forts, including St. Augustine and Amelia Island, while Federals held on to forts at Key West and Fort Jefferson in the Dry Tortugas.

It was in this remote brick fortress that Dr. Samuel Mudd was imprisoned. Unjustly convicted as a conspirator in the assassination of Abraham Lincoln, for setting the broken leg of assassin John Wilkes Booth, Mudd was imprisoned for years after the war at "Devil's Island".

Today, the island fort with its ghosts and legends can be visited by boat or seaplane, or overnight campers who must supply their own drinking water.

Each side held one of the two forts that guarded the narrow entrance to Pensacola's harbor during the Civil War. According to local legend, an entire night was spent firing at each other. Distances were too great. Every shot fell short. By morning, both forts were undamaged but the waterway between them had a new artificial reef formed by cannon balls.

One of the South's great victories occurred at the Battle of Natural Bridge, saving Tallahassee which was the only Confederate capitol east of the Mississippi that did not fall into Union hands. Still, the Union prevailed. By May, 1865, the Stars and Strips once again flew over the Capitol. And by 1868 voting rights were granted to all Floridians, regardless of race. By 1877, the hated Yankee "car-

petbagger" government was gone and a golden era of development began. By 1880, the state's population was 270,000; double what it had been at the onset of the war.

Except for a cross-Florida railroad that had been built from Fernandina Beach to Cedar Key in 1860, there was almost no overland access to the state. Steamships ran the St. Johns River from Charleston to Sanford three days a week; all other commerce called at ports along the ocean, gulf, and navigable rivers.

Two railroad magnates are credited with bringing the state out of the swamps and into the locomotive age. Both were given enormous land grants in exchange for laying rails through a wet wilderness that was alive with mosquitoes and alligators. The precedent is carried on in modern Florida with the zoning and environmental concessions granted to developers such as Disney, the company that turned thousands of acres of central Florida scrub into the most successful amusement park in the world.

Henry Plant's line stopped in Tampa. To lure wealthy northern tourists, Plant built a flamboyant hotel. It was so big that guests were trotted through the halls in rickshaws. Today the ornate, minaret-topped relic is the Henry Plant Museum, part of a bequest to the University of Tampa.

Henry Flagler built a railroad running down the state's east coast, confirming his position as one of the titans of Florida development. He wanted his railroad to outshine Plant's and lure greater numbers of tourists to the Atlantic side. This was accomplished by building lavish hotels from St. Augustine to Key West, transforming bug-ridden pest-holes into plush winter havens for wealthy northerners.

Surviving Flagler hotels, as luxurious today as they were in their heyday, include the Casa Marina in Key West and the landmark Breakers in Palm Beach. Another Flagler hotel, the Ponce de Leon in St. Augustine, is now a part of Flagler College. The Flagler mansion, Whitehall, in Palm Beach, ranks with the most extravagant stately homes of Europe, and is open to the public as a museum. Flagler's plan was to end his rail line in Palm Beach, but a killer freeze struck the area's orange groves.

A plucky Miami pioneer named Julia Tuttle had been campaigning unsuccessfully to get Flagler's railroad to come as far south as the remote outpost. Seizing the opportunity, she reportedly dispatched a messenger by boat to carry a fresh orange blossom to Flagler, a fragrant reminder that Miami's oranges had survived. Message received. The Florida East Coast Railroad continued south. The effort to continue the railroad beyond Miami and through the Keys proved Flagler's undoing. A hurricane in 1926, followed by the Depression of 1929, ended a dizzying real estate boom in South Florida.

Florida was flattened by the Labor Day Hurricane of 1935, one of the most intense tropical disturbances ever recorded. It smashed through the Keys, carrying away Flagler's railroad, much of the roadbed, engines and rail-cars, as well as more than 400 human lives, countless cattle and wildlife. The railroad was never rebuilt, although its remains became a part of the Overseas Highway which at last linked Key West to the rest of the United States.

The much-publicized Cuban-immigration following the Castro takeover was not the state's first migrant wave. At Key West at the turn of the century, Cuban cigar makers were turning out 100 million stogies a year. Their simple, three-room "shotgun" houses were so named because you could shoot from the front door through to the back without hitting anything. Examples of these old houses still remain today.

With labor problems deepening in Key West, Vincente Ybor moved his cigar works to Tampa. Restored and transformed into shops and restaurants, Ybor City today is a tourist attraction where hand rolled cigars can still be purchased. Ironically, they cannot be smoked in the historic Columbia Restaurant, which today is entirely smoke free.

The cigar industry brought waves of new Cubans into Tampa, where they were spurred on by local speeches by Jose Marti, as well as by the inspired presence of Teddy Roosevelt and his Rough Riders. They worked feverishly to fund the revolution against Spain.

The battleship *Maine* called at Fort Jefferson for fuel and proceeded to Cuba where it was blown up. The Spanish-American War began, its soldiers exhorted to "Remember the *Maine*", as they charged up San Juan Hill. Military tent cities sprang up in Florida. Clara Barton set up a Red Cross station. The British press sent a young and unknown reporter named Winston Churchill to cover the war from Tampa.

It was during this same era, just after the turn of the century, that one of the state's most colorful festivals was founded. Gasparilla Days, held in Tampa each February, are named for pirate Jose Gaspar. He was one of several pirates who reportedly found shelter, and possibly safe burial sites for gold booty, most unrecovered, in Florida coves and lagoons. During this splashy event, pirates land in Tampa Bay, parading, shouting, shooting and swashbuckling. Locals and tourists make merry, to the delight of Bay Area cash registers. Pirate legends pop up in almost every coastal community, but so elusive were the likes of Gaspar, Anne Bonney and Blackbeard, that it has become impossible to separate truth from the elaborate myths that have grown up around their names.

Jean Lafitte headquartered in New Orleans but his career began at Pensacola. During the war of 1812 he was offered $30,000 and a commission in the British

Right: Relaxing with one's own history.

Navy to betray the United States. Loyal to his American homeland, he went instead to the governor of Louisiana to warn them about British ambitions. Ironically, his roguish reputation preceded him. His story was not believed. At the Battle of New Orleans, Lafitte fought alongside the Americans. Eventually he and his buccaneers were pardoned by President James Madison. Their honor reinstated, they returned to pirating with a proud new vigor.

Sanctioned salvagers and home-grown pirates were the wreckers of Key West, where the recovery of shipwrecks was a legal and very profitable enterprise. Some of today's Key West fortunes had beginnings in the days when tall ships were driven onto the treacherous reefs of the Straits of Florida. Treasure by the ton, from mahogany pianos to linens and crockery – some of it on view today in Key West museums and private collections – found its way into Key West homes. Local legend says that when business slowed, false lights were hung to

lure ships to their doom. Whether this is a lie will never be known.

Real Estate Madness

Most of the gold-rush-like madness of Florida's current real estate boom is simply a continuation of the state's favorite sport, real estate speculation. The bubble has burst time and again as land values zoom during good times and plunge after a freeze or war or crop failure or hurricane.

The end of slavery spelled the end of the plantations, with their palatial manor houses. Lands that had sold for as much as $12,000 an acre in Confederate funds sold for $1 an acre in gold. An article in an 1870 issue of *Harper's Magazine* told of a farmer living in a Florida paradise for which he had paid a nickel an acre.

The coming of the highway system signaled the doom for some riverside developments whose economies were based on steamboat traffic. The decline of rail traffic led to the abandonment of

Central Ave. looking West.

settlements along useless tracks. Still today, the beat goes on as populations shuffle and shift, and grow, grow, grow.

It was after the Spanish-American War that one of the most colorful boom-bust eras occurred. Soldiers returning from Florida told stories of moist, moonlit nights on Tampa Bay, and oranges free for the picking. Railroad transportation was in its heyday, and the state had begun a massive road building system. Reaching Florida no longer involved a long sea voyage. After mosquito control programs brought an end to the yellow fever epidemics that for years had raged through Florida's coastal settlements, the health-promoting merits of sunshine and fresh air became marketable.

Rash speculation was the religion of the 1920s, not just in real estate but in a soaring stock market. The American dream was going daffy. Addison Mizner

Above: Who said "St. Pete" didn't change?
Right: Bridges – like this one near Jacksonville – are a sight to behold for the tourist.

moved to Boca Raton. Determined to make Palm Beach look like a slum, he built a highway 20 lanes wide and hired a publicity flack. The clever motto created was "Get the big snob and the little snob will follow."

Land sales averaged $2 million a week. "I am the greatest resort in the world", blared newspaper ads run by the Mizner Development Corporation in 1925. Potential customers were invited to call Miami Beach 888. Detractors pronounced Mizner's Boca Raton as Beaucoup Rotten, perhaps rightfully so, as the financier's whiz-bang maneuvering displaced the Finnish farmers who had originally settled the area.

Starting in 1915, Carl Fisher dredged and filled to turn the swampy farmlands of Miami Beach into a grid of high-priced lots. Coral Gables, the nation's first fully planned community, sold like hot cakes, thanks to the persuasive, early-celebrity endorsement of famed orator and one-time presidential candidate William Jennings Bryan.

Excess became commonplace. Barron Collier sailed into Useppa Island, in Pine Island Sound, built lavish "cottages" for his winter visitors, and awarded Tiffany diamond stick-pins to winners of tarpon fishing tournaments. John Ringling, best known as a circus showman, was also responsible for real estate developments in Sarasota that forged his fortune.

The wildest stories were carried north to a limitless list of eager buyers. A barber had turned $80 in tips into a million dollars overnight. St. Petersburg developer Walter Fuller wrote a book revealing how he had bought $50,000 worth of land and sold it for $270,000. Unfortunately, most of the wealth was in paper, mortgages and options, including deeds for worthless swampland, and $3000-a-week salaries that were spent on more paper.

The boom slowed when hit by a series of natural disasters, including a freeze and a hurricane. Soon the pool of buyers began to dry up. The stock market crashed, the Depression dug in to stay, and the looniness of an era depicted in the Marx Brothers' movie *Cocoa Nuts* came to a close.

Of Wings and Wheels

During the 1880s, roads were still so rare in South Florida that mail was delivered by a barefoot mailman. He walked a regular route, on the beach, between Palm Beach and Miami. It took three days down, a day for rest, and three days back. At the time, the only other way to post a letter between the two communities was to put it on a schooner to Key West. From there it went to New York via Cuba and back south via railroad and riverboat. By the beginning of the twentieth century, good roadbeds were still rare, so when automotive pioneers looked for places to set speed records, the endless miles of hard packed sand at Daytona Beach beckoned them.

Today's space events at Cape Canaveral are a direct descendant of a love affair with gallantry and speed that began

on those tide-flattened sands, where records were set by such greats as Barnie Oldfield and Sir Malcolm Campbell, starting in 1903, when Alexander Winton set a 68 mph world record here. Florida's automotive racing heritage has resulted today in the Daytona International Speedway with its world famous events.

The state's aviation history goes back to 1911 when the first night flight in history was made over Tampa. In 1914 the world's first scheduled airline carried one passenger at a time across Tampa Bay. An exacting, full scale replica of the tiny Benoist seaplane used in the project is now on display at Heritage Park in Largo. Pablo Beach, south of Jacksonville, was the take-off point for Jimmy Doolittle when he set a transcontinental speed record in 1922. He made it from Florida to

Above: Unbelievable sight in an automobile-drivers paradise: ships have the right of way! Right: Inside the Naval Aviation Museum at Pensacola.

San Diego in 24 hours. By 1929, commercial flights operated between Key West and Havana, a forerunner of what would become Pan American World Airways. America's first scheduled jet service linked New York and Miami.

It was the beaches that were Florida's first runways and race tracks, and Florida weather that has kept the state in the aviation spotlight for as long as airplanes have been flown. Clear weather year-round has made Florida an important training area for pilots ever since World War I. Today, the state is dotted with very good, paved, private airports that were built during World War II to train pilots by the hundreds. One trainee was movie star Clark Gable. Quiet and overgrown, once-busy bases house flight schools, sightseeing rides, soaring, parachute jumping, air shows, aerobatics, and other airborne activities, thus making Florida a mecca for aviation buffs from all over the world.

Pensacola's Naval Aviation Museum is the largest of its kind in the world. The

Valiant Air Command Airshow held each March in Titusville is the largest all-warplane show in the nation. Funds are being raised to create a year-round VAC museum here. A significant collection of vintage fighters, bombers, and aviation memorabilia is housed today in the Flying Tigers Warbird Air Museum in Kissimmee.

In 1950, when a German V-2 rocket carrying a WAC missile was launched from Cape Canaveral, Florida entered the space age. From Canaveral, in 1958, the first US space satellite, Explorer I, was launched. In 1965, Major Edward White became the first American to walk in space and, in another 1965 mission, a successful space rendezvous was made between Gemini 6 and Gemini 7. In 1971, Apollo 14 blasted off from the Cape for the moon. Canaveral remains the focus of international attention as its space probes come and go from the Kennedy Space Center.

Despite the US space program's first tragedy, which occurred in 1967, when three astronauts died in a fire aboard Apollo I, two years later men walked on the moon. After the Challenger tragedy in 1986, in which seven astronauts died, shuttle flights again resumed with new resolve. Visitors are often surprised to find that, in addition to highly publicized shuttle launches, there are equally spectacular launches of communications, weather, and experimental vehicles that get little attention from national media. The local newspaper, *Today*, is the best source of launch information. On any day, the Kennedy Space Center is a tourism blockbuster, one of the best free shows on earth and the fourth largest tourist destination in the state.

Florida's Tourism History

Tourists first came to Florida via steamships and sailing ships, before railroad days, when some of the state's most

extravagant resorts flourished. As roads were built, people began driving down in their Olds and Packards, pitching tents because there were too few hotels. Locals called them Tin Can Tourists and set about finding ways to fleece them.

In 1925 alone, in the last insane madness of the real estate boom, more than 400 hotels and apartment complexes were built in Miami. By the end of World War II, the state was attracting 2.5 million tourists a year. Polls of Florida visitors show that 97% want to return, and state tourism promoters spend $10 million a year to tempt them to do so.

No matter how extravagant the numbers, however, every influence pales when compared to the impact of Walt Disney World, which covers 50 square miles and attracts millions of people from all over the world. Although Disney does not reveal its gate counts, it admits to hosting more than 20 million visitors each year. The 100-acre Magic Kingdom opened in 1966 and the 260-acre Epcot in 1971. Recent growth has been giddy, including an entire new theme park based on the movies, a fourth Disney theme park in the works, an enormous Victorian hotel, a new beach resort, and two massive new hotels which will serve the largest convention center east of the Mississippi. Almost every county and community in the state lists tourism among its biggest industries. Some of New York's biggest public relations agencies represent Florida clients.

While the beaches and theme parks steal most of the thunder, a quiet explosion has also been going on in the state's cruise ports. Two million cruise passengers a year pass through the Port of Miami. By 1995, four million passengers a year are expected. New super-liners, carrying more than 2000 passengers, are being added each year to a list of ships that includes the fabulous, 2284-passenger *Sovereign of the Seas* and the 2600-passenger *Ecstasy*. In Miami alone, nine ships are taking on passengers on one side of Dodge Island while four more mega-ships are loading or unloading on the other side. A new, five-lane bridge had to be built to accommodate the constant flow of cars, chartered buses, cabs, and food trucks.

Fort Lauderdale's Port Everglades is another leading cruise port. Tampa hosts such ships as Holland America's *Nieuw Amsterdam*. Port Canaveral is home port to Premier Cruise Line, the official cruise line of Walt Disney World. Some ships even call at little Key West.

A Look Ahead

In recent years Florida's taxes have risen faster than those of any other state. Although some believe the most rapid growth rate has leveled, the population is still swelling by hundreds of families per

month. Roads and other vital human services can be badly out of sync with the needs of a rocketing citizenry.

The Everglades, once thought to be a worthless swamp ripe for draining and development, are now known to be the source of drinking water for all South Florida. Yet encroachment has been escalating since as early as 1898, when a contract was given for the draining of 8 million acres. Now reduced to half the area they enclosed before developers arrived, the Everglades continue to be threatened by man and nature.

Some environmentalists say it is already too late, and that South Florida will eventually have to be abandoned for lack of drinking water. Others warn that a major hurricane will wipe out many of the state's most densely populated areas. Doom-predictors aside, there is much in Florida that is bright, that is happening now, and that bodes well for a shining future. Talk of a bullet train that will link the major cities and relieve highway congestion is heard more often and more forcefully these days.

Environmental legislation is taking hold. Alligators, once hunted close to extinction, are once again so abundant that they can be harvested legally for meat and leather. Pelicans, which suffered greatly before DDT was outlawed, have made a comeback.

Plumed birds, which were almost wiped out by hunters who took only their feathery topknots and sold them to milliners for the making of elaborate hats at the turn of the century, are again nesting safely in rookeries. There is also hope for the tiny Keys deer, even a faint hope that the Florida panther and the manatee may endure.

Best of all, thousands of unspoiled acres are already set aside as parks, wildlife refuges, state and national forests, and pristine wetlands in which life struggles to go on in harmony with the human population.

Right: Flamingo Hotel, Miami Beach, 1923 – holding a party.

Timing Your Own Florida Visit

Arriving at the right part of Florida, at the right time of year, has been a large part of historic success or failure for visitors to Florida long before people came here for vacation.

Let's explode some myths. Although Florida is still called the Sunshine State, it has an annual average rainfall of 50-65 inches. During a hurricane, 30-inches, or more, may fall in a 24-hour period. During the summer rainy season, there is a 50-50 chance of rain every day.

October is the driest month in northern Florida, one of the wettest in the Keys. Never forget the distances mentioned previously. Florida spans from sub-tropic to tropical climate zones, which means that it can be snowing in Tallahassee while people are basking on beaches in Fort Lauderdale. Yet in summer, when it is "high" season at steamy Panhandle beach resorts, it may be a few degrees cooler in Miami where hotel rates are chopped in half.

If you want to save money, go to South Florida in summer, where l00-degree temperatures are almost unknown. Record highs in New York, Minneapolis, Ottawa, Boston, Paris, Rome, and Athens average higher than those in Miami.

Weather is one thing and costs are another. If you're looking for rock bottom rates, go to southern Florida and to the Keys in summer and to the Panhandle in winter. In other areas, rates rocket up and down according to other factors such as school holidays, when family tourist traffic is heaviest, special events such as the races at Daytona or the Gator Bowl in Jacksonville, and big conventions that can fill a city to overflowing even though the weather is at its worst.

If climate is your most important criterion, south is best in winter. During brief but bitter cold snaps, Miami may fall into the 30s while Key West's overnight low remains in the 40s. February and March are warm, breezy, flower-filled months in central and northern Florida. Generally, cities that face the Gulf are muggier during the warm periods, while the Atlantic beaches are cooled by ocean breezes.

The hurricane season, which means cloying heat and flooding rains, runs officially from June through October. Storms are likeliest to occur in August and September. But the chance of your being involved in a hurricane is rare; the chance of heavy rain and almost unbearable humidity during these months is very good.

Beating Florida's Bugs

Although the state has ambitious and effective mosquito control programs, they remain a problem in some areas. Avoid the Everglades in summer, and have repellent with you at any time of year when venturing outside cities. Big, biting green flies are a scourge in spring; sand flies or "no-see-ums" give nasty bites on still days in sandy areas.

"Love" bugs collect in spring and fall on warm highways where they are smeared thickly onto speeding cars. Inexpensive protective netting can be placed over the snout of a car, making the clean-up of some of Florida's historic characters a bit easier.

Living History Re-enactments

History comes alive all over Florida. Living history exhibits have always been popular with Florida visitors. Among the major historic reenactments on view in the state is **Fort Foster**. This fort recreates the installation that was built here during the Seminole Wars. Tours leave from Hillsborough River State Park on Saturdays, Sundays, and holidays to tour an "occupied" fort filled with "troops" who must be on constant guard against Seminole attack.

Right: A reminder of the pirates' heyday in Florida.

Fort Clinch State Park. Although this massive brick fort saw service in a number of events, its living history interpretation is that of 1864 when the fort was occupied by Union troops. Costumed artillerymen will show you how they train and drill, and will answer questions about their lives back home in the Ohio or Michigan or New York of 1864.

Kissimmee Cow Camp. You should always keep in mind when you talk to the men here that, to them, the word "cowboy" is a derisive term. These are men who happen to be cow hunters, and don't you forget it. Brought to Florida by the Spanish in 1521, cattle thrived in the Florida scrub and roamed freely until they were rounded up each spring by these cow hunters. Their tools were the whip, the cow dog, and the lariat. The year is 1876. Tours are provided on Saturday, Sunday and holidays at the camp 15 miles east of Lake Wales.

Dade Battlefield. Each year on the scene of the massacre at Bushnell, the Seminole attack on Major Francis Dade and his 108 officers and men, is reenacted on the Saturday nearest December 28. Half the men fell when the Indians fired their first rounds from ambush. Survivors of the first attack hastily cut trees and tried to built a breastwork, but were cut down by deadly fire. Only two soldiers made it back to Fort Brooke to tell their story; and it took more than six weeks before the bodies of Dade and his men were found.

Battle of Natural Bridge. At the battlefield 6 miles east of Woodville off US 363, this Confederate victory is replayed on the Sunday closest to March 6 each year.

Battle of Olustee. On the Sunday nearest February 20 each year, Florida's biggest Civil War battle is reenacted by men in authentic blue and gray. The original battle was a Confederate triumph. The site is located only two miles east of Olustee on US 90.

FLORIDA'S
SPICY CULTURAL MIX

Take time to leave the beaches and theme parks. Reach out into Florida's neighborhoods and savor the spicy bouillabaisse of the state's population mix. It is no surprise to see black beans and rice on the menu of a Chinese restaurant, or to see bearded Hasidic Jews in frock coats on the same Miami beaches as young European sunbathers wearing tiny string bikinis.

Key West has a highly visible and vocal homosexual community. Jacksonville has one of the largest Arab communities in the United States. Jamaican music rules the airwaves on Saturday mornings in the little college town of De-Land, where the owner of your motel may well be a Pakistani.

Almost every community has at least one Spanish language radio station. Most cities have one or more Spanish language TV channels. Almost every hamlet in the state has at least one Spanish language church, and many have a Spanish church for each major denomination. A Cuban-born Floridian represents Miami Beach in Congress. Even English language stations broadcast certain commercials, as well as public service announcements, in Spanish.

No longer is Miami the only center of Hispanic culture in Florida, and no longer do Cubans have a monopoly on Florida's love of all things Latin. Florida residents include Puerto Ricans, Mexicans, Panamanians, Costa Ricans, Nicaraguans and Hondurans – plus pockets of Argentines, Brazilians, other South and Central Americans, and the occasional Spanish family from Spain.

Left: Greetings from Ybor City – rum, reggae and heroin.

In some hotels and neighborhoods, especially in Miami, it can be difficult to find anyone to give you street directions in English, understand that you need extra towels in your room, or take a complicated restaurant order. So thoroughly Latin has Miami become that many travelers feel a real culture shock when they arrive. Those hotel workers who aren't Hispanic are probably Haitian, speaking Creole.

On sunny days in Tarpon Springs, men hunch over coffee and speak spiritedly in Greek. In Surfside or Daytona Beach, French Canadian newspapers are sold on every corner. On Indian reservations, school lessons are taught in the Seminole language.

In Miami Beach, Yiddish is the everyday language of the many old-world Jews who continue to winter here. In the fields, the melodic English of the Bahamas is spoken by temporary workers who are brought in on a contract basis. Many of the state's nurses are well-educated Jamaicans, speaking their own, highlands-tinged Caribbean patois as well as English.

The New Smyrna Colony was founded in 1768 by a group of Minorcans led by Dr. Andrew Turnbull. He named the new community after the birthplace of his Greek wife. Minorcan Easter cakes, called "fromajardis", are still served in New Smyrna homes. It is believed that the fiery hot datil pepper also arrived with the Minorcans. It is now a staple ingredient in the cooking of some Florida kitchens.

In Volusia County, acres of ferneries are worked by Mexicans who impart their own brand of the Hispanic culture to that area. Ordinary supermarkets sell rice by the 25-pound bag and jalapeno peppers in 5-pound packages. Proud, hardworking men bring their wives and babies to share the spectacle and ritual of shopping for food in a land of plenty. The slap-slap sound of women making *tortil-*

las by hand is commonplace in migrant housing complexes.

Florida's Immigrants

Ever since the earliest explorers, Florida has been a refuge for the stateless. Hounded from their homelands during the religious wars of the sixteenth century, French Protestants settled near present-day St. Augustine. British Loyalists escaped to Florida rather than fight against the Crown during the American Revolution. José Marti, leader of the Cuban war of independence against the Spaniards, took refuge in Tampa.

Today's refugees come from Haiti, Panama, Nicaragua, Cuba, Southeast Asia. There are more Nicaraguans in Miami than in any other city except

Above: Besides existencial anxiety latinos also brought their cheerfulness: Hispanic Festival in Miami. Right: Florida's black population fought long and hard for rights.

Managua. In 1980, 140,000 Cuban refugees were absorbed into south Florida.

Others are escapees from winter: Midwestern retirees, New York vacationers, Canadian pensioners, European beachgoers, and families from everywhere whose kids want to meet Mickey Mouse.

The result is a mix of all ages, hues, religions, languages, costumes, and habits. The state's calendar is peppered with ethnic events: Greek festivals, Oktoberfests, Hispanic holidays, and Scottish clan gatherings.

Miami's Carnival has all the glitz of a Rio. The St. Patrick's Day mayhem in Pensacola is second only to New York's. Vizcaya, an Italian Renaissance villa in Miami, is the scene of an Italian Renaissance festival. Teenage boys dive for a golden cross which is thrown into the waters at Tarpon Springs on Epiphany. The event recreates events from a Greek fishing village. So numerous are the Britons who have bought motels in the state, that they have formed their own British Motel Owners Association.

Florida's Black Culture

Florida's black communities have an especially rich heritage that combines influences of descendants of the earliest slaves with newcomers from the North and the Caribbean. In Spanish times, blacks mingled and married with whites and Indians alike. Until the Civil War, most of Florida was a haven for escaped slaves, many of them allied with the Seminoles. Other blacks were purchased by the Seminoles, who incorporated a version of slave society in which servants were required to give only token service.

Although Jacksonville remained a hotbed of contraband slave trading, even after slavery was outlawed, the state granted blacks freedoms that were denied in other parts of the South. During some antebellum eras blacks could vote and serve on juries. The census of 1860 listed 61,000 slaves in the state, but also a total of almost $100,000 in properties owned by free blacks.

Badly outnumbered, white plantation owners became increasingly afraid that their slaves might rise up en masse. By the 1840s, laws involving blacks became ever tighter. Freedmen had to have white guardians; visiting ships were not allowed to put black crewmen ashore.

When Florida joined the Confederacy, 1200 blacks went north to join Union forces. After Reconstruction, the state had 19 blacks in its legislature, and a black secretary of state was appointed in 1868.

Strictly enforced racial segregation became acceptable practice in Florida, where it lingered as firmly as in any other Dixie state. Drinking fountains, hotels, restaurants, and schools were segregated. Blacks were not allowed on the island of Miami Beach after dark, nor were they allowed to swim in the sea along the Palm Beaches.

True emancipation didn't come until the 1960s, with the passage of the Civil

Rights Act. Eatonville, a community near Orlando that was incorporated in 1888, was probably the first black community in the nation. At Daytona Beach, black education pioneer Mary McLeod Bethune lived and worked until her death in 1955. Her spacious home, filled with memorabilia including the room where Eleanor Roosevelt slept while visiting here, is now open to the public on the campus of Bethune-Cookman College.

Also in Daytona Beach is the home of Dr. Howard Thurman, who was named by *Life Magazine* in 1950 as one of America's ten most celebrated twentieth century preachers. Author of 14 books, professor of systemic theology at Howard University, and Phi Beta Kappa, Thurman was the principal contact in the United States for Mahatma Ghandi. At the time of writing, funds are being raised for the restoration of his home and the creation of a library. The house can be seen at 641 Whitehall St., and if anyone is on the grounds they will show you around.

Jackie Robinson, the first black to play major league baseball, played his first spring training game with the Montreal Royals at Daytona's City Island Park. Recently renamed Jackie Robinson Park, the site of major league baseball's first integrated game is marked with a large, bronze statue of Robinson. It was made from the same casting used for his statue in Montreal.

Black Music Month is celebrated each June in Miami with jazz, folk, gospel, rhythm and blues, Caribbean, and Afro-Cuban entertainers. Headquarters for the festival is Model City Center.

On the first Saturday of February, Black Awareness Day in Boynton Beach includes a beauty contest, dancing, a parade, an oratorical contest, and theater. Among legendary black musicians born in the state and surely inspired by Florida's unique pleasures and cadences, is Ray Charles. Blinded as a child in an

Above: There are over 400 horse farms around Ocala.

unsuccessful bid to save a brother from drowning, he was educated at a state school for the blind in St. Augustine.

Cowboys and Indians

It comes as a surprise to many Florida visitors that cowboys and rodeos are an important part of the rural scene. Cattle were introduced by the Spanish. In the 1600s an enormous cattle ranch covered all of what is now Payne's Prairie. More than 7200 cattle brands are officially registered with the state, and the raising of beef, dairy, and breeding stock cattle accounts for a big chunk of the state's agricultural income.

The earliest wranglers, who preferred to be called cow hunters rather than cowboys, used long, cracking whips. This is thought to be one reason that native Floridians are called Crackers – although other theories have also been advanced. Working cow hunter exhibitions are given at Lake Kissimmee State park, 15 miles east of Lake Wales, off Camp Mack

Rd. where, on weekends and holidays, the camp comes alive with real cow hunters who live, work, and speak as though the year is l876. It is fun to play the game their way, lapsing into the language of the times.

Artist and writer Frederic Remington, best known for artwork that preserved the spirit of the vanished Old West, visited Florida in l985 and reported finding the same sort of cowboys he had immortalized in the west, complete with broad brimmed hats, six-gun slung on the hip, and long hair.

Davie, near Fort Lauderdale, has had rodeos for 40 years. Kissimmee's Silver Spurs Rodeo, the state's oldest professional rodeo, is held twice a year. A championship rodeo is held in Homestead each February. A professional rodeo takes place each September in Titusville. Fort Myers holds a two-day championship rodeo in January.

For tourists who are interested in Indian history, Florida spreads a bountiful buffet of events and showplaces. Seminole villages are open to the public in Tampa and Fort Lauderdale. A Museum of the Sea & Indian has extensive Indian collections in Destin. Fort Walton Beach has a museum devoted to a ceremonial mound, which was once a gathering ground for tribes from miles around. Artifacts excavated here have a distinct Mayan look. Miccosukee tribes celebrate a yearly festival in Miami. Always held in the last week of December, it takes place in the Miccosukee village where dancing, singing and crafts of the tribe are shared with outsiders. The Miccosukee tourist "village" at Shark Valley in the Everglades has daily demonstrations of tribal cooking, sewing and alligator wrestling.

A Seminole tribal fair is held each February in Hollywood. An Indian Pow-Wow at Fort Pierce in March features Indian foods, dancing, clothing and artifacts from tribes all over the United States. A particularly good Calusa and Seminole collection is on display at the Lawrence Will Museum in Belle Glade.

Today, Seminoles number about 1500 and Miccosukees about 600. Most live on reservations which are shown on state maps but which otherwise look the same as any other stretches of the Everglades and Big Cypress Swamp. Wrangles with Washington over land, hunting rights and reparations continue. In the meantime, exempt from state and local laws, some reservations are making profits by holding high-stakes bingo games and by selling cigarettes sans state tax and therefore at irresistible prices. Most Indians live ordinary Florida lives; others continue placidly on ancient paths, farming, ranching, and wearing the brilliantly colored clothing that is their trademark.

Florida Horse Country

Ever since the Spanish introduced horses to North America, Florida has been a center for equestrian events.

The area around Ocala is green with pastures where thoroughbred foals frolic through the mild winters, strengthening young legs that will run at the nation's most famous tracks. Palm Beach has become so important as a polo center that Prince Charles may be seen playing here.

An Olympic class equestrian contest goes on for three weeks each March in Tampa. The Winter Equestrian Festival in West Palm Beach, in February, attracts more than 1500 of the world's finest horses to three grand prix events, one of them a World Cup qualifier.

Religion

Florida's religions are as diverse as its people. In dark corners of Caribbean enclaves, ancient rites of *obeah* are still practiced. It is no surprise to find stores carrying omens, symbols, chicken feet and all the paraphernalia. From special candles to magic furniture polish, these

are the commonplace and arcane articles that can be used in one's personal war against evil spirits.

The Church of Scientology remains a powerful presence in Clearwater. The Mormon Church is one of the state's largest land owners.

In 1894, a group led by Chicagoan Cyrus Teed settled near Fort Myers where they lived a celibate, communal life based on a belief that the world is hollow and they were living inside it. The group died out but their cult newspaper, *The American Eagle*, is still published by descendants of those Teed followers who stumbled on the road to celibacy and produced offspring. The settlement has been preserved as the Koreshan State Historic Site. A group of spiritualists left New York State late in the nineteenth century and settled at Cassadaga near Deltona. Their community, lined with neat, narrow

Above: Synagogues are typical for Miami Beach. Right: Free entrance to the open air theater in St. Petersburg.

brick streets, is still owned by the group and contains a hotel where visitors can get a hearty, old-fashioned meal followed by a spiritual reading. The first Christian to die for his faith in the New World is thought to have been a Spanish priest slain by the Indians he was trying to convert near Tampa Bay.

It seemed only natural that the fertile, Bible Belt soil of Florida would provide a final refuge for discredited evangelist Jim Bakker. The couple have faded from the news, but his wife Tammy continues to lead Bakker's followers in services.

Florida's communities, like those anywhere in America, cluster around churches and synagogues, many of them open daily to tourists. In St. Augustine, a church endowed by Henry Flagler holds the elaborate marble burial vaults of his daughter and grand-daughter. Historic churches are found in Fernandina Beach. Mount Pisgah Church outside Tallahassee is one of the state's oldest. A tiny chapel in St. Augustine marks the place where the first mass in the New World is

thought to have been said. Our Lady of Charity Shrine in Coconut Grove is a soaring 90-foot modern tower with a mural that depicts the history of Cuba. Plymouth Congregational Church in Coconut Grove has gates that were brought here from a seventeenth-century monastery in the Pyrenees. In Dade County alone, four churches are on the National Register of Historic Landmarks. Duval County and Leon County each have three. Others include St. Gabriel's Episcopal Church in Brevard County, St. Margaret's and St. Mary's in Clay County, Holy Trinity in Lake County, and First Baptist in Madison County.

It is not just the churches alone, but their cemeteries and the eloquent stories they tell that make historic churches so important to the tourist who delves into Florida's cultural history.

The Arts

The beauty of Florida is more than skin deep. The arts are taken seriously here.

The state boasts several operas and ballets, plus 24 symphony orchestras including half-a-dozen in the Fort Lauderdale-Miami area alone. Tallahassee has two symphony orchestras. Naples, Sarasota and Venice have symphony orchestras. Miami has a monthly guide to the arts, sold on newsstands. Jacksonville has an arts hotline where you can get updated information on concerts, plays, and museums. Phone 904/ 353-5100.

Internationally known artists are featured at annual jazz festivals. The largest are in Jacksonville, Pensacola, Tampa and Miami. Thanks to the state's diversity of peoples, its popular music ranges from Gospel to salsa, bluegrass to reggae. Every city has its hangouts for those who like rock, country and western, folk, Dixieland or whatever.

Arts and crafts festivals attract artisans and artists from all over the United States. Among the biggest and best events are those at Mount Dora, Lake Buena Vista, Winter Park, Pompano Beach, Coconut Grove, Miami and Fort

47

Lauderdale. Unique events held in one of the state's most rural areas are the Jeanie Festival and the Florida Folk Festival, both in Stephen Foster Country on the Suwannee River at White Springs. Artists and authors who lived and worked in the state, and who are remembered in annual festivals or events include Tennessee Williams, Ernest Hemingway, John James Audubon and Winslow Homer. Mary Roberts Rinehart, the mystery writer, often visited Useppa Island, which was an aloof and plush private compound. The entire club was abandoned and fell into ruin before it was restored in the 1970s. At the neighboring island of Cabbage Key, the home built by her son is now a ramshackle inn where boaters can stop for a cold beer, a meal, or an overnight stay.

Marjorie Kinnan Rawlings made an important contribution to the under-

standing of – and love for – the central Florida scrublands which for years had been looked upon only as a wilderness that needed taming. Best known is her Pulitzer-prize-winning book, later a movie, *The Yearling*. A more incisive look at the land and its people may be found in her book *Cross Creek*, written in 1942. Her simple home at Cross Creek near Gainesville is now a state historic site, open to the public.

Harriet Beecher-Stowe's book *Uncle Tom's Cabin* fired northern fury against slavery and helped win support for the Abolition that led to the Civil War. She had a winter home at Mandarin, near Jacksonville. The house burned down long ago, but the community is worth visiting for its art show, held each Easter weekend. Still available is Stowe's less famous, but more appropriately Floridian book, *Palmetto Leaves*, published in 1873 and later reprinted.

In modern times, John D. MacDonald lived and wrote in Florida. Many of the Travis McGee mysteries were written in

Above: Known to insiders only: Hemingway's first pub. Right: The palazzo, brought to Sarasota by Ringling.

Fort Lauderdale where MacDonald, like McGee, lived full-time on a houseboat. Later, MacDonald moved to an island near Sarasota, which was the setting for his novel, *Condominium*. Few writers have so fully captured the grit and grist, sham and shame of the Sunshine State as MacDonald was to do in his books.

Playwright Tennessee Williams spent most of his time in Key West, where the movie version of his play, *The Rose Tattoo* was filmed. His plays continue to be seen in the Performing Arts Center that bears his name in Key West.

Annual Shakespeare and Bach Festivals are also found around the state. Orlando's Shakespeare Festival goes on for three weeks in April. Coral Gables offers the Bard year-round at the Minorca Playhouse. The Bach Festival, in Winter Park, is one of the nation's most notable.

The British composer Frederick Delius lived for a time near Jacksonville, where he tried his hand at orange farming. The rhythms and harmonies of black Florida laborers inspired him to write works that brought him international acclaim. Today, a Delius festival is held yearly, in March, in Jacksonville. Lecturers and musicians celebrate Delius' works, including his *Florida Suite*. His home, restored and open to the public, is on the campus of Jacksonville University.

Florida's modern music idol is Jimmy Buffett whose songs such as *Changes in Latitudes, Changes in Attitudes*, and *Margueritaville* capture the Florida scene perfectly. Buffet got his start singing in Key West saloons, and is often seen in Florida aboard his boat.

Theater thrives throughout Florida, not just imports from Broadway but professional local productions. The Asolo State Theater in Sarasota is an eighteenth-century theater which was dismantled, imported, and reassembled here. The Coconut Grove Playhouse, built as a movie palace in the 1920s, became a state theater in the 1950s.

Tampa's Center for the Performing Arts is one of America's great complexes, featuring state-of-the-art acoustics and backstage machinery for its theaters and concert halls. Miami's Gusman Center for the Performing Arts is home to the Miami City Ballet, directed by Edward Villela. Miami also hosts a film festival in February.

Among the state's most important art museums are the Ringling in Sarasota, which houses one of the world's largest collections of baroque art, and Ocala's Appleton Museum, which is amassing one of the state's largest art collections. The Cummer Gallery, in Jacksonville, has one of the largest collections of Meissen porcelain in the world. The Bass Museum of Art is in Miami. Lowe Art Museum, in Coral Gables, has a collection including American, primitive, baroque, and Renaissance pieces. The Norton Gallery in West Palm Beach has a French impressionist collection. The Jacksonville Art Museum is known for stunning jade.

Fort Lauderdale's Museum of Art has an important collection of CoBrA movement (Copenhagen, Brussels, Amsterdam) paintings. Impressive Boehm collections are housed in the Plant Museum at the University of Tampa and in the Alexander Brest Museum at Jacksonville University.

The Morse Gallery in Winter Park has an extensive Tiffany collection, and the Salvador Dali Museum in St. Petersburg contains the largest Dali collection in the world. The Universalist Church in Tarpon Springs houses an impressive collection of paintings by Florida landscape artist George Inness Jr. Housed in the Daytona Beach Museum of Arts and Sciences is the largest collection of pre-Castro Cuban art in the United States. For those who like architecture there are time-warp neighborhoods of period buildings, some of them in the most unlikely places.

Above: Cultures meet in Ocala's Appleton Museum – the motor champ Don Garlits and an Asiatic war-lord.

The Deco District in Miami Beach is the largest, purest Deco neighborhood in the nation, with block after block of fine examples of Moderne buildings. Between the end of World War II and the mid-1950s, more hotels were built in Miami than in the rest of the states combined. Some of them comprise Flabbergast Row, the extravagant high-rise hotels along Collins Avenue on Miami Beach. Street after street of Victorian homes remain intact in Fernandina Beach. A National Historic District comprises 30 blocks. Jacksonville has entire historic neighborhoods of homes which have been caringly maintained or restored. Pensacola's North Hill Preservation District is filled with wooden gingerbread mansions built at a time when the city was exporting 200 million feet of lumber per year. Coral Gables is a sprawling neighborhood of Spanish mediterranean homes built in the 1920s. It is anchored by the Biltmore Hotel, which stood vacant for 20 years before it was restored to its original splendor.

The world's largest concentration of buildings designed by architect Frank Lloyd Wright may be found at Florida Southern College in Lakeland.

Stop at the Administration Building to pick up a free map to a self-guided tour. On the campus of the University of South Florida's New College at Sarasota are several buildings designed by I. M. Pei. Saint Leo Abbey in Dade City is an ornate Lombardic-Romanesque design that includes a faithful reproduction of the Grotto at Lourdes.

Florida's Funny Side

Zany, off-the-wall happenings typify a slightly lunatic mixture that is also part of Florida. See the nightly sunset at the Mallory Docks in Key West. Tourists gather to watch the sun set into the sea, while gaggles of hucksters, peddlers, and loonies sell their wares or simply show off. The city's annual Fantasy Fest is another insane and indescribable fun-fest. And each year the Keys celebrate the Conch Republic, commemorating the day in the 1980s when Florida's Keys seceded from the United States.

Other inspired silliness occurs at the King Mango Strut in Miami – the people's version of the ultra-commercial Orange Bowl parade. Every Labor Day, there are anything-goes raft races on the St. Johns River, near DeLand.

The Gasparilla invasion in Tampa is preceded by the Ybor City Naval Invasion, to clear the waters. A festival in Wausau, in August, focuses on attractive features of baked possum.

More serious events which have spread throughout the state are annual Blessings of the Fleet and night-time Christmas Boat Parades. Both are lovely, lively pageants that celebrate all Florida's favorite place, the waterfront. When colored Christmas lights are reflected back from the water, the mirror effect is one of the season's most beautiful.

Lifestyles of the Rich and Richer

Even during the steamy, stultifying days before the invention of air conditioning, Florida drew its share of visitors and settlers who were rich, royal, famous or all three. Prince Achille Murat, a nephew of Napoleon Bonaparte, lent glitter to the social life of Tallahassee in the early nineteenth century. He and his wife, who was a grand-niece of George Washington, are buried in the city's Episcopal cemetery. John Ringling's palatial home in Sarasota, John Deering's Italian Renaissance estate, Viscaya in Miami, and Henry Flagler's echoing marble Whitehall rival the world's greatest mansions.

Although Thomas Edison's home and laboratory in Fort Myers convey a simple and even austere lifestyle, experiments that were done here made world history. His office remains much as he left it. Harry Truman's winter White House was in Key West. During his presidency he was a familiar figure on local streets, taking his early morning walks and stopping for breakfast at a local coffee shop. Truman Specials are still served by the restaurants he favored.

John F. Kennedy spent winter vacations in the family compound at Palm Beach. Other residents and visitors form a Who's Who of old money, new money and show-biz money or political power.

A neighborhood newcomer is billionaire Donald Trump. President Richard Nixon's home was on Biscayne Bay. George Bush spent his first vacation after the presidential election fishing in the Florida Keys. Prince Charles is a not-infrequent visitor to Palm Beach.

Less visible, but leading lives so opulent they boggle the mind, are the many oil-rich princes and sheiks who have been quietly buying up some of South Florida's most extravagant estates.

Quietly gaining its own neighborhoods of the mega-rich, most of them living low-profile lives, are other cities includ-

ing Naples, Boca Raton, Fort Lauderdale, and Sarasota. Ocala has its own aristocracy of wealthy horse breeders. Orlando is attracting a growing list of movie super-stars and business moguls. It is increasingly common to see movie stars around town, taking time off from filming at Disney or Universal Studios. John Travolta, who flies his own jet airplane, lives in a fly-in community near Daytona Beach. Burt Reynolds and Loni Anderson live near Jupiter.

The Flavors of Florida

So thoroughly is America on the move today that regional cuisines are blending one into the other until there is no single style that Florida can claim as exclusively its own. Among the influences that are most significant, unique and delicious is Cuban cuisine. America may have gone

Above: Hurricane Restaurant at St. Petersburg – cooking done by the chef himself!
Right: You may take this literally!

goofy for Mexican and Tex-Mex, but there are new discoveries ahead for the traveler who is encountering Cuban cookery, which is subtly different from any other Latin cuisine.

At the turn of the century, Columbia Restaurant was opened in Tampa. It remains a cultural and culinary Cuban landmark, with clones in other Florida cities, too. Miami has its own Little Havana area, and Cuban restaurants can be found as far north in the state as Orlando and Jacksonville. Cuban classics, some sold in hole-in-the-wall restaurants at pittance prices, include *ropas viejas,* chicken *alicante, paella,* black beans and rice, Cuban coffee, and crusty Cuban bread which is still baked in the old style - creased with a palm leaf – in South Florida bakeries.

Continental cuisine has long had adherents in Florida. The state is a major destination for business travelers, overseas tourists and jet setters. There has always been a very critical demand for the best in dining prepared by chefs trained

in traditional and nouvelle continental disciplines.

There are only ten five-star restaurants in the entire United States. One of them is in Florida. One of only seven five-star hotels is here. Two of the nation's 12 five-star resorts are in Florida. Miami has two four-star restaurants. Tampa has one.

Except for the most remote rural areas, you are never more than a 30-mile drive from a good to great continental restaurant. Ethnic foods, in addition to Cuban restaurants, are available in Florida restaurants ranging from Lebanese to Thai, Italian to Chinese, for starters.

Miami has a rich Jewish heritage with a wide choice of good, modestly priced kosher restaurants. Tarpon Springs is known for Greek restaurants. Jacksonville has a group of authentic Arab eateries. In Little Haiti, a 200-block area in Miami, Haitian foods are available in restaurants, bakeries and markets.

Showcase restaurants at Epcot Center are operated by native Chinese, Canadians, Moroccans, French, Italians, and

Norwegians, with Russians on the way. Ethnic flavors that may be new to you in Florida include Jamaican "jerk" cooking and Bahamian conch dishes.

Florida native cooking takes many forms. Among the state's most lauded, totally homegrown restaurants are Chalet Suzanne, Lake Wales, which serves continental meals with a Florida twist. The Yearling, at Cross Creek serves cooter pie, venison, and other local country specialties. The Colony, on Longboat Key, near Sarasota, is where traditionally trained chefs create Florida renditions of gourmet favorites. Bern's Steak House in Tampa is where meltingly tender steaks are served with organically grown local vegetables. Key West rivals even San Francisco in the range and quality of its eateries.

Seafood anchors Florida's strongest claim to culinary greatness, in any season, shape or recipe. Fishing boats dock daily, spilling their silvery catches into seaside kitchens. The state has hundreds of seafood restaurants, all of them with

and white cornbread. It is likely that your breakfast will be served with grits, unless you ask for hashed browns, even when you stay in a big city hotel.

Florida hasn't forgotten that it is a Dixie state. You can usually get good baking powder biscuits, pecan and sweet potato pie, cornbread dressing, fried chicken, pit barbecue, greens with fatback, and many other southern classics cooked to perfection. Tropical influence on Florida's citrus crops leads to a glorious colorful cornucopia of grapefruit, tangerines and varieties of different oranges making a debut at many different seasons during the year.

Juicy Key limes, mangoes, and the occasional find of less frequently cultivated citrus fruits such as ugli fruit, kumquat, and calamondin were introduced by the Spanish. Crown law required that each sailor departing for the New World bring 100 seeds. Later, they began bringing seedlings instead. Descendants of those early trees are sometimes found deep in the scrub or the Everglades.

Key lime pie is a Florida passion, resulting in equally passionate arguments over whether it should have a pastry or graham cracker crust, a whipped cream or meringue topping. Only one thing is certain. Key limes are tiny and yellow, with a faint vanilla scent. Real Key lime pie is never green.

There are still secondary roads in the state where citrus can be found at roadside stands. Tune in to the seasons, to discover honeybelles which have a short, sweet harvest, or naval oranges, which appear, grapefruit-sized and zipperskinned, right after the first cold snap. Only in late summer does the citrus market slumber. The harvest is much longer lived and more varied than nonnatives realize.

An offshoot product is orange blossom honey which is harvested here and sold worldwide. One Volusia County producer alone ships 2 million pounds a

lengthy menus of fish and shellfish, which can be ordered boiled, broiled, poached, mesquite or charcoal grilled, en papillote, sauced, or fried.

Favorites include Apalachicola oysters, stone crabs, Florida lobster, smoked mullet, all the snappers, fresh tuna, bay or sea scallops, swordfish, catfish, grouper (called scamp in some areas), shark, freshwater crab, and alligator. Some restaurants also fly in fresh salmon or cod from northern waters. Menus may also list seasonal or occasional catches such as tile fish, monk fish, bluefish, or jack.

Faithful southern cooking is found only in the most rural counties.Perseverance is rewarded with consistently Deep South favorites such as perloo, "dirty" rice, country ham with redeye gravy, greens of fresh collard, mustard or turnip, served with pot liquor, corn pudding, congealed salads, okra, chicory coffee,

Above: For the name of this fish look in your encyclopedia. Right: At Port Canaveral, doing a man's job!

year, most of it going to Europe and Japan. In addition to orange blossom honey, Florida bee-keepers gather honey from ti-ti, palmetto, sunflower, gallberry, pepper, alfalfa, sweet clover, and blueberry.

Dictionary of Florida Foods

Alligator pears are an old-time Florida name for avocadoes, which grow abundantly in south Florida. Alligator, meaning the reptile, is often seen on menus. It has a meaty taste that some people find delicious. Blackeye peas and hog jowls are a soul food classic. The dish is traditionally eaten by Floridians on New Year Eve to bring good luck. Blue crab is served boiled whole or in heaping, steaming dishes. The crusty creatures require lots of labor but are worth the hours of picking and cracking. All-you-can-eat blue crab specials are an excellent buy for crab devotees.

Bollos, pronounced "boy-ose," are the spicy, deep-fried balls made from mashed peas, which are sold on Key West streets. Cactus is a sweet red "pear," served as a fruit; marinated it can be served as salad.

Carambola, also known as star fruit, has a tart, puckery tang, suitably served as a garnish in drinks. Catfish served in Florida are probably farmed rather than caught in the wild. Many restaurants offer all-you-can-eat catfish specials. Fingerling catfish are served whole. Tiny and bristling with bones, they have the sweetest meat of all.

Chayote is a bland, crisp fruit sometimes served cooked as a vegetable. It's called christophene in the West Indies. Conch, pronounced "konk," is a rubbery shellfish served in chowder, fritters, or "cracked", dipped in cracker crumbs and fried. The word also refers to a person who was born in the Keys.

Coontie is wild cassava root made into a flour much like arrowroot. This is the Seminoles' basic starch. The bread baked from it is bright orange.

Cooter is a land tortoise, served in turtle soups and fricassees. Coquina is a

55

tiny clam, used in broths and chowders. Dirty rice is a soul food favorite among blacks and rural whites made from a blend of white rice boiled with chicken gizzards, hearts, and livers. Dolphin is called *dorado* in Mexico, or *mahimahi* in Hawaiian waters. It is one of Florida's meatiest fishes, but it is not prepared from the bottle-nose dolphin, or porpoise, which is not harvested here for food. Flan is a caramel-trimmed custard popular in Cuban restaurants.

Florida lobsters are spiny lobsters, otherwise known as crawfish, and quite unlike the Maine lobster. Only the tail of the Florida lobster, which may weigh as much as 2 pounds, is eaten. Menus often list it simply as lobster. Ask which lobster is being served. Some people who eat Maine lobster are allergic to the Florida crustacean, which is generally unavailable fresh from April to July.

Grouper is called scamp in Florida's Panhandle. It is a name used for many types of grouper and jewfish. It is a mild, firm fish that tastes much like the most delicate breast of chicken.

Guava is a tangy fruit, sometimes available fresh at roadsides. Guava ice cream is sold in Key West. Heart of palm is also called swamp cabbage. It may be offered cold in salad or cooked as a vegetable.

Jerk cooking is Jamaican in origin. Spicy, barbecue jerk pork, beef, chicken, fish or goat is served in Florida's increasingly popular Caribbean restaurants.

Jicama is popular in Mexican cooking. A bland and crunchy vegetable (pronounced HEE-come-ah) it is found commonly in Florida markets.

Early Keys residents, who had no refrigeration and consumed canned milk, discovered that Key lime juice could be added to sweetened condensed milk to make a sweet custard. Many imitations

Right: This fish-head is bigger than a man's back.

are made, but real Key lime pie is made from yellow limes and canned milk.

Loquat is also called Japanese plum, a yellow plum-like fruit.

Mangoes are sweet, peach-like fruits that grow only in south Florida. The flesh is juicy and delicious; some people are allergic to the sticky sap. Wash it off your hands.

Okra grows abundantly in Florida. A southern favorite, it is used in many ways by Cracker cooks, who favor it stewed with tomatoes.

Old sour is made when salt is added to the juice of sour oranges. Allowed to ferment, it is then served as a condiment.

Papaya can be grown in yards in South Florida. It is seasonally available on restaurant menus.

Purloo is probably a corruption of *pilau* or *pilaf*, a rice dish that varies according to the cook. Sea grapes look and taste like grapes.

Soffkee is the Seminoles' everyday stew with meat, grits, and vegetables.

Snapper is a popular fish which may be red, yellowtail, or mangrove snapper.

Stone crab is Florida's unique crab. It grows a hard, glassy shell, which protects a nugget of sweet, white meat. Only the claw can be legally harvested. The crab is thrown back to grow another. Served hot or cold, stone crab is available fresh only from mid-October through mid-May. Frozen claws are served during other months by some restaurants.

Surinam cherries are often grown as a landscaping hedge, and they can be made into jellies or sauces.

Persimmons are cultivated in Florida and sold on roadside stands.

Plantains look like large bananas, but don't try to eat them raw. They are not sweet, but taste fine served fried or boiled, with a bland starchy taste that only hints of banana.

Tomatillo is a vine-grown green tomato-like vegetable found commonly in Florida supermarkets.

SOUTHERN FLORIDA

MIAMI
MIAMI BEACH
FORT LAUDERDALE
PALM BEACH
FLORIDA KEYS
EVERGLADES

MIAMI

Ask anyone for an image of Miami and Miami Beach and you're bound to get a variety of views. Some know it as a retirees' haven, the sunny place you went to visit grandma as a child. Others see a more current Miami, of glass and steel skyscrapers, and a humming business mood. Still others know the Miami of TV's *Miami Vice* - dangerous, swaggering, a place of drug dealers, nightclubs, and cigarette boats. Others see a colorful mix of Latin cultures, retained by Central American, South American and Caribbean immigrants.

In reality, the area is all of these things but additional flavors mix in all the time. The last decade, for instance, has brought a number of new aspects. Cultural facilities have increased as the area strives to be taken seriously as an artistic center, not just a place to lie on the beach. A new fashionable area has emerged, **South Beach**, built around the spectacular Art Deco buildings of the 1930s and 1940s. Another fashionable stretch, **Coconut Grove**, has expanded its outdoor café

Preceding pages: Evening mood at Sandestin Beach. Fascinating night and day – Miami's skyline. Left: Most popular style at Miami Beach – Art Deco.

population, becoming a prime place to watch people.

And some veteran hotels have been demolished, while others have been reborn. To get a sense of the area overall, you will need at least a couple of days to explore leisurely – the only way. And to get into the proper spirit, drive around. Rent a convertible and put the top down.

The Origins

The discovery of Florida does put the Mayflower settlers to shame - Ponce de Leon first stepped off here seeking his fountain of youth in 1513. Miami's history, though, is considerably more recent – it was so far down the state's east coast that no civilized souls wanted to venture down here. Julia Tuttle was a spirited exception. The wife of a wealthy industrialist from Cleveland, Mrs. Tuttle arrived in Miami on a mail boat in 1875. What she found was not particularly auspicious: the ruins of a US Army camp and an Indian trading post, operated by the local Seminoles. Still, she thought the sunny, scenic area had possibilities, a fact she tried to impress upon Henry Flagler, the Standard Oil co-founder, railroad tycoon and developer of the east coast of Florida.

Flagler resisted. But the weather intervened in Julia Tuttle's favor. A ferocious freeze hit during the winter of 1895, wiping out most of Florida's citrus industry. Down south, though, in uncivilized Miami, orange blossoms were flourishing without a touch of frost. Tuttle sent Flagler a bouquet of them and the railroad czar got the message. His railroad was extended downward, arriving in town a year later. Flagler came down with it and built a hotel **The Royal Palm**. The development of "America's sun porch", as he called it, was on. As often happened with Flagler's march down the Florida coast, where he went the rich and famous followed. But they all settled in Miami proper.

In 1912, millionaire Carl Fisher of Indianapolis decided to stretch the horizons. He looked around **Biscayne Bay**, bought a vast sandbar from an avocado farmer (named John Collins, remembered in **Collins Avenue**) and dredged it until he saw land. He filled it with plants, birds, golf courses and hotels. **Miami Beach**, famed the world over, was born.

Fisher wasn't the last visionary in the area either. In 1921, a local boy, George Merrick, took his father's Miami farm and designed a European-feel city within it. Observers are hard pressed to figure out which European or Asian city it resembles, though: there is a mixture of Venetian-style canals and Chinese- and French-style houses. The result, **Coral Gables**, is still one of the city's most exclusive addresses. It may not be the most unique in appearance, however. That distinction could go to Opa-Locka, an Arabian Nights fantasy of spires, domes and parapets developed by former aviator Glenn H. Curtiss. Like his other developments, Hialeah and Miami Springs, **Opa-Locka** was intended as a destination for frostbitten northerners, and today, although a residential area inhabited primarily by blacks, you can still see the somewhat run-down but outstanding architecture. The tradition of wintering in Miami was now well-established.

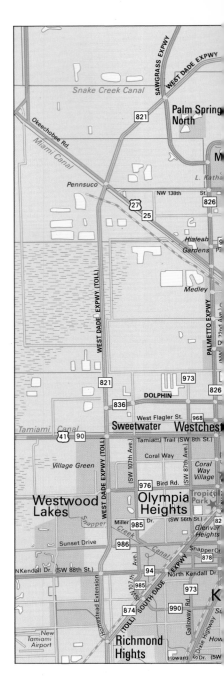

Miramar

821

Buccaneer
Estates

847

Carol City

PALMETTO 826

Bunche Park

mory

Locka
Opa-Locka
ort

9

th St.

953

le River Canal
9th St.

9th St.)

HIALEAH

aleah

S
th St.)

mi.
rnat.
port
WY

968

90

953

oral
iables

Douglas
Road

uth Miami

Hallandale Beach
Rd.

County Line

Rd.

858

91

860

826

9A

817

441

NW 135th St.

953

Gratigny Rd.
(NW 119th St.)

924

932

934

Northside

Martin
Luther
King

944

AIRPORT EXPWY

25 27

MIAMI

(TOLL)

EAST-WEST EXPWY

972

9

976

Coconut
Grove

Silver
Bluff

Pembroke
Park

832

854

Ives
Estates

5

A1A

856

Hallandale Beach

Golden Beach

Golden Beach

Sunny Isles

North
Miami Beach

Haulover Beach

N. Miami Recr. Facility, Florida Int'l University

Bal Harbour
Bay Harbor Islands

Surfing

Surfside

North Shore Park

65th St. Park

Ocean Front Park

Indian Beach Park

Miami Beach

Collins Park

Lummus Park

VIRGINIA KEY

Virginia Beach
Southeast Pt.

ATLANTIC   OCEAN

KEY
BISCAYNE

Fairchild Tropical Garden

Matheson Hammock
County Park

Cape
Florida

MIAMI – MIAMI BEACH & VICINITY

0   4   8km

0   2   4 miles

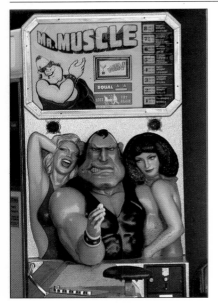

Well-heeled "snowbirds" were not the only ones flocking south, though. Other tourists, drawn by the warmth and the beauty, also learned that there was money to be made in real estate deals. Speculators were soon taking the train down with dollar signs in their eyes. The result was that the population boomed – from 30,000 to 100,000 in five years, with an additional 300,000 visitors in winter.

Obviously, not all cashed in on the deals. Scamps abounded, some developments went bust. Then Miami saw a crippling hurricane in 1926 and the Depression in 1929. The Depression did not finish Miami, though; some of its most enduring legacies, in fact, were built during this time.

The WPA came to Florida and built the Art Deco hotels - smooth, modern, tropical in feel. Retirees also started to stream to the area; land was cheap, there was no

Above: Kitsch? Art? Business? Right: Miami Beach's hundreds of Art Deco buildings were saved from dilapidation.

inheritance or income tax and the weather was much easier on one's body and soul.

After the Second World War, the area went through another real estate boom. It also went through a public relations boom, due to the presence of two television celebrities. Arthur Godfrey broadcast his show from Miami Beach starting in 1953. Jackie Gleason proclaimed Miami Beach the "sun and fun capital of the world" in the 1960s. The city became a celebrity playground, something of a domestic St. Tropez.

Celebrities were not the only new faces in Miami in the 1960s, though. The influx of refugees – approximately 265,000 – fleeing Castro's Cuba changed the sights and the sounds of the city immeasurably. Now, 45% of the city is Hispanic – Colombians, Guatemalans, Nicaraguans and Panamanians followed the Cuban migration.

But the ethnic mix does not stop there. French-speaking Haitians, who have their own section, Little Haiti, Brazilians, Germans, Greeks, Iranians, Italians, Swedes, etc., all fill the streets and shops, creating a polyglot that distinguishes the area from any other. When you visit Miami, you could, seemingly, be in any of a number of different countries at once.

Downtown

The downtown business district of Miami flaunts its success the way many American cities do - with tall glass skyscrapers. These reflect the sun during the day and variously colored lights at night. Depending upon the time of year, the **CenTrust Building**, 100 S.E. 1st Street, changes its outdoor lighting colors accordingly: red and green for Christmas, purple and pink for Easter, orange and green for really important occasions - home games of the town's two football teams: the Miami Dolphins and University of Miami Hurricanes.

To take in the whole spread, drive **Brickell Avenue** from north to south. It has more than skyscrapers; after the few business buildings, innovative, colorful residential buildings appear.

To tour the other sights of downtown, though, you should leave your convertible somewhere else; like most cities, the inner business sanctum area has little parking and what there is priced to discourage ever parking there again.

This is a good opportunity to use **Metrorail**, the train service that was begun with great fanfare in 1984. Once being downtown, you can hop on **Metromover**, an elevated transit system that circles the section. But it is advisable to get off from time to time and take in the street scene: the lawyers and businessmen mixing with street vendors of all nationalities.

Points of Interest

The **Dade County Courthouse**, at 73 W. Flagler Street, is one of the veteran

buildings amid all this glass. It dates all the way back to 1928 and was once the tallest building south of the nation's capital. Now the tallest building in the city, and in the whole state, is the 55-storey high **Southeast Financial Center**, 200 S. Biscayne Blvd.

For a little art among all this commerce, the **Metro-Dade Cultural Center**, 101 W. Flagler Street, was opened to the public in 1983. It is a 3.3 acre complex encompassing art, history and scholarship. The **Center for Fine Arts** possesses no permanent collections; curators acquire temporary shows. The **Historical Museum of South Florida** is, as the name implies, a collection of historical artifacts pertaining to the area. The **Main Public Library** offers 700,000 volumes and occasional art exhibits.

For performing arts, an interesting place to look at, and actually attend performances, is the **Gusman Center for the Performing Arts**, 174 East Flagler Street. It is a very baroque former movie palace that might seem more at home in

Morocco. Inside, the Miami City Ballet performs, a company given real status by its director Edward Villella, a former star of the New York City Ballet.

For lounging and shopping, a prime stop is the **Bayside Marketplace**, an extravaganza of a mall on the waterfront at 401 Biscayne Blvd. Next door is the Miamarina, roosting point for luxury yachts and a 36-foot Venetian gondola that gives rides.

Another ship nearby also takes visitors but stays at the pier: the reproduction of the **H.M.S. Bounty** that was built for the 1962 film *Mutiny on the Bounty*.

Little Havana

Southwest of downtown, in the neighborhood bordering S.W. 8th Street, is the Latin section called **Little Havana**, the area where, starting in the 1960s, Cuban immigrants settled. This is a popular area for strolling, with its brick sidewalks, tree-lined streets, outdoor food stalls and Cuban cafés. At **Domino Park**, S.W. 8th and 14th Avenue, you can also watch residents try to outwit each other in domino games.

Those are tame activities, though. Wilder goings-on occur the first week of March every year during the **Carnival Miami**, a nine-day festival culminating with **Calle Ocho**, a twenty-three block long party. Bicycle races, numerous concerts, a masquerade ball in the streets, conga lines, live music, sambas, mambos – lots of different rhythms can be heard in the streets during this festivals.

Little Haiti

About 60,000 Haitian emigrants live in this section, a 200 block area in northeast Miami. On the side-streets are elegant Mediterranean-style homes, originals from the land boom era of the 1920s, and on the main drag, N.E. 2nd Avenue between 45th and 79th Streets, is a panorama of brightly painted buildings – in purples, reds, pinks, greens, yellows.

In these florid buildings are shops selling foods and crafts. And in the middle of all extends the **Caribbean Marketplace**, 5927 N.E. 2nd Avenue, in which thirty-odd merchants sell fruits and vegetables, baskets and other crafts.

Coral Gables

George Merrick's planned community calls itself "The City Beautiful". It is not hard to see why: this wealthy section built along golf courses and canals appropriates the best of European styles and transplants them side by side. The main gates, fountains and plazas are in Spanish style, but Merrick thought residents should have a choice, so "atmospheric" neighborhoods called The Villages were created. If Spanish wasn't your style, you could choose French Country, French Provincial, French City, Dutch South African, Colonial and Chinese. Regardless of a person's choice of architecture, all Coral Gables residents had, and still have, one structure in common: the **Venetian Pool**, 2701 De Soto Blvd., probably the most deluxe community swimming pool in the world. Originally the site of a coral rock quarry, it was sculpted from the coral into a veritable lagoon in 1924. Vast and romantic - with a waterfall, caves and lush foliage all around, it definitely transports you to another time and place.

So do the **Coral Gables City Hall**, 405 Biltmore Way, a Spanish Renaissance structure built in 1928 and the showplace **Biltmore Hotel**, 1200 Anastasia Avenue. The lavish (and some say haunted) hotel, built in 1926, has a beautiful tower modeled after the Giralda Tower in Seville, more Spanish style to fit Merrick's motif. The hotel did not have a successful run, though, and was vacant for nearly twenty years before renovation started in 1986. Now it is a palace with opulent chan-

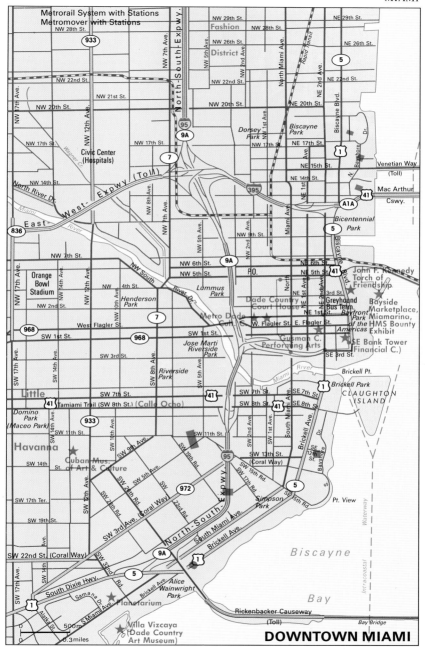

MIAMI

Metrorail System with Stations
Metromover with Stations

NW 28th St.
NW 29th St.   NE 29th St.
933
Fashion
NW 26th St.   NE 26th St.
NW 7th Ave.   5
District
NW 5th Ave.
North Miami Ave.   NE 2nd Ave.
Rapid Transit
NW 22nd St.   NE 22nd St.
95
NW 22nd St.
NW 21st St.
NW 20th St.   NW 20th St.   NE 20th St.
9A
Biscayne Blvd.
NW 7th Ave.
NW 12th Ave.
NW 17th St.   NW 17th St.   Dorsey   Biscayne   NE 17th St.
Park   Park   1
7   Ave.   NE 15th St.   Venetian Way
Civic Center   (Toll)
(Hospitals)   NE 14th St.
West Expwy. (Toll)   41   Mac Arthur
395   A1A   Cswy.
North River Dr.
NW 14th St.   Miami Ave.   Bicentennial
NW 8th Ave.   Park
East-   NW 7th Ave.   5
836   River   NW 9th St.
Miami   NW 5th Ave.   Biscayne
NW 7th St.   NW 2nd Ave.
NW 6th St.   9A   NE 6th St.   John F. Kennedy
Orange   NW South   NW 5th St.   P.O.   NE 5th St.   41   Torch of
Bowl   River Dr.   Lummus   North   Friendship
Stadium   NW 4th St.   Park   3rd St.   Greyhound   Bayside
Henderson   Dade County   NE 1st St.   Bus Term.   Marketplace,
NW 2nd St.   NW 10th Ave.   Park   Court House   Bayfront   Miamarina,
7   Metro Dade   NE 1st St.   Park   of the HMS Bounty
West Flagler St.   W. Flagler St. E. Flagler St.   Americas   Exhibit
968   SW 1st St.   SE Bank Tower
968   Gusman C.   (Financial C.)
SW 1st St.   Jose Marti   Performing Arts   SE 3rd St.
Riverside
SW 3rd St.   Park   Miami   River
Riverside   Brickell Pt.
Park   SW 5th Ave.   1   Brickell Park
Little   SW 7th St.   SW 7th St.   SE 7th St.   CLAUGHTON
41   SW 8th St.   41   ISLAND
Tamiami Trail (SW 8th St.) (Calle Ocho)   South Miami Ave.   SE 8th St.
Domino   933   Brickell Ave.
Park   SW 11th St.
(Maceo Park)
Havanna   SW 13th St.
Cuban Mus.   (Coral Way)
SW 14th   of Art & Culture   95
St.   5
SW 17th Ter.   972   Simpson
Park   Pt. View
SW 19th St.
North-South Expwy.   Biscayne
SW 22nd St. (Coral Way)   9A   South Miami Ave.
5   1   Brickell Ave.
SW 17th Ave.   South Dixie Hwy.   Alice   Bay
1   Brickell Ave.   Wainwright
Planetarium   Park   Rickenbacker Causeway
0   500m   (Toll)   Bay Bridge
Villa Vizcaya
0.3 miles   (Dade County   DOWNTOWN MIAMI
Art Museum)

69

deliers, painted ceilings and a decadently oversized pool.

Coconut Grove

The Grove, South Florida's oldest settlement, was established a full twenty years before Miami, so although annexed by the city in 1925, it has never quite integrated itself. Its reputation as a Bohemian center also sets it apart: first settled by Bahamian blacks, Key Westers and transplanted New England intellectuals, it was originally a no-class divisions, artists and writers community, the Greenwich Village of the South, an image that still applies today. But the Grove is an eclectic area; the tropical vegetation is steadfastly maintained so that the overall effect is arty, quaint and jungle.

People come here to sit in open air cafés and watch the parade of well-

Above: Attending Coconut Grove Arts Festival. Right: Sailing – one of the great passions.

dressed pedestrians stride by. They also come to shop, go to galleries, and generally spend money. Browsing can be done, though, at the **Farmer's Market** every Saturday on Margaret Street. A rich variety of handicrafts and multi-ethnic foods are on display.

Also worth a look on the edge of Coconut Grove is the estate we all wish we could borrow for the winter, **Vizcaya**, 3251 S. Miami Avenue. James Deering, the heir to the International Harvester fortune, built it for his winter retreat and he did not stint – he spent $15 million back in 1912 for this 70-room Italian Renaissance palace. The 10 acres of sculpted gardens add a lot to the sense of luxury and romance.

Key Biscayne

Take a drive over the Rickenbacker Causeway from Coconut Grove and you wind up on a very exclusive island, **Key Biscayne**. Gulls and herons were about the most famous residents here until the late 1960s when another temporary resident began coming south for the winter – then US-President Richard Nixon. The **Florida White House**, as it was known, is at 485 W. Matheson Drive – but Nixon, fortunately for the publicity-shy neighbors, is nowhere in sight.

This is not a place to do anything - it is a place to languish on one of the beaches or in **Bill Baggs State Park** and watch the sailboats or local fishermen casting for grouper or snapper. If you are feeling mobile, the best idea might be to rent a bike and pedal around.

MIAMI BEACH

Miami Beach has had sweeping ups and downs over the years. From its mangrove swamp status in 1910 it became the Riviera of the United States in the Roaring Twenties, a wild, drinking and gambling-filled playground. The big hotels

from that era were supplemented in the post-war era with huge, flashy, intentionally exotic- sounding new hotels such as the renowned Martinique, the Monmartre, the Barcelona, and the Bombay. Motels began to spring up on **Collins Avenue** in North Miami Beach.

Now middle class America came to Miami Beach for vacation. In the 1960s and 1970s, though, Miami Beach as vacation spot took a sharp downturn; the older vacationers of past seasons bought houses of their own in the area, abandoning the hotels, and their children, bored with Miami Beach and curious about more faraway places, took advantage of the new jet flights to explore.

Some of the fancier hotels fell into disrepair. But lately a number have come back impressively and with the their revitalization and that of other neighborhoods, Miami Beach is lively and fashionable again.

Start your drive into Miami Beach by taking the **MacArthur Causeway** across the Intracoastal; on your way you will

pass a couple of islands, **Star Island**, **Hibiscus Island** and **Palm Island**, that are more notable for their residents than their location: Al Capone lived on Palm Island, author Damon Runyon lived on Hibiscus Island and *Miami Vice* star Don Johnson lived on Star Island.

The Causeway will bring you into **South Beach**, the area from the southern tip to 23rd Street. You will cross on 5th Street; if you are a boxing fan you should pay attention to the corner of Washington and 5th: the 5th Street Gym has been the site of workouts by Muhammad Ali, Sonny Liston, Roberto Duran and Joe Louis, among other champions.

Fifth Street is also the beginning of the revitalized Art Deco district. From 5th to 15th Streets on **Ocean Drive**, block after block of imaginative, whimsical, freshly repainted structures face the beach. Tourists often just stroll on their own, stopping in the hotel restaurants for a snack or crossing over to **Lummus Park**, relaxing in a grassy park that runs parallel to the area and the beach.

Once you have walked the district, you might want to do one of the area's truly great drives, up **Collins Avenue** to 163rd Street, the length of the island. As this street changes, you will see the cultures change, from the communities of Hasidic Jews to the once and in some cases presently glamorous hotels, to the exclusive beach communities up north and "Motel Row" cluster of funky motels.

At Collins Avenue and 44th Street, you will see a unique mural signaling a similarly unique hotel. The giant arch, Roman figures, waterfalls and lagoon look real but are not – they are just covering a blank wall that shields the immense Fontainbleau (mispronounced locally as Fountain Blue) Hotel.

This mammoth conventioneers' haven is what most people think of when they think of Miami Beach – it fronts a huge,

18 acres stretch of beach, it caters to outrageous frivolities, exemplified by the Poodle Lounge, decorated with pink poodles. It may be kitsch but it is worth a stop at 4441 Collins Avenue, Miami Beach. Also worth a stop is the pink and purple lobby of the **Eden Roc**, 4525 Collins Avenue, and the elegant, glassy **Doral**, 4833 Collins Avenue. Farther up Collins, past the down at heel **Surfside**, you come to **Bal Harbor**, an elegant, quiet stretch with shops and luxurious homes tucked behind secure gates. The tawdry stretch of motels along **Sunny Isles** follows. Then at the top of **North Miami**, you find the quietest, most exclusive enclave of all, **Golden Beach**. Drive by for a look at the mansions.

Nightlife

Day-tripping is one thing almost everyone comes to Miami for; the sunshine is an intoxicant in itself. But Miami has always had a reputation as a pretty swinging town, and with the massive

Above: "The" event for hundreds of thousands: the Orange-Bowl competition. Right: A touch of the Caribbean at Key West. Far right: Glamor girls.

wealth pouring into the area from all over the world being used to revitalize neighborhoods, that is even truer now. And the mix of nightlife reflects the mix of cultures. For an elegant club with a Latin beat, Miamians have been going to **Les Violins**, 1751 Biscayne Blvd, for 25 years. For nostalgic rock n' roll, younger dancers go to the newer **Biscayne Baby**, 3336 Virginia Street, Coconut Grove. **Regine's**, 2669 South Bayshore Drive, Coconut Grove, located atop the Grand Bay Hotel, caters to affluent members, guests of the hotel and those who sound important when they call to put their name on the list. **Club Decos** is a Deco dancing palace at 1235 Washington, Miami.

After Nightlife

In the city one need not look hard to encounter low-life. Crime, drugs and record-setting murder rates committed in the humid heat of the tropics makes for serious law enforcement operations, and there is no better place to house the

American Police Officer Hall of Fame and Museum. This is the nation's only memorial honoring US law officers who have died in the line of duty. Newly opened in May 1990 in the former **FBI headquarters** at 3801 Biscayne Boulevard, the museum had outgrown its previous quarters in Sarasota. The collection includes more than 10,000 police and law enforcement artifacts and exhibits and a 400-ton marble memorial is being built. On it, the names, ranks and affiliations of officers killed in the line of duty since 1960 will be inscribed. The new location also includes an interdenominational chapel and crime prevention center. Exhibits include law enforcement paraphernalia, vehicles, an electric chair, a guillotine, jail cells and a mock crime scene where visitors are challenged to "solve the murder". The memorial is operated as a trust of the National Association of Chiefs of Police, a non-profit organization composed of more than 11,000 command rank officers throughout the United States.

MIAMI / MIAMI BEACH
Accommodation

LUXURY: **Grand Bay Hotel**, Five-star elegance overlooking Biscayne Bay, 2669. S. Bayshore Dr., Coconut Grove, 33133, 305/858-9600. **Mayfair House**, European-style boutique hotel, 3000 Florida Avenue, Coconut Grove, 33133, 305/441-0000. **Grove Isle**, a small luxury hotel with the added security feature that it is on an island, at 4 Grove Isle Dr., Coconut Grove 33133, 305/858-8300. **The Biltmore Hotel**, 1200 Anastasia Ave., Coral Gables 33134, 305/ 445-1926. Historic extravaganza, but some of the guest rooms are not up to the main rooms' decor. **Hyatt Regency Coral Gables**, ia a tall, new building that integrates its just built glitziness with the old world feel of the neighborhood, 500 Alhambra Plaza, Coral Gables 33134, 305/ 441- 1234. **Sonesta Beach Hotel and Tennis Club**, self-contained resort on a fabulous beach at 350 Ocean Drive, Key Biscayne 33149, 305/361-2021. **Alexander Hotel**, sophisticated and antique-filled hotel with ocean or bay views from every room. 5225 Collins Avenue, Miami Beach 33140, 305/ 865-6500. **Turnberry Isle Yacht and Country Club**. Ideal if you want to run into tennis players; Jimmy Connors and John McEnroe have condos here, 19735 Turnberry Way, North Miami Beach 33163, 305/932-6200. **Sheraton** Royal Biscayne Beach Resort and Racquet Club. A beachfront resort surrounded by coconut palms. 555 Ocean Drive, Key Biscayne 33149, 305/361- 5775.

MODERATE TO BUDGET: **Hotel Place St. Michel**, small and private with antiques from all over the world. 162 Alcazar, Coral Gables 33134, 305/444-1666. **Park Central Hotel**, a jewel of an Art Deco hotel, located at 640 Ocean Drive, Miami Beach 33139, 305/538-1611. Other choice Art Deco District hotels: **The Avalon**, 700 Ocean Drive, Miami Beach 33139, 305/538-0133. **The Carlyle, Leslie** and **Cardozo**, are located at 1250, 1244 and 1300 Ocean Drive, respectively, owned by the same group. Phone 305/534-2135 for information. And the **Cavalier**, another small hotel built in the Deco-style, is favored by photographers. 1320 Ocean Drive, 305/531-6424.

Restaurants

Joe's Stone Crab, 227 Biscayne Street at Washington Ave., Miami Beach, 305/673- 0365. The most famous and therefore most crowded restaurant in town, serving the area's indigenous stone crab as it has been doing since 1913. Joe's closes when the crab is not in season, from mid-May to mid-October. Plan to wait on line for at least an hour for a table, a hassle, but worth it for a great meal. Hint: Savvy diners order stone crabs cold with Joe's mustard sauce. **Monty Trainer's Bayshore Restaurant**, Lounge and Raw Bar, 2560 South Bayshore Drive, Coconut Grove, 305/858-1431. Seafood emporium with an outdoor marina-side raw bar. **Chef Allen's**, 19088 N.E. 29th Avenue, North Miami Beach, 305/ 935-2900. Sublime, sophisticated and expensive New American cuisine. **Versailles**, 5535 S.W. 8th Street, 305/445-7614. A lively, casual Cuban restaurant. **The Malaga**, 740 S.W. 8th, 305/858-4224, also serves Cuban food in a slightly more upscale environment. **Tropics International**, Edison Hotel, 960 Ocean Drive, Miami Beach 305/531-5335, a fun place with an open-air patio for people watching in the breeze. **Cafe Chauveron**, 9561 E. Bay Harbour Drive, Bay Harbor Islands, 305/866-8779. A romantic French restaurant. **Wolfie's**, 2038 Collins Avenue, Miami Beach, 305/538-6626. Huge, open 24-hours-a-day, this Jewish delicatessen is a Miami Beach landmark. **Rascal House**, 172nd Street and Collins Avenue, Miami Beach. No need to call here; there is always a line of customers waiting for a table at this cavernous 37-year old Jewish delicatessen, which is among the top-ten grossing restaurants in the United States. Open 7 am-2 am daily. Huge servings, monster corned beef on rye, mountainous slabs of cherry cheesecake.

Getting Around

The first thing that any visitor needs to know is that Miami and Miami Beach are separate entities. The city of Miami is on the mainland; Miami Beach is actually a cluster of islands linked to the mainland by a range of causeways. Altogether, 26 separate communities comprise what is known as Greater Miami, organized on a grid quadrant system, SE, SW, NE and NW.

To keep from being overwhelmed, visitors might want to take a tour for an overview. There are a number available. **Miami Vision**, 2699 Collins Ave., Miami Beach, telephone 305/532-0040, does the whole city tour and throws in a couple of attractions. Guides speak English, German, French, Portuguese, Spanish and Italian. The **Old Town Trolley** tour transports tourists around Miami and Miami Beach in, as they say, an old trolley, Box 12985, Miami, 305/374-8687. **The Miami Design Preservation League**, 1201 Washington Avenue, Miami Beach 33119, phone 305/672-2014, has a Saturday morning walking tour of the Art Deco District.

GUIDEPOST MIAMI / MIAMI BEACH

Sightseeing

Metrozoo, 12400 S.W. 152nd Street, Miami, 305/251-0400. White Bengal tigers, gorillas, koalas, etc., wander in man-made approximations of their natural habitats in this 290-acre zoo. **Miami Seaquarium**, Rickenbacker Causeway, Key Biscayne, 305/361- 5703. Home to more than 10,000 sea creatures including sharks and dolphins. **Planet Ocean**, 3979 Rickenbacker Causeway, Key Biscayne, 305/361-9455. A marine science museum that is very interesting. **Spanish Monastery**, 16711 W. Dixie Highway, North Miami Beach, 305/945-1462. A real monastery, and a real Spanish one, built in Segovia in 1141. Publishing tycoon William Randolph Hearst bought it and brought it over here in pieces. **Hialeah Park**, 105 E. 21st Street, Hialeah, 305/885-8000. A thoroughbred racetrack with a French Mediterranean-style clubhouse on 220 flowered acres. Daily free tours when racing is not in session.

Sports Activities

Boating, fishing, swimming, golf, tennis – it would not be a trip to Florida without partaking of at least one of these activities. Sailors should head for Dinner Key in Coconut Grove for hourly or daily rentals of 19- and 22-foot sailboats. Lessons are available. Phone **Dinner Key Marina**, 305/858-4001. Speed boaters may contact **Beach Boat Rentals**, Inc., 2380 Collins Avenue, Miami Beach, 305/534-4307, for 18-foot power boats. For grander designs, **Florida Yacht Charters & Sales**, 1290 5th Street (in the Art Deco District), Miami Beach, 305/ 532-8600, can provide sailboats ranging from 28 to 70 feet, or power boats from 40 to 150 feet. Captains, if you wish, can be chartered along with the vessels. For deep sea fishing, the **Blue Sea II**, 1020 MacArthur Causeway, 305/358-3416 can be chartered for half-day cruises. **Kelley Fishing Fleet**, 10800 Collins Avenue, Miami Beach, 305/945- 0944, offers half- or full-day deep sea fishing trips, as well as 2-3 day jaunts to the Bahamas. **Ocean Type Fishing Charters**, 4035 S.W. 11th Street, Coral Gables, 305/446-8445, rents out a day on the water that can be used as you wish - for trips to the coral reefs for snorkeling, island-hopping, beach-hopping. **Tropic Dive and Sail**, 8346 NW South River Drive, G, Medley, 305/888-3002, has a 15-passenger ship, the *Tropic Diver*, that offers coral reef snorkeling. It leaves from Watson Island, just off the MacArthur Causeway. And, for those who prefer to go solo, windsurfing and jet ski rentals are available at Hobie Beach, 3501 Rickenbacker Causeway, Key Biscayne, 305/361-1225.

Shopping

Mayfair Shops in the Grove, 2911 Grand Avenue, Coconut Grove, a beautifully designed open air mall with 74 intensely upscale shops. **Bayside Marketplace**, 401 Biscayne Boulevard, downtown. Everything for everybody. **Bal Harbour Shops**, 9700 Collins Avenue, Bal Harbour. Haute shopping at haute prices. **Miami Fashion District**, 5th Avenue from 29th to 25th Street. The opposite of Bal Harbour, factory outlets and discount shops.

Tourist Information

The Greater Miami Convention and Visitors Bureau, Suite 2700, 701 Brickell Avenue, Miami 33131, 305/539-3000.

Access and Transportation

Miami International Airport, 6 miles west of downtown Miami, is the area's big commercial airport. To reach the city center, take the **Metrobus**, metered taxicabs, the **SuperShuttle**, which moves between the airport and hotels, or limousine services.

Guided Tours

For those who decide to forgo that convertible, a number of multi-lingual guided Tours are available in the Greater Miami Area. **Miami Vision**, 2699 Collins Ave. Suite 113, Miami Beach, 305/532-0040, offers a variety of itineraries throughout Miami and Miami Beach, with pickup service available at many hotels. Guides who speak English, French, German, Italian, Portuguese and Spanish are available. *Heritage of Miami* is a gaffrigged wooden schooner that can accommodate about 40 passengers on daily two-hour tours of Biscayne Bay. Contact **Dinner Key Marina**, Miami, phone 305/858-6264. An Art Deco District Tour is conducted one day a week, on Saturdays. It is a walking tour, so wear good walking shoes, and be prepared for hot weather. The tour starts at the welcome center of the **Miami Design Preservation League**, 1201 Washington Street, Miami Beach, and lasts 90-minutes. Fee is $5 and reservations are necessary. Contact **MDPL**, 1236 Ocean Drive, Miami Beach, 305/672-2014. Also available is an **Art Deco District Guide** featuring self-guided walking or driving tours.

Miami Freebies

An organization known as **PACE** (Performing Arts for Community and Education) sponsors a wide-ranging year round schedule of free musical events featuring top names who perform on beaches, in parks or community centers. Phone 805/681-1470 for information and a current schedule of upcoming performances.

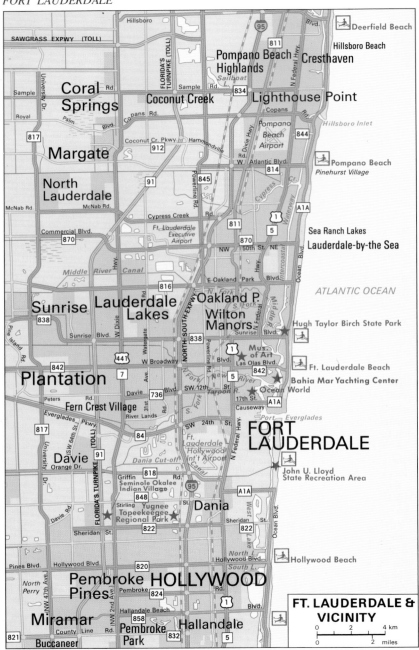

FORT LAUDERDALE

Deerfield Beach

SAWGRASS EXPWY (TOLL)

Hillsboro

811

Blvd.

Hillsboro Beach

Pompano Beach
Highlands

Cresthaven

Sailboat

834

Lighthouse Point

Sample Rd.

Coral
Springs

Coconut Creek

Sample Rd.

Copans

Hillsboro Inlet

817

Royal

Palm

Blvd.

Copans Rd.

Pompano
Beach
Airport

844

Margate

Coconut Cr. Pkwy

Hammondville

912

W. Atlantic Blvd.

Pompano Beach
Pinehurst Village

North
Lauderdale

91

845

814

McNab Rd.

McNab Rd.

Cypress Creek Rd.

Dixie Hwy.

A1A

Commercial Blvd.

870

Ft. Lauderdale
Executive
Airport

811

1

Cypress Cr.

5

Sea Ranch Lakes
Lauderdale-by-the-Sea

Middle River Canal

NW 50th St. NE

870

Pine Island Rd.

816

E Oakland Park Blvd.

ATLANTIC OCEAN

Sunrise

838

Lauderdale
Lakes

Oakland P.
Wilton
Manors

Ocean Blvd.

Hugh Taylor Birch State Park

Sunrise Blvd.

Sunrise Blvd.

838

441

W Broadway

1

Mus.
of Art
Las Olas Blvd.

842

Ft. Lauderdale Beach

842

Plantation

7

Davie Blvd.

SW 12th St.

New River

5

Bahia Mar Yachting Center

736

Ocean World

Fern Crest Village

River Lands

17th St.
Causeway

A1A

Peters Rd.

31st Ave.

S. Fork Tarpon

Everglades Pkwy.

SW 24th St.

Port

Everglades

817

84

FORT
LAUDERDALE

Davie

91

Dania Cut-off

Ft.
Lauderdale
Hollywood
Int'l Airport

N Federal Hwy.

Orange Dr.

Griffin Rd.

818

John U. Lloyd
State Recreation Area

Seminole Okalee
Indian Village

848

Stirling
Topeekeegee
Yugnee
Regional Park

A1A

Dania

822

Sheridan St.

822

West Lake

Sheridan St.

Pines Blvd.

North
Perry

Hollywood Blvd.

820

North L.
Hollywood Blvd.
South L.

Hollywood Beach

Pembroke HOLLYWOOD
Pines

824

Pembroke

1

Blvd.

Miramar

858

County Line Rd.

Hallandale Beach

Hallandale

821

Pembroke
Park

832

5

Buccaneer

FT. LAUDERDALE &
VICINITY

0   2   4 km

0   2   miles

76

FORT LAUDERDALE AND BROWARD COUNTY

Anyone who has seen the 1960s movie *Where the Boys Are* has seen **Fort Lauderdale** – the old Fort Lauderdale. In that kitschy movie, girls came down to the beach during spring break from college to meet boys who were acting like morons. Art, as it were, was following life – spring break had been a huge tradition here for years. Recently, though, the celebrations – meaning the moronic behavior – got so out of hand that the city fathers raised the legal drinking age. And so the college party boys went north – to Daytona Beach. Fort Lauderdale has not been the same since.

Despite the loss in revenues, though, not many are complaining. Fort Lauderdale is a quiet place, it does not have the sprawl, the multi-attractions of Miami. That means it does not have as many tourists - although it has the same scenery and water sports and weather.

Fort Lauderdale Origins

The city sounds like it should be an armed camp. It is not – no military encampments remain. But it was named for an actual fort, built in 1838 by Major William Lauderdale during the Seminole Indian Wars. Years later, in 1893, a trader named Frank Stranahan, regarded as the father of modern Fort Lauderdale, came to the sunny area for his health. The settlement was then known as New River Camp, and he had come to run it.

It did not seem like a big job, the camp consisted, at that point, of three men and the Seminoles, so he started thinking of other ideas. His best was a trading post; he bought pelts and hides from the Seminoles and resold them. Soon native Americans from the Everglades were

Right: Yachting – the favorite sports in Fort Lauderdale.

canoeing down the river to do business. Stranahan loved the quiet life on the river, but it did not remain quiet for long. When Henry Morrison Flagler extended his Florida East Coast Railway from West Palm Beach to Miami, passing through his small settlement, people were drawn to the area and many farming communities sprang up.

One, **Hallandale**, was founded by Swedish settlers in honor of their leader Luther Halland. A few miles north, a group of Danes named their tomato farming acreage **Dania**. In 1904, Dania was incorporated as the first town in what is now **Broward County** and tried to annex its neighbor Fort Lauderdale. The attempt failed but Fort Lauderdale was rattled enough to incorporate itself out of self-protection in 1911. **Pompano Beach** followed, named by a local surveyor after its native fish.

Full-scale progress occurred when former gun runner Napoleon Bonaparte Broward won the governorship in 1904 and embarked on his campaign to drain

the Everglades to create acreage for farming. The first settlement of land that resulted was named **Zona** for reasons nobody knows, then **Panama**, because dredgers had previously worked on the canal. Ultimately, it was renamed, as often happens, after the area's largest landowner, a man named **Davie**.

Through the boom years in the rest of South Florida, the Roaring Twenties, Broward County also prospered, giving rise to the vast development **Hollywood-by-the-Sea** and to the Venice-like islands subdivision of Fort Lauderdale. In the 1950s, though, some canals were dredged and land filled for development, resulting in the new communities of **Plantation, Cooper City, Coral Springs, Sunrise** and **Tamarac**. Today, the population is still growing, with the numbers expected to hit 1.3 million in the 1990s, double what it was 20 years ago. Many of those

Above: A leisurely walk in the evening – the individualist's hour. Right: Enthusiasm for baseball is alive and well.

residents are retirees and many services are geared to that clientele.

For example, nearly every restaurant offers an "Early Bird Special", which is a bargain-priced dinner for diners who arrive between 5 pm and 7 pm. Since many of the elderly residents are not night owls, this works quite nicely, and savings are equal for tourists as for residents. The area does not want the reputation as a final resting place, though, and so is building up its business community. To many, it seems as if Fort Lauderdale and Broward County are just building, which can make driving around here a nightmare. Many of the roads are being widened, and the airport was recently enlarged. Actually, driving in the cities around Fort Lauderdale with their large number of retirees can be hazardous.

An Overview

Fort Lauderdale likes to call itself "the Venice of America" because it has so many canals – 300 miles of inland canals. Cruising on them can be the best introduction to the area.

You could take the *Jungle Queen*, a would-be old steamboat that travels through the center of Fort Lauderdale. It leaves from Bahia Mar dock on Route A1A: The *Paddlewheel Queen*, another cruiser carries sightseers along the Intracoastal Waterway from 2950 N.E. 30th Street.

Another possibility is taking a water taxi; if you have a knowledgeable and talkative skipper, you will get all the sightseeing you need. Taxis can be hailed from the shore along A1A, picked up at hotels or called. And at Christmas time Fort Lauderdale hosts a boat parade on the intra-coastal that is one of the highlights of the season.

For many, though, seeing is less important than sunning. The area has 23 miles of beaches and the sand remains the prime destination. Now that the hard-

drinking kids are gone, the famous beach on the Fort Lauderdale strip from Las **Olas Boulevard** to **Sunrise Boulevard** is a beauty. The shops along the strip, though, are a nightmare: garish and junky, as the student revelers liked. This is where you can stock up on t-shirts or tacky souvenirs. Anyone for a rubber alligator? The area is in the midst of a transformation, to make it more appealing to the more discriminating tourist.

Another beach is in the middle of a park, the **John U. Lloyd Beach State Recreation Area**, located at 6503 N. Ocean Drive, Dania. Besides swimming, fishing and canoeing are available, in one of the more natural areas left amid the urban megalopolis that is growing from Miami to the Palm Beaches and beyond, along the southeastern coast of the state. For more serious fishing, head north to **Pompano Beach** and the rebuilt **Fisherman's Wharf**; extending 1080 feet into the Atlantic, it is believed to be the longest fishing pier in Florida. If you want your fishing in even deeper seas, though, you can charter a boat in Pompano Beach at the **Hillsboro Inlet**, or at the **Bahia Mar Yachting Center** in Fort Lauderdale.

Fish are not the only items of interest under the sea. Divers here look for wrecks, or for the sea life attracted by intentionally sunk wrecks. Perhaps the most famous of recent years is the **Mercedes**, a 200-foot freighter that had the bad luck to wash ashore on a Palm Beach socialites' beach. Numerous unsuccessful removal efforts made headlines for weeks. It is now submerged in 100 feet of water a mile off Fort Lauderdale Beach. Nearby is another vessel, the **Poinciana**, lying tilted on its side. Sinking boats is not just a perverse diversion, though; there actually are beneficial effects – coral grows on sunken ships, and where the coral grows, fish will appear, regenerating a depleted coral reef. There are currently 17 reef sites for inspection.

Would-be divers interested in several hour dives or dive/hotel packages can report to Lauderdale Diver, 1334 S.E. 17th

Street Causeway, Fort Lauderdale 33316, or Pro Dive, which works in conjunction with the Bahia Mar Resort and Yachting Center, A1A, Fort Lauderdale, 33316.

This is also a major area for golf, with many resorts such as the **Diplomat** in Hollywood and **Inverrary** offering golf packages. There are also a number of public courses on offer .

For rainy day amusements, go indoors and indulge – the area has two major spas and spa facilities are open to the public on a daily basis: The **Sheraton Bonaventure Resort and Spa** in Fort Lauderdale, 250 Racquet Club Drive, and the **Palm-Aire Spa Resort** in Pompano Beach, 2501 Palm-Aire Drive N. Exercise programs, herbal wraps, massages and facials can be arranged, as can longer stays.

Other non-sun activities include a visit to the **Seminole Okalee Indian Village**, a reservation of the Seminole tribe, where crafts are sold, alligators are wrestled for the public's amusement and a hot bingo

Above: Retirees can be found at all places.

game is held three times a day, at 4150 N. Route 7, Hollywood.

Nearby is another preserve of the Seminole, the **Anhinga Indian Museum and Art Gallery**, where artifacts are displayed and contemporary art and crafts are sold, at 5791 S. Route 7.

And for smokers, the Seminoles sell cigarettes at prices lower than retail stores. Just drive along **Hollywood Boulevard**, north of the city of Hollywood, and watch for the garish signs.

If native Americans are based in Hollywood, would-be cowboys hold forth in Davie. The popularity of horses around here gave rise to an all pervasive Western flavor, complete with a town hall flanked by cactus – not a native plant – hitching posts. And swinging saloon doors serve as the entrance to the Town Council chambers. Even the local McDonald's has hitching posts and a ride-through for customers on horseback.

If you want to get into proper gear, the town has plenty of Western wear stores. Then you can head to the rodeo, held every Friday night at the domed **Davie Rodeo Arena**, located at 6591 S.W. 45th Street, Davie.

Nightlife

Besides the rodeo, the area has a very popular destination at night: the **Dania Jai-Alai Palace**, where you can bet on one of the fastest moving sports – it looks like suped-up racquetball, at 301 East Dania Beach Blvd, Dania.

If your taste runs more to music than gambling, try the **Musician's Exchange Downtown Cafe**, a small club that features local bands as well as big name jazz, rock, folk and reggae artists and groups just passing through. 729 W. Sunrise Blvd., Fort Lauderdale.

For theater, pre- or post-Broadway productions can be seen at the **Parker Playhouse**, 707 N.E. 8th Street, Fort Lauderdale.

FORT LAUDERDALE / BROWARD COUNTY
Accommodation

LUXURY: **Pier 66 Resort and Marina**, 2301 S.E. 17th Street, Fort Lauderdale 33316, 305/525-6666. Circular high-rise overlooking the Intracoastal Waterway and fantasy pleasure boats. **Westin Cypress Creek**, 400 Corporate Drive, Fort Lauderdale 33334, 305/772-1331. Flashy business hotel with a lobby inspired by an Egyptian temple. **Inverrary Hotel and Conference Center**, 3501 Inverrary Blvd. Lauderhill 33319, 305/485-0500. Fountains, marble, crystal chandeliers. **Marriott's Harbor Beach Resort**, a deluxe tower set against 16 acres of oceanfront at 3030 Holiday Drive, Fort Lauderdale 33316, 305/525-4000.

EXPENSIVE: **Diplomat Resort and Country Club**, huge all-facilities area classic, located at 3515 S. Ocean Drive, Hollywood 33019, 305/457-8111. Riverside Hotel, small, European style hotel on Fort Lauderdale's best shopping street, at 620 E. Las Olas Blvd. 33301, 305/467-0671. **Bahia Mar Resort and Yachting Center**, 801 Seabreeze Blvd, Fort Lauderdale 33316, 305/764-2233. Terrific views of the Intracoastal and the ocean. *MODERATE TO BUDGET:* Holiday Inn **Fort Lauderdale Beach**, 999 North Atlantic Blvd., Fort Lauderdale 33304, 305/563-5961. **Hollywood Beach Hilton**, on the Intracoastal, at 4000 S. Ocean Drive, Hollywood 33019, 305/458-1900.

Restaurants

Cap's Place, Cap's Dock, 2765 N.E. 28th Ct., Lighthouse Point, 941-0418. Fresh seafood in an island beach shanty; the restaurant's launch takes you out. Popular with Roosevelt and Churchill during World War II; JFK after. **Burt and Jack's**, Berth 23, Port Everglades, Fort Lauderdale, 305/564-3663. One of area resident Burt Reynolds' contributions – a Spanish villa with steaks and seafood. **Le Dome**, 333 Sunset Drive, Fort Lauderdale, 305/463-3303. Chic, rooftop restaurant with nouvelle American cuisine. **Cafe Max**, 2601 E. Atlantic Blvd., Pompano Beach, 305/782-0606, California cuisine. **Shirttail Charlie's**, 400 S.W. 3rd Avenue, Fort Lauderdale, 305/463-3474. Casual dockside cafe with fresh seafood. **Shooter's Waterfront Cafe U.S.A.**, 3033 N.E. 32nd Ave, Fort Lauderdale, 305/566-2855. Lively restaurant with seafood and Mexican food. **La Rumba**, 6224 Johnson Street, Hollywood, 305/989-6250, Cuban cuisine.

Sightseeing

Butterfly World is a 2.8-acre property which houses a screened-in tropical rain forest that is home to 150 species of butterflies. Guided tours are available. 3600 W. Sample Road, Coconut Creek, 305/977-7400. And there is a wonderful sea creature that calls the warm waters off Fort Lauderdale home. These are manatees, which are large mammals that grow up to 15 feet long, weighing as much as 1000 pounds, or more. These gentle creatures love to play near the surface of the water and a particularly good spot to see them is at the Port Everglades power plant of the Florida Power and Light Company. The power company discharges warm water which attracts the manatees when the temperature of the sea water drops below 68° F. A free observation deck is open to the public year-round.

Shopping

This is mall country and the spiffiest is the **Galleria** on Sunrise Boulevard, just west of the Intracoastal. All the top shops plus upscale department stores such as Neiman-Marcus, Lord and Taylor, and Saks Fifth Avenue are here. For other upscale shops, walk Las Olas Boulevard from S.E. 5th Avenue to one block past the Himmarshee Canal. The brick sidewalks and palm trees also make it scenic.

Tourist Information

The main tourist office is the **Greater Fort Lauderdale Convention and Visitors Bureau**, 500 E. Broward Blvd, Suite 104, Fort Lauderdale, FL 33394, 305/765-4466. **Greater Fort Lauderdale Chamber of Commerce**, PO Box 14516, Fort Lauderdale 33302, 305/462-6000. **Coral Springs Chamber of Commerce**, 7305 W. Sample Road, 110, Coral Springs 33065, 305/752-4242. **Dania Chamber of Commerce**, PO Box 838, Dania 33004, 305/927-3377. **Davie-Cooper City Chamber of Commerce**, 4185 Southwest 64th Ave, Davie 33314, 305/518-0790. **Greater Deerfield Beach Chamber of Commerce**, 1601 East Hillsboro Blvd, Deerfield Beach 33441, 305/427-1050. **Greater Hollywood Chamber of Commerce**, PO Box 2345, Hollywood 33022, 305/ 920-3330.

Parks

Hugh Taylor Birch State Recreation Area, 3109 East Sunrise Boulevard, Fort Lauderdale 33304, 305/564-4521. **John U. Lloyd Beach State Recreation Area**, 6503 North Ocean Drive, Dania 33004, 305/923-2833

Access and Transportation

Flying into Fort Lauderdale takes you to the Fort Lauderdale Hollywood Airport, once a sleepy little airport, now an ever expanding monster. There is slight bus service. Many travelers prefer limousine service to all points in Broward County, or taxis.

81

THE PALM BEACHES

If ever a name was synonymous with society, it is **Palm Beach**. Elegant, expensive, exclusive, it is a land of mansions, Rolls Royces, glittering balls that harken back, in scale, to the Gilded Age.

Henry Flagler, the Standard Oil co-owner and owner of the Florida East Coast Railway who was so instrumental in developing Florida's coast, essentially created Palm Beach as a winter resort for his friends, the rich and famous of their time. He built a hotel for them, the **Royal Poinciana**, in 1894 and in 1896 built another called **The Breakers**. It was wood – Flagler had a passion for wooden hotels – and so it burned down. It was rebuilt and burned down again. In 1926, the heirs of Flagler's widow decided to put an end to inflammable hotels and rebuilt the hotel in stone. Today it stands as the centerpiece of Palm Beach's grandeur.

The area is not all high end, though, which is the reason people stress the name as the Palm Beaches, not just Palm Beach. Flagler built **West Palm Beach**, a city across **Lake Worth**, to house the servants of the Palm Beach mansions; today it is the commercial center and the place where the more down to earth reside. To the south **Boca Raton**, upscale but not rigidly affluent, is a showcase of the Spanish Revival style of pioneering architect Addison Mizner. To the north **Palm Beach Gardens** is a paradise for golfers. Farther north, Jupiter houses the **Burt Reynolds Dinner Theatre** and is relatively undeveloped

But first in interest and curiosity is the inevitable Palm Beach. To fit in, dress conservatively and be very quiet – this is a town that takes its noise laws very seriously. Car horns are not honked here. Even the tennis ball machines are not operated indiscriminately; there are rules for the times in which that noise may

Left: Palm tree – a welcome beach parasol.

occur, 9 am-5:30 pm in season, December through April; 8 am-6 pm the rest of the year. Never, never in the evening. Residents take pains to stay within the laws too; one woman, afraid of violating the rules, even had her parrot's decibel level tested by the police. To test him, the police ventured forth from what may be the prettiest precinct house in America – an elegant pink stucco house, surrounded by palms – and stood outside her kitchen window. The parrot just passed.

To get the true sense of Palm Beach, the best place to start may well be **The Breakers**. It may remind you of a grand Italian villa, or – if you have traveled in Italy – several specific villas: the exterior is copied from the Villa Medici in Florence, the gardens and courtyard are similar to the ones at Villa Sante in Rome, and the Mediterranean Ballroom is inspired by Genoa's Palazzo Deg'l Imperial.

To learn more about the hotel, the area and Henry Flagler, guests can take the tour conducted by Jim Ponce, the hotel historian, every Wednesday. The tour begins in the south loggia on the ground floor, with a discussion of Flagler's development of the east coast of Florida: from his first hotel, the Ponce de Leon in St. Augustine in 1888, to his railroad, the Florida East Coast Railway. Flagler's goal for the railroad was Key West, the state's, and the country's, southernmost point, and when his trains reached it in 1912, he announced that he could now die happy. He did, the following year.

Moving through the rooms, Ponce also points out the lavish decorations – from handpainted ceiling frescoes to fifteenth century Flemish tapestries – and the hotel's brushes with historic events. A private club met during Prohibition above the Florentine dining room – the reason that windows looking out but providing no looking in are visible near the ceiling; and the hotel served briefly as a (lavish) hospital during World War II.

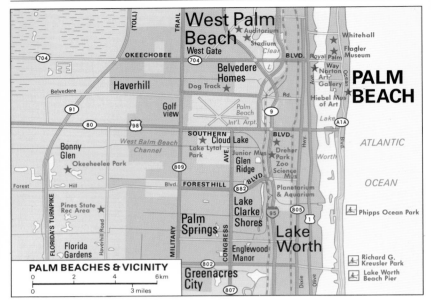

During this time, German submarines also cruised just off the beach.

To get a more in-depth look at lavishness as it applied to Henry Flagler, go over to **Whitehall**, Coconut Row at Whitehall Way. This 73-room mansion is opulence incarnate, a palace built by Flagler, then 71, in 1901 at a cost of $2.5 million (it's now assessed at over $12 million) as a wedding present for his third wife Mary Lily Kenan. He then spent another $1.5 million furnishing it with Baccarat crystal chandeliers, silk damask wallpaper, seven different types of Italian marble and much antique furniture from Europe. As you walk through it, you are awed by the luxury of it, made even more remarkable by the fact that this was intended as a vacation house, for use only in January through March.

If Whitehall whets your appetite for mansions, there is an unending string of them on Ocean Boulevard; you can drive

Right: One of the posher hotels in the United States – The Breakers.

slowly and stare. Standing out in a pretty grand field is **Mar-a-Lago** at 1100 S Ocean, breakfast cereal heiress Marjorie Merriweather Post's 128-room mansion built in 1927 on 16 acres of land. Tycoon Donald Trump bought the estate a few years ago and immediately discovered that despite its extravagance, it was noisy – it is straight in the flight path to the West Palm Beach Airport. Reportedly, he tried to have the flight path moved but scored a rare defeat.

On the north end of the street is an estate owned by a family held in much higher regard, the Kennedys. Their estate at 1095 N. Ocean Boulevard served as the Florida White House during John Kennedy's tenure as President, and traffic usually jammed as the curious lined up to take a look. They also often stopped for a drink – JFK nieces Maria Shriver and Sydney Lawford, showing their grandfather's entrepreneurial spirit, set up a lemonade stand in front of the estate.

For a more relaxing view of different mansions, you can take a paddleboat up

the Intracoastal starting from **Phil Foster Park** on **Singer Island**, north of Palm Beach. (Island Queen Riverboat Cruises, 1250 E. Blue Heron Blvd., Riviera Beach, 407-842-0882.) These mansions front Lake Worth and their famous owners are identified. One belonged to John Lennon and Yoko Ono.

Also identified is a small island of some historic note: **Peanut Island**, where a bomb shelter was built for the obviously pessimistic Kennedys during the Cuban Missile Crisis.

Also of some historic note, and definitely of shopping note, is **Worth Avenue**, extending in from Ocean Boulevard. It is hard to top such concentrated wealth: every major name in upscale retailing is here, from Porthault, Pratesi, Laura Ashley, Hermes and Chanel to a disproportionately large number of fine jewelers. Of special note: Hamilton Jewelers, where the largest impulse buy on the street was recorded: a diamond necklace for $1.6 million.

It is also hard to imagine looking at

"The Avenue" that it had very humble beginnings. At the turn of the century it was the site of **Joe's Alligator Farm**, a tourist attraction whose proprietor "Alligator Joe" Frazier collected 6000 alligators and wrestled a number of them for spectators. Towards the end of World War I, though, "Alligator Joe" sold the land to local resident and sewing machine heir Paris Singer who planned to build a veterans' hospital on it.

Singer hired his friend, society architect Addison Mizner to design it but Mizner took so long with his plans that by the time he finished, the war was over and few veterans wanted to use it. So they turned the hospital into the exclusive Everglades Club and Mizner built elegant, Spanish style shops and apartments leading up the Avenue to it.

Today, those shops are filled not just with famous names but also with one of a kind items. Worth checking out: **The Summerhouse** at 319 Worth stocks antique porcelain, silver and accessories; **Donald Bruce** at #237 stocks an eclectic

variety of indulgences, from quail eggs to an $1100 14k gold stole. Bruce, whose family came to Palm Beach in 1928, is also an unofficial, irreverent historian of the area. At **Frances Brewster**, 259 Worth, you find outrageously opulent evening gowns, perfect for society galas. At **D. Kylene**, you find upscale women's sportswear, Yankee, a parrot with a scandalous vocabulary, and owner Kylene Barker Brandon, Miss America, 1979. As you walk, pay attention to the offshoots of the street, designed and named, like tiny Italian streets - Via Parigi, Via Roma, Via de Mario, etc. Exquisite shops and cafés are tucked away at the ends of Mizner's quaint streets.

To see more of Addison Mizner's designs, a good place to stop, as well as to stay, is the **Boca Raton Resort** in the town of the same name. This somewhat outrageous pink complex was Mizner's dream, "the greatest resort in the world, a happy combination of Venice and Heaven, Florence and Toledo, with a little Greco-Roman glory and grandeur thrown in", as he described it.

It was, when it opened as the Spanish-styled Cloister Inn in 1926, the most expensive 100-room hotel in the world. Mizner furnished it elegantly, with his own Spanish antiques, and celebrities flocked there – in part because of Mizner himself. Totally charming and eccentric, he would walk the grounds dressed in silk pajamas, leading around a few of his pets – monkeys, macaws, chows, chimpanzees. Mizner's reign ended after one season, though, when the Florida land boom went bust and he went bankrupt. His Cloister Inn re-opened under a new owner as the Boca Raton Hotel and Club.

Nightlife

If you are looking for activity after (or during) dinner, a popular spot is the **Palm Beach Kennel Club** (a.k.a. the dog track) in West Palm Beach, near the air-

Above: Beauty-contest: who will win? Right: Honeymoon at the beach.

port, at 1111 Congress Avenue. It may sound and seem cruel but the kennel personnel insist that the dogs really need to race. Some may have doubts. Betting is also rather complicated. You can ignore the whole thing and just concentrate on dinner, all American hearty steaks in their restaurant, the Paddock.

Other possibilities for nightlife include the traditional – bars like **Bradley's**, on Bradley Place in Palm Beach, a subdued place with an open air patio, or **Alligator Joe**, 132 North County Road, which has live music and dancing.

Another activity is slightly more adventurous. If it is the right time of year (May through September) you can go on a nocturnal tour up on **Jupiter beach**. The Loggerhead turtles come ashore during those months to deposit their eggs in the sand, and observation trips – observing from a distance without bothering the turtles – are arranged through the Jupiter Beach Hilton, on Indiantown Road and A1A, Jupiter. Consult them for times.

Turtles for Posterity

Even in this age of Teenage Mutant Ninja Turtles it probably seems at least a little strange that some 200 of the most prized residents of this bastion of the ultra-wealthy are supporters of several perilously endangered species of giant sea turtles. But guilt can do strange things to people. There is no doubt that at least part of the blame for the turtles near demise comes from the rampant development along Florida's Atlantic coast, destroying annual breeding grounds in the march of progress. Yet somehow, the **Jupiter Beach Hilton** beach front remains smooth and rock-free, gently sloping and well-protected by coastal vegetation, just the way these remaining loggerhead, leatherback and green sea turtles – some fifty years old and weighing 350 pounds – like it. Swimming ashore from deeper water, some from far distant waters of New York, South America and the Caribbean, females enter the hotel harbor-reef to dig their nests in the sand.

The hotel takes great pains to promote the environmental and conservation concerns surrounding this prehistoric ritual, along with no effort spared to toot their own horn for the obvious potential of visitors at a special time of year – a traditionally "soft" time of year, too, and so all the better to fill rooms at a time when bookings are generally at their lowest. It is all in their best interest, of course. The slow-moving creatures chose this beach long before bipeds seeking sun and sand for recreation.

In fact, the seasonal appearance of the giant sea turtles lumbering out of the depths for procreation used to startle unwary guests from late-May through September in the days before the "Turtle Watch" became a certified attraction.

To mention nothing of what the sight and curiosity of humans did to upset the turtles. Out of every 100 eggs produced, only a few survive. Humans, of course,

Above: Turtles are said to reach a biblical age.

poking and prying, pose one of the greatest threats to the turtles, along with predatory animals, storms, ocean currents and perhaps saddest of all, coastal pollution.

The "Turtle Watch" program is one effort to reinstate nature's balance. Overseen by Florida's Department of Natural Resources, it is headed by a licensed marine researcher. Along with endeavors to preserve and protect the turtles, programs offered from human visitors include evening slide lectures, giving background information on the turtles, their habits and the ongoing work to protect them, guided nocturnal tours of nesting sites along the hotel's beach, daytime patrols of egg hatcheries where protective incubation pens have been set up, and organized releasing of baby hatchlings into the sea, always a popular event.

In addition to "Turtle Watch", the **Marine Science Center** in **Juno Beach** is a small marine biology museum and aquarium featuring exhibits especially designed for children.

THE PALM BEACHES
Accommodation

LUXURY: **The Breakers**, 1 S. County Road, Palm Beach 33480, 407/655-6611. Elegant and formal. **The Brazilian Court**, 301 Australian Avenue, Palm Beach 33480, 407/655-7740. Low-key, low-rise yellow Mediterranean style buildings with private, leafy courtyards. The management takes pride in its discretion – as a result, David – son of Robert - Kennedy's death from a drug overdose here was very unwanted publicity. **The Colony**, 155 Hammon Avenue, Palm Beach 33480, 407/655-5430, small, elegant European style hotel recently reopened, just off Worth Avenue. **Boca Raton Resort and Club**, 501 E. Camino Real, Boca Raton 33432, 407/395-3000. Pink palace with all sporting facilities. **PGA Sheraton Resort**, 400 Avenue of the Champions, Palm Beach Gardens 33418, 407/627-2000. A golfer's paradise with five PGA courses. **Palm Beach Polo and Country Club**, 13198 Forest Hill Blvd., West Palm Beach 33414, 407/798-7000. You do not have to play polo to stay in one of the luxury villas.

MODERATE TO BUDGET: **Singer Island Oceanfront Holiday Inn Resort**, 3700 North Ocean Dr., Singer Island 33404, 407/848- 3888.

Restaurants

Charley's Crab, 1000 N. Federal Highway, Jupiter, 407/744-4710. A huge waterfront seafood extravaganza. One of several in the area. **Chuck and Harold's**, 207 Royal Poinciana Way, Palm Beach, 407/659-1440. An outdoor cafe in the center of town, also open for breakfast and lunch. The **Dining Room** of the Brazilian Court is a sophisticated, expensive restaurant with dishes based on local ingredients. 401 Australian Avenue, Palm Beach. **The Breakers**, specifically for Sunday brunch.

Sports and Outdoor Activities

It is possible to stay in this area and only look at bastions of wealth - but it can, after a while, drive you crazy. This is where nature, the great leveler, comes in. Palm Beach is located at the tip of the Everglades and there is a short (half-hour) but interesting wildlife-spotting ride through the Loxahatchee Wildlife Reserve south of Palm Beach in Delray Beach. You travel in airboats, ear splittingly noisy things that require earplugs for passengers but do not seem to bother the animals. It is best to go early. More wildlife sightings occur during the morning, but even if you go in late afternoon, you are bound to see at least a few alligators and birds. And by see, that means up close. You get so close to the alligators that you can count the scales on their backs. For complete information contact **Loxahatchee Wildlife Reserve**, Lox Road, west of Rte. 441, 305/426-2474. If it is polo season, January through April, you might want to take in a game at **Palm Beach Polo**, a club of such note that polo fanatic Prince Charles plays there and stays there when he is in town. 13240 Southshore Blvd., West Palm Beach, 407/798-7605. Croquet is also fun although the real game is harder and more exacting than the backyard variety; it takes real muscle and strategy. Professional croquet lawns and lessons are available at the **Sheraton PGA Resort** in Palm Beach Gardens, north of Palm Beach. Players are advised to wear white. 400 Avenue of the Champions, Palm Beach Gardens, 407/627-2000. If fish are more one's interest, you can also charter a boat for deep sea fishing north of Palm Beach at **Sailfish Marina**, 98 Lake Drive, Palm Beach Shores, 407/844- 4356, as well as at the B-Love **Fishing Marina**, 314 East Ocean Avenue, Lantana, 407/588-7612.

Shopping

Besides glittering Worth Avenue, there is a glittering mall on Worth Avenue: The Esplanade near the end of the street. This small structure houses stores such as Saks Fifth Avenue, Ralph Lauren, all the right names.

Access and Transportation

Flyers arrive in Palm Beach via Palm Beach International Airport, another tiny airport that expands by the year. Palm Beach Transportation provides taxis and limousines.

Tourist Information

For more information about Palm Beach County, contact the Palm Beach County Convention and Visitors Bureau, 1555 Palm Beach Lakes Boulevard, Suite 204, West Palm Beach, FL 33401, 305/471- 3995.

Museums

Norton Gallery of Art, 1451 South Olive Avenue, West Palm Beach, 33401, 407/832-5194, is considered one of Floridas's major cultural attractions. Permanent exhibits are supplemented by a temporary exhibits year-round. Open Tuesday through Saturday, 10:00 am to 5:00 pm, Sunday, 1:00 pm to 5:00 pm. Admission free. French or Spanish speaking tour guides are available. **South Florida Science Museum**, 4801 Dreher Trail North, West Palm Beach, 33405, 407/832-1988, features permanent and temporary hands-on science exhibits for children and adults, science demonstrations, planetarium shows and the **South Florida Aquarium**. Open Tuesday through Saturday, 10:00 am to 5:00 pm, Sunday, noon to 5:00 pm, Friday, 6:30 pm to 10:00 pm. Admission free.

THE FLORIDA KEYS

We profess a long standing love affair with the Keys: for the pale turquoise of the shallows and the ink-blue gulfstream; for skies that make the palm fronds greener and the coral rock and sand beaches whiter. For bougainvillaea's pinks, corals, and purples, for thatch palm, gumbo limbo and seagrape; for soaring eagles, man-of-war birds, formation-flying pelicans, and kingfishers on telephone wires; for seafans, corals, angelfish, grouper.

We love the gingerbread houses built in the Bahamas and the sense of history at Indian Key Archaeological Site, Mel Fisher's Treasure Museum, and Fort Jefferson in the Dry Tortugas; for the tranquility of an afternoon sail in Florida

Bay, the rhythmic dip of the paddle through mangrove channels, and the excitement of the first big strike while trolling at the edge of the gulfstream.

We look forward to the sunset celebrations in Key West, frozen Margaritas and Jimmy Buffett tunes. The Keys, from *cayo* meaning little islands in Spanish, can be divided into Upper, Middle, Lower Keys and Key West.

Hotels, restaurants and attractions are easily located with the mile marker (MM) system. Key West for example is at MM 0 and Jewfish Creek at MM 108 on Key Largo. Just look for the green and white markers.

As in the rest of Florida, a great deal of development has been allowed to happen along the commercial corridor of the highway, destroying much of the old-fashioned charm the Keys once held.

Diving and fishing are the main activities here besides indulging in every form of laziness. All along the Overseas Highway you'll find marinas where you can rent small boats by the hour or charter a

Preceding pages: Sunset on the Keys. Above: Here man made nature his partner – Seven Mile Bridge. Right: Being different – a must on Key West.

captained boat for deep-sea fishing, diving or back-country exploring.

Upper Keys

Not counting the boat-access only islands of **Biscayne National Park**, the **Upper Keys** begin at **Key Largo** with its crocodile refuge at the northern end and many small, old-fashioned lodges that Miamians prefer along the bay side.

Its main claim to fame is **John Pennecamp Coral Reef State Park** (MM 102.5). It protects a good portion of the only living coral reef in the contiguous United States (see the article on "Natural Areas"). Shipwrecks and reefs with evocative names like The Elbow, Grecian Rocks, and Molasses can be explored by taking one of the park service or private dive charter boats.

For diving, snorkeling and the glass bottom boat trips to the reef, the winds should be calm for the best viewing conditions. Morning hours are usually best, especially in the summer when afternoon thunderstorms are common.

Farther along the road are commercial tourist attractions including the **Theater of the Sea** (MM 84.5), the second oldest marine park in the world, which introduced the bottle-nose dolphins to thousands of visitors. It is a good show if you have never seen performing dolphins or if you like trained animal acts.

Upon leaving **Islamorada**, the highway literally goes out to sea. Originally built to carry the railroad designed by Henry Flagler early in the century, the present highway opened in 1938 after a disastrous hurricane that destroyed much of the track and wreaked incredible havoc in the Keys. Many of the bridges were recently rebuilt, leaving the old ones as convenient fishing piers.

Harking back to earlier times are some nice, old-fashioned picnic shelters and little beaches, perfect spots for wading and swimming. If you venture out with

fins and snorkel, be sure to tow along a small float with a dive-flag so that passing boaters can spot you!

Just past Islamorada off Indian Key Fill (MM 79) are **Indian Key State Historic Site** and **Lignumvitae Key State Botanical Site**, which can be reached by a private rental or park service boat. Lignumvitae Key is a naturalist's paradise with an intact tropical habitat that contains many of the local plant species, birds, butterflies and tree snails.

Long Key, the next large island after leaving Lower Matecumbe, is the site of the **Long Key State Recreation Area** (MM 67.5). Shaded by tall Australian pines, it's a fine spot for a picnic. Put on your bathing suits and enjoy splashing in the shallow waters. Bird watchers may want to take the nature trail or rent a canoe from the rangers to explore the natural riches along the marked trail.

It was here at Long Key that Henry Flagler built his famous fishing club where Western author Zane Grey and other luminaries came to fish.

Middle Keys

This is the area of the long bridges with **Long Key Viaduct** on one end and **Seven Mile Bridge** on the other. In between lies the beauty of the waters.

During the eight long years of building the railroad known as "Flagler's Folly", a worker, upon having to rebuild one more time a roadbed washed away by a hurricane, reputedly exclaimed, "What is this, a Marathon!" Thus a town was named. Eight thousand people live in **Marathon**, which explains the presence of shopping centers and trailer parks along the highway. This strip of commercial development includes the convenience of an airport with daily flights to and from Miami.

Visitors come for the deep-sea fishing tournaments and back-country fishing. Reefs like **Sombrero Reef**, **Coffin's Patch** and **Looe Key**, with their large brain and lettuce corals, as well as multitudes of reef fish, attract many divers.

Lower Keys

Leaving the Middle Keys presents a stunning sight: the Seven Mile Bridge, with a length of 35,830 feet, swings out to sea in a high arch to accommodate the deep ships' channel, paralleling the old bridge, the world's longest fishing pier. At MM 37 you enter **Bahia Honda State Recreation Area** with the finest ocean beach in the Keys. There are cabins for rent here but they are high priced and close to the road. Beach campsites are better, and for a bonus there is the high rising skeleton of the old railroad and car bridge, an impressive sight.

Big Pine Key shelters the **National Key Deer Refuge**. Off the main highway, sightings of this tiny deer are frequent in morning and evening hours, but their numbers are diminishing fast, victims of road accidents and habitat destruction.

Looe Key National Marine Sanctuary, only 6 miles from land, and acces-

sible by dive boat from either Marathon or **Ramrod Key** (MM 27) is, according to many divers, more beautiful than the Penne Camp Reefs.

The Lower Keys have a quiet beauty. The many islands, like **Lower Sugarloaf** and **Saddlebunch Keys**, the **Coupon Bight State Aquatic Preserve** and **Watson Hammock** on Big Pine Key can be explored by canoe or small power boat - a respite before crowded Key West.

Key West

It is ebullient, a haven for artists, writers, free spirits, homosexuals, hippies and at least one million tourists a year. It has a violent history, like the rest of Florida.

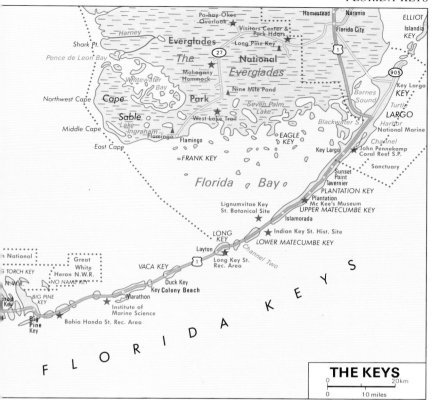

THE KEYS

0   20km

0   10 miles

Possession of the island passed back and forth between the Spanish and British several times. Incredibly lucrative salvage prizes from the many ships that grounded on the reefs and shoals, sponging and cigar-making made **Key West** the richest city per capita in the United States in the nineteenth century.

Yet in the 1930s Key West went bankrupt and its citizens suffered abject poverty from the lethal combination of hurricane destruction of the railroad, depression, labor troubles, sponge disease and the closing of the naval base. People were so poor that many of the old wooden, tumble-down houses here, shadowed by the about a hundred years old Royal Poincianas, remained un-touched until the restoration of the **Audubon House** in 1961 inspired a re-newal of "conch" houses. A number of the early houses had been shipped piecemeal from the Bahamas, others were built from materials as they became available from wrecks. They incorporate the fancies and skills of ship carpenters and a wide variety of architectural and environmental influences, like wide porches, steep roofs, cisterns, shuttered window and rooftop hatches. Some houses have been turned into Bed and Breakfast Inns, the place to stay unless you prefer the elegance of Henry Fla-gler's restored **Casa Marina Resort**.

An influx of new permanent residents, the yuppie and well-to-do individualists

looking for a free and easy lifestyle, is slowly changing Key West to a city of somewhat contrived charm that is encouraging many old "conchs" (natives) who cannot or will not adjust to leave.

Try "sunset" in the early evening at **Mallory Pier**. Where once ferries departed for Cuba, bagpipers, jugglers, fortune tellers and a blend of tourists and locals gather to see the day out before moving on to the many eating and drinking establishments around town.

To see the town, board the **Conch Train**, one of the few relics of old-time tourism. You'll visit the site of the naval base, center of activity during the Spanish American War, the Cuban missile crisis and the Mariel boatlift, as well as **President Harry Truman's Little White House**, the shrimp fleet, beaches and some of the historic houses to which you may want to go back: **Audubon House and Gardens, Wrecker Mu-**

Above: Cocktails and sunset on Key West.
Right: Destroyed by a hurricane.

96

seum, **Mel Fishers' Treasure Museum**, and **Hemingway House**.

Amble through town or acquire a tan on the beach, rent a bicycle, "hang out", eat some eclectic food, spend a day fishing, snorkeling or diving, participate in one of Key West's outrageous festivals, like **Fantasy Fest** in October or **Hemingway Days** in July and you'll know why Key West has our vote for the most unusual vacation spot in Florida.

Dining in Key West

Nowhere is the international appeal of Key West more apparent than in the wide range of dining options available. It is just a hop, skip and jump from Key west to South America, and the flavors of that continent are available in a restored house at 600 Fleming Street at the newest international restaurant in the city, **Cafe Marquesa**. Spicy specialities come from Argentina – Delmonico Steak and Argentine chimichuri; Brazil – black bean and pork stew; as well as Central American

influenced dishes served with red salsa. Reservations are recommended for dinners which average in the $30-$35 range.

Cafe des Artistes is notable for several reasons: the French cuisine that favors local seafood served in the continental style is very good, and dinners can claim bragging rights to eating in what may be the city's most expensive restaurant. Located on the corner of Truman Avenue and Simonton Street, reservations are necessary for those wishing to sample local Florida lobster, grouper or yellowtail tuna, lamb, veal or filet mignon served in one of the more formal dining environments anywhere in the Keys. Bring money. Dinner for two will set you back $100 or more.

Louie's Backyard serves European-style cuisine, with a strong French influence, spiced by the island. Dining is available indoors, but the outdoor patio at 700 Waddell Avenue, overlooking the Atlantic Ocean, is a virtual must for visitors, well worth making sometimes problematical reservations at this popular dining spot where dinner for two should cost a hair under $100.

Also on the list of the best of Key West dining are the following restaurants listed in briefly. **Antonia's**, at 615 Duval Street, specializes in pasta dishes from northern Italy, featuring local seafood, as well as other Mediterranean inspired dishes. Reservations required. Dinners should cost under $30 per person. **Din Sum**, on Key Lime Square, features Indian, Thai, Burmese and Indonesian food. Reservations recommended. Dinners should cost under $25. **El Siboney**, at 900 Catherine Street, is considered Key West's best Cuban restaurant, and a relative bargain, to boot. Dinner costs under $15. **Yer Sake**, on Duval Street, serves Japanese *sushi, teriyaki* and other traditional fare. Reservations are suggested for meals that should cost around $20 per person. For Mexican food try **Pancho and Lefty's Southwestern Cafe**, **El Loro Verde** or **Viva Zapata**. **Bagatelle** serves Caribbean cuisine which may be eaten at a table set on a balmy balcony.

FLORIDA KEYS
Accommodation
Our choice is based on quiet, off the highway location and/or special Keys charm. Listings in
each category are in order of mile marker (MM)
distance from Key West.
LUXURY: **Sheraton Key Largo**, MM 97, Key
Largo 33037, 305/852-5553, 800/325-3535
(US). **Cheeca Lodge**, MM 82, Islamorada
33036, 305/664-4651. **Hawks Cay Resort**, MM
61, Duck Key, 33050, 305/743-7000, 800/327-
7775 (US). **Little Palm Island**, ferry at MM
28.5, Little Torch Key, 33043, 305/872-2524,
800/343-8567. **Marriott's Casa Marina Resort**, 1500 Reynolds St., Key West, 33040, 296-
3535, 800/228-9290 (US).
EXPENSIVE: **Marquesa Hotel**, 600 Fleming
St., Key West 33040, 305/292-1919. **Pier House**,
One Duval Street, Key West, 305/294- 9541,
800/327-8340.
MODERATE TO BUDGET: **Rock Reef Resort**,
MM 98, Key Largo 33037, 305/852-2401. **Kona
Kai**, MM 97.8, Key Largo 33037, 305/852-4629.
The Islander, MM 82.1, Islamorada 33036,
305/664-2031. **Ocean Beach Club**, near MM 54,
399 E. Ocean Dr., Key Colony Beach, 33051,
305/289-0525. **The Buccaneer**, MM 48.5,
Marathon, 33050, 305/743-9071, 800/237-3329
(US). **The Barnacle Bed and Breakfast**, MM
33, Long Beach Road, Big Pine Key, 33043,
305/872-3298. **Looe Key Reef Resort**, MM 27,
Ramrod Key 33043, 305/872-2215. **Duval
House**, 815 Duval St., Key West 33040,
305/294-1666. **Eaton Lodge**, 511 Eaton St., Key
West 33040, 305/294-3800.
Drinking Spots
Bars, from loud and boisterous to quietly sub-
dued are a Key West tradition. **Captain Tony's,
Sloppy Joe's, The Bull** and the **Whistle,
Holiday Inn La Concha, Roof Top Bar.** Open
air bars at the Pier House, Louie's Back Yard.
Festivals
January-March: *Old Island Days*, Key West.
April: *Indian Key Festival*, Indian Key.
July: *Hemingway Days*, Key West.
October: *Fantasy Fest*, Key West.
Restaurants
EXPENSIVE: **Marker 88**, MM 88, 305/852-
9315. **Louie's Backyard**, Key West, 305/294-
1061. **La-Te-Da**, Key West, 305/294-8435.
MODERATE: **Italian Fisherman**, MM 104,
305/451-4471. **Lorelei**, MM 82, 305/664-4657.
Green Turtle Inn, MM 81.5, 305/664-9031.
A&B Lobster House, Key West, 305/294-2536.
BUDGET: **Papa Joe's**, MM 80, 305/664-8109.
El Siboney, Key West, 305/294-2721.

Parks and Attractions
John Pennecamp State Park, MM 102.5,
305/451-1621, 800/432-2871 (FL). **Theater of
the Sea**, MM 84, 305/664-2431. **Indian Key
State Historic Site and Lignumvitae Key**, MM
79, 305/664-4815. **Long Key State Recreation
Area**, MM 67.5, 305/664-4815. **Bahia Honda
State Park**, MM 37, 305/872-2353. **Looe Key
National Marine Sanctuary**, MM 27, Ramrod
Key. **Audubon House**, 205 Whitehe ad, Key
West, 305/294-2225. **Hemingway House**, 907
Whitehead, Key West, 305/294-1575. **Mel
Fisher Maritime Heritage Society Museum**,
200 Greene, Key West, 305/296-9936. **Wreck-
ers Museum**, 322 Duval, Key West.
Shopping
Fastbuck Freddy's for kitsch, costumes and
some good gift items; **Mel Fisher's Gold
Museum Gift Shop** and the **Haitian Art Co.**, the
best Haitian gallery in Florida.
Sightseeing
Conch Tour Train, Key West. **The Trolley**, Key
West. **Key West Sea Plane Service**, 305/294-
6978.
Tourist Information
Florida Keys Information – 800/FLA-KEYS,
For brochures, maps: **Chamber of Commerce
Key Largo**, MM 103.4, Key Largo, 33037,
305/451-1414. **Islamorada**, MM 82.5, Islam-
orada 33036, 305/664-4503. **Marathon**, MM
48.5, 3330 Overseas Highway, Marathon 33050,
305/743-5417. **Lower Keys**, MM 31.9, Big Pine
Key, 305/872-2411. **Key West**, 402 Wall Street,
Key West 33041 305/294-2587.
Access and Transportation
From Miami, Turnpike Extension to US 1, south
to Key West. A scenic detour is Cardsound Road,
south of Florida City, to Route 905 which rejoins
US 1 in the middle of Key Largo. **By Plane**:
Commercial service to Marathon and Key West.
Watersports, Boat Rentals Charters
Wind Surfing of the Florida Keys, MM 104.1,
305/451-3869. **Atlantis Dive Center**, MM
106.5, 305/451-3020. **Divers World**, MM 99.5,
305/451-3200, or 800/445-8331. **Whale Habor
Marina**, MM 83.5, 305/664-4511. **Bud N',
Mary's Fishing Marina**, MM 79.5, 305/664-
2461. **The Diving Site**, MM 53.5, 305/289-1021,
or 800/634-3935. **Faro Blanco Resort**, MM 48,
305/748-9018. **Looe Key Dive Center**, MM 27,
305/872-2215. **Key West Pro Dive Shop**, Garrison Bight Marina, 305/296-3823, or 800/426-
0707. **Princess Fleet**, A & B Lobster, House
Docks, Key West, 305/296-3287, glass bottom
boats. **Yankee Fleet**, Lands End Marina,
305/294-7009. Fishing in Tortuga Banks.

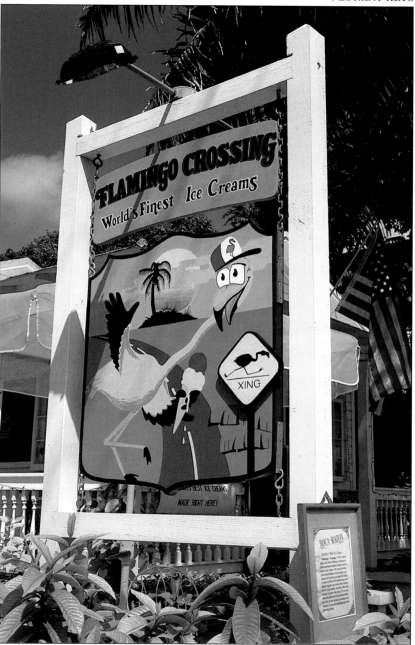

THE EVERGLADES

Forget about Miami, Fort Lauderdale, Palm Beach and Naples. What South Florida is really all about is the **Everglades** – a swath, 60 miles wide and about 120 miles long, of slow-flowing, grass-covered surface water, from **Lake Okeechobee** in the north to the **Ten Thousand Islands** and **Florida Bay** in the south and southwest. At least, that's the way it was until the beginning of the century. It took nature thousands of years since the last ice age to build the saw-grass prairies, the hardwood hammocks, pine-lands, mangrove islands and estuaries, cypress swamps and freshwater sloughs, but in less than a hundred years, we have come close to destroying the entire system!

Today, half of the living Everglades are gone. What we have left are a million and a half acres in **Everglades National Park**. For these precious wetlands, we owe thanks to a few visionaries early in the century who acquired **Paradise Key** and **Royal Palm Hammock**, for the public, in order to save at least a small piece from the loggers and plume hunters who had decimated the wading bird population to a perilous degree.

Not until 1947 were land purchases completed and the National Park, as it exists now, dedicated. Your travels through south Florida will reveal what happened to the rest if you look for it. Sugarcane fields around the lower crescent of Lake Okeechobee pollute the waters downstream. Two major highways, **Alligator Alley** and the **Tamiami Trail**, US 41, cut through and effectively alter the natural flow of water on which the life of the Everglades, Florida's drinking water, and the state's climate depend.

Preceding page: When it comes to publicity, never short on gags. Left: Nature is the dominant factor in the Everglades. Above: Not a rarity – forest-fires in the Everglades.

Florida cities have grown to the edge of the wetlands and beyond. In efforts at flood control, the water supply to the park has been severely compromised, with potentially lethal consequences to life cycles in the Everglades which depend on natural dry spells and flooding at the proper times. Fortunately, the idea that the Everglades are for birds, alligators and a few crank bird watchers, is disappearing. No one denies that this is the eleventh hour for the fragile Everglades, and the challenge to preserve this truly unique wilderness remains. The number of voices heard in defense of conservation is growing, along with people who love and appreciate the stillness and immensity of the grassy waters.

The park service rangers take great pains to introduce first time visitors to the park. Their advice: don't expect imposing vistas, go into slow gear, watch and listen, let the quietude surround you. There is only one road, 38 miles long, from the visitors' center southwest of **Homestead**.

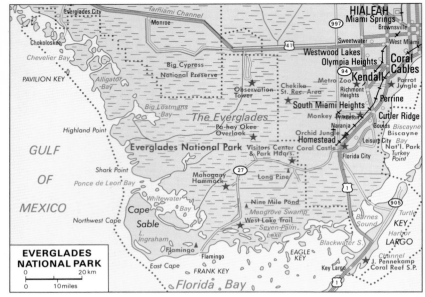

Intelligently written explanations, with pictures, can be found along the road, pointing to views of a particular habitat or community. You can look and become more aware of what you are seeing. You will soon be differentiating between the sawgrass prairie and the dwarf cypress forest, or know the red from the black mangroves and the buttonwoods. It takes practice to recognize the telltale bumps sticking out of the water at **Nine-Mile Pond** as an alligator, even after you have seen his little brother on the **Anhinga Trail** earlier.

You will see birds, anhingas, of course, along the Anhinga Trail boardwalk, together with several varieties of egret: the stately American, the tri-colored, great and little, blue, reddish, green. Less common is the Great White Heron. Farther down, towards Flamingo, on the wide flats of **Snake Bight**, you might, with luck, see a few flamingos that have flown

Right: A peaceful encounter with an alligator in the Everglades swamps.

in from the Bahamas or Hialeah Race Track. The sandbars just in front of the visitors' center and restaurant in Flamingo are especially fertile birding grounds, for sandpipers, black skimmers, the ubiquitous brown pelican squatting on pilings at the marina, or a flock of white pelicans doing their communal fish herding.

To give you an idea why the Glades are so dear to bird watchers: nearly 300 species of birds have been recorded here, made up of winter and year round residents and those who only stop by during spring and fall migration.

The big wading birds are the easiest to identify and the rangers, who lead regular nature walks in the cooler months, will be happy to point them out to you. A good field guide, which you can pick up at the visitors' center book store, and a pair of binoculars will come in handy.

Flamingo is the southernmost outpost on the mainland and the starting point for a full range of outdoor activities, including fishing, birding, canoeing, and hik-

ing. At the marina store you can pick up the bare necessities for a picnic or full day's outing, like coke and beer, matches and sterno, packaged sandwiches, beef stew, and mosquito repellent, which is necessary almost year round, especially when the wind dies down at night.

In Flamingo you camp right on Florida Bay or stay in the modest motel or housekeeping cabins. In the winter months you need to call ahead for a reservation.

Ride the tram or paddle your rental canoe to **Snake Bight** for incomparable wading-bird sightings, or take it up **Buttonwood Canal**, the start for the 7-10 day canoe trip through bays, sloughs and mangrove channels to the park's western gateway in **Everglades City**.

This is an excursion that should not be undertaken lightly. Strenuous paddling, possible adverse weather conditions, primitive camping on platforms or in the mangroves, absolutely no facilities, but what rewards. An easier alternative is a houseboat rental. If you can drive a car, after a one-hour lesson you will be able to

maneuver in protected waters. For a few days you can lose yourself in the channels and wide open stretches of **Coot** or **Whitewater Bay**. Chances to see eagles are excellent with 50 nests recently reported in the park.

Canoeing in the Everglades

There is something utterly relaxing about the gentle "glurp-glurp" sound of a paddle pressing through calm waters, and in many ways that peacefulness makes canoeing in the Everglades an especially intimate way to explore this natural wonderland of the world. Flat-water canoeists flock to many of South Florida's waterways, and nowhere more so than within this national park, so do not expect perfect solitude. In winter, when the temperatures are cooler and the mosquito population dwindles, you will find many other paddlers out there. The seasons of April-May and October-November are recommended. You probably would not want to canoe here in

103

summertime, due to heat, rain and insects, but if you do, you will experience the park and wetlands in as close to their pristine natural state as it is possible to encounter in this day and age. Just do not forget the strongest insect repellent you can find, along with the strongest sunblock. Bring plenty of water. Wear a hat. Forget about a tan. Stay covered up.

Now that you are sufficiently prepared to tackle mother nature, obtain a free permit for overnight camping at Flamingo or Everglades City. Although a permit is not required for day-trips, it is wise to leave word of your plans in case you do not return at the specified time. It is flat water, but still easy to get lost. A word to a friend staying behind, a park ranger, or even a note left behind in your car can prevent a disaster.

Everglades National Park contains five marked canoe trails in the Flamingo area, as well as the southern end of the 100-mile long Wilderness Waterway which

Above: Happy family life in the Everglades.

stretches to Everglades City. Maps, as well as pertinent information on weather predictions and other canoeing conditions, are available at park ranger stations as well as from private outfitters who rent canoes, including the following. Flamingo Lodge Marina and Outpost Resort offers the most services within the park, including 40 canoes that may be rented. In Everglades City, Everglades National Park Boat Tours offers canoe rentals by the half or full-day. They also offer a shuttle service to carry canoeists and canoes to Flamingo, but it is a seven-hour trip costing around $100.

Guided Canoe Trips

As for guided canoeing, North American Canoe Tours at **Glades Haven** offers guided canoe excursions from November 1-March 31. Children under eight years are not accepted, but for those old enough to qualify these trips are approved by the National Park Service. Year-round canoe rentals are also available.

Main Entrance
Access
Drive south on the Florida Turnpike Extension to US 1. Turn west on Palm Drive and follow route 9336 for 11 miles to reach the park Visitors Center.

Visitors Center
Park services and information are administered daily from 8 am to 5 pm. Free services include natural history displays, a short film about the park and advice. Maps and books are available for sale. Phone 305/247-6211.

Admission
The National Park charges a $5 per car entry fee, but the receipt is good for as many as 14 days. Activities (some seasonal): Flamingo park rangers lead back-country hikes, canoe trips of varying duration, bird walks and camp fire programs. A tram tour is available to Snake Bight. Whitewater and Florida Bay boat trips are offered, as well as sunset cruises under power or sail, skiff or canoe rentals.

Accommodation
There is no expensive or luxury accommodation in the Everglades. Moderate priced Flamingo Lodge Marina & Outpost Resort is the only place to stay, other than camping. For information contact P.O. Box 428, Flamingo, 33030, 305/253-2241. The complex is made up of 102 bay view rooms and individual housekeeping cottages. Screened pool, laundry, restaurant. Fifty-slip marina. Reservations are essential in high season from November to May.

Camping
Long Pine Key Camp Ground also offers hookups and sites for tents or mobile homes, located near main park entrance. Primitive tent sites are situated in back country areas. Permits are required. These are available for free at ranger stations, or the Visitors Center. Canoe, motorized skiff or house boat rentals are available at Flamingo Resort.

Restaurants
Flamingo Restaurant, located at the Visitors' Center, Flamingo, is the only restaurant in this part of the park, and it is closed from May-October. Phone 305/253-2241 for information.

Additional Sightseeing
Then there is Florida Bay, immensely rich spawning and feeding ground for fish, playpen for bottle-nosed dolphin, full of sandbanks, turtle grass, deep channels, mangrove islands and the shell-strewn beaches of Cape Sable. Sign up for an evening sail, watch the roosting flight of heron and ibis, or arrange with a nature/fishing guide to take you well out into the bay, through Lake In-

graham, and around Cape Sable where mangrove islands dot the horizon and dolphins gambol. Experiencing this unspoiled, primitive wilderness we hope that the words, uttered so optimistically by President Truman in his dedication speech in 1947, will hold true, "we have permanently safeguarded an irreplaceable primitive area."

SHARK VALLEY
Access
Driving, take the Tamiami Trail, US 41, for 30 miles west of Miami. Phone 305/221-8776 for information.

Admission
$3 per car, is good for 7- days entry, or the fee can be applied towards main park admission.

Activities
Tram tours are offered year round, phone 305/221- 8455 for information, also details on bicycle rentals, hiking, natural history displays and book store.

Accommodation
None inside the park. Restaurants: None inside the park. For moderate dining just outside park boundaries try the **Miccosukee Restaurant**, Tamiami Trail, near Shark Valley entrance, phone 305/223-8389. **Coopertown Restaurant**, 22700 SW 8th St., on the way to Shark Valley, is also located outside the park, on the Tamiami Trail, 305/226-6048.

EVERGLADES CITY
Gulf Coast Ranger Station: Phone 813/695-2591 for park information, details on boat tours, canoe rentals, natural history displays and maps.

Access
Follow Route 29 south from US 41. Privately-operated activities: Contact Capt. Dave Pricket 813/695-2286, expert fishing and nature guide, island charters, half- and full-day.

Accommodation
None inside the park. Moderately priced at the Rod and **Gun Club**, Everglades City, 813/695-2101. **Barron River Marina**, Everglades City, 813/695-3331, offers villas, cabins, trailer rentals, RV sites, marina.

Additional Sightseeing
Everglades National Park Boat Tours are available for $10 per half day. The tour boats are kept near the Gulf Coast Ranger Station in Everglades City. Phone 813/695-2591, or 800/455-2400 from within Florida. **North American Canoe Tours** at Glades Haven offers canoe rentals as well as guided Everglades tours, 800 South East Copeland Ave., Everglades City, 33929, phone 813/695-2746.

WEST COAST

TAMPA
ST. PETERSBURG
CLEARWATER
NAPLES
FORT MYERS
SARATOSA

The **Tampa Bay** area is Florida's fastest growing area and the eighth fastest growing region in the United States. Many people are lured by 28 miles of beaches stretching along the gentle coast of the Gulf of Mexico, while others come for the booming job market that is created along with unprecedented growth. Many of the 1.7 million residents came first to vacation and decided to stay.

What this means for the typical visitor is that real life goes on here, not simply tourism, and thus many travelers find prices of accommodation, dining and attractions to be more reasonable than in other areas of Florida.

The first outsiders to move in were Spanish *conquistadors* in the sixteenth century, pressing on the traditional homeland of early Timucuan Indians. These were followed by Catholic missionaries, Cubans who were drawn to the bountiful fishing grounds, or to make cigars, and the colorful Greek sponge divers who found the gulf waters reminiscent of their Mediterranean homeland.

Henry Plant's railroad reached **Tampa** in 1884, and this was followed by the construction of a luxury hotel modeled

Preceding pages: The skyline of highrise buildings in Tampa. Left: Anything metallic will be found.

on the Alhambra in Spain, complete with 13 silver minarets. Guests were transported around the grounds on rickshaws. Now part of the University of Tampa, you can still see Plant's handiwork.

The development of **St. Petersburg** followed, also in the 1880s. A Russian named Peter Demens built his Orange Belt Railroad and produced a master plan for the backwater community that he named after his home town.

Then came Cubans seeking a deepwater port for large ships. They established **Ybor City**, which is today classified as an historic district. You can still see Cuban cigar-makers at work, hand-wrapping the golden tobacco leaves exactly the way their ancestors did more than 100 years ago.

Tampa Bay Communities

Cities on both sides of Tampa Bay offer tremendous resources for the tourist. Aside from the moderately priced accommodation available there are numerous luxury resorts that are virtual Florida landmarks. The **Don Cesar Hotel** on St. Petersburg Beach is an enormous pink stucco presence, one of the top hotels on the Gulf Coast. North of there, in **Clearwater**, the **Belleview Biltmore** is a rambling structure, the largest occupied

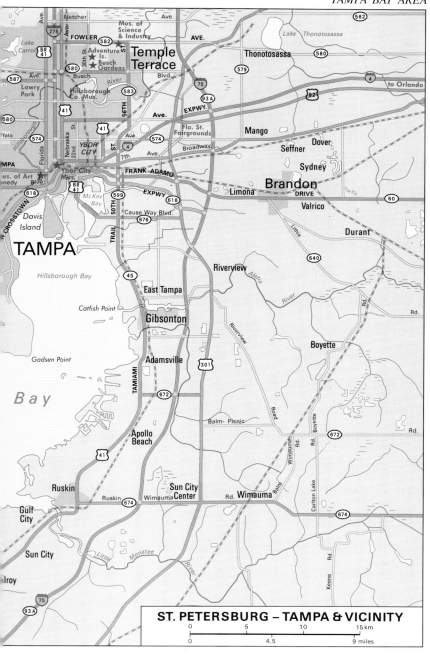

ST. PETERSBURG – TAMPA & VICINITY

| 0 | 5 | 10 | 15 km |

| 0 | 4,5 | 9 miles |

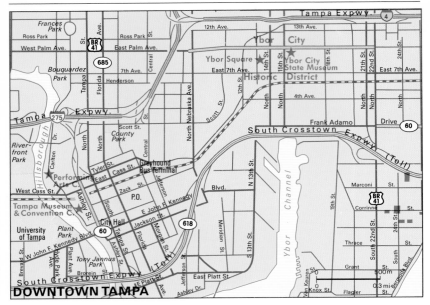

DOWNTOWN TAMPA

wooden building in the world. And for golfers and sports-lovers, **Innisbrook Resort**, sitting amidst acres of lush landscaped grounds, provides the perfect environment for those seeking peace and quiet in the midst of a burgeoning urban landscape, as well as some of the nation's top golfing on highly rated courses.

Culturally speaking, the area boasts some of the most diverse attractions available anywhere in Florida. Aside from the Ybor City Historic District, across the bay, visitors can find a **Salvador Dali Museum** in St. Petersburg, housing the largest collection of the work of the late artist in the world. A **Museum of Fine Arts** is also located in St.Petersburg, as well as a tremendously popular hands-on museum for children, **Great Explorations**.

Visitors to St. Petersburg can also find the **Shuffleboard Hall of Fame**, located at the St. Petersburg Shuffleboard Club.

Right: A top address is the Don Cesar Hotel in St. Petersburg.

Here, mostly elderly residents and visitors partake of the sport that epitomizes the lure of Florida – easy days, no hassles, just one endless game of shuffleboard. And in the same vein, the **Haas Museum** consists of old homes and buildings out of Florida's past. One structure, **The Lowe House**, was built in 1850, and there is an old-time barber shop, a blacksmith shop, and an old railway depot.

In **Tarpon Springs** visitors can find a bustling Greek community that still makes a living off the gulf sponge beds. Exhibits include a Sponge-o-rama Museum, complete with mannequins with painted-on mustaches to make them look Greek. This may well be where you can find more varieties of sponge than you ever knew existed, and there are also the local pastry shops and markets where authentic Greek culture thrives within the context of modern-day Florida.

Visit the **St. Nicholas Greek Orthodox Church** on a Sunday morning when traditionally clothed women in

long dark dresses amble down the narrow streets. The chapel is a replica of St. Sophia's Church in Constantinople. It is one of the best American examples of New Byzantine architecture, with an interior of sculpted Grecian marble, wonderful icons and stained glass.

Water Activities

The seaways and ports of this area are the lifeblood of the community. Deep-water ports are now home to cruise ships, including **Sea Escape** and the **Ocean Spirit**, a modern 457-foot mobile scuba diving complex that carries passengers to the Bay Islands of **Roatan** and **Guanaja**, located south of the Belize reef in Central America, one of the world's top diving sites. The weather here is most conducive to water sports, with an average of 361 days of sunshine a year, and an average temperature of 75 degrees F.

St. Petersburg Beach is one of Florida's broadest and best maintained. It stretches for seven-and-a-half miles from **Blind Pass** to **Passe-a-Grille Beach**, the oldest settlement in the area, where early Spanish fishermen came to cook the fresh catch, even though they had to share cooking grills, hence the name.

Along with sunny urban areas, nature lovers can enjoy the pristine beauty of **Fort DeSoto Park**, which has an old-time fort to explore, or Caladesi State Park, said to contain one of Florida's best undeveloped beaches. Reached by ferry from Dunedin, **Caledesi** offers a quiet escape from the hustle and bustle of the cities. The park contains nature trails and boardwalks winding through sand dunes flecked by sea oats. Activities include swimming, sailing and wind-surfing and hiking, or simply picnicking at one of the shaded picnic tables scattered throughout the preserve.

And for those seeking more action, **Clearwater Beach**, in the heart of the city, fills with young people, who fill the air with frisbees, the sound of boom-box radios and the youthful murmur of fun in the sun punctuated by the lapping tides.

Surfing, though not especially common in calm Florida waters, is best along a sand bar that runs the length of **Indian Rocks Beach, Indian Shores** and **Reddington Beach**. These are not the Big Kahuna waves of Hawaii, though, making this a particularly good spot for novices seeking to test their surfing prowess. Surfboard rentals are available.

Windsurfing is also increasing in popularity. Beginners can try the bay side of **Sand Key**, north of the **Belleair Causeway Bridge**. Reliable winds sweep across the Bay, although the waters remain calm. Experienced wind-surfers are more likely to be found in the open gulf waters beyond the sandbar near the Don Cesar Hotel. Two- to three-foot swells are the largest in the area.

And families can usually be found congregating at several area beaches noted for especially calm waters. Indian Rocks Beach is protected by a sandbar that keeps waves small and also warms the water. Another beach that is well suited to children's activities is the **Ben T. Davis Municipal Beach**, situated between Tampa and Clearwater on State Road 60, on the Courtney Campbell Causeway. Shallow water reaches far into the bay before it tops little ones' heads.

Seashells

Florida actually contains 1000 miles of beaches filled with shells, but the very best place for finding them in this part of the state is on the beach at **Caladesi Island**. Most serious seekers come out at the morning's low tide. Winters are considered best, and shelling after a full moon is recommended by experts.

Land Activities

Out of the water, opportunities for good times are manifold. From Ybor City, with its parade of history, to Busch Gardens or the **Suncoast Seabird Sanc-tuary**, a world-renowned facility where injured waterfowl are brought from all over the state, there is more than enough to see and do to fill several vacations here with pleasurable activities.

Starting in **Ybor City** you can visit Ybor Square downtown. This is the name given to the Historic District, where, among other things you can find three old-time cigar factories that have been transformed into a modern tourist complex that is worth a visit.

Ybor City State Museum was once the Ferlita Bakery. Today it houses exhibits and artifacts of the cigar industry and the Hispanic community. **Cigar-Workers House Museum** and Tampa Rico Cigars offer, respectively, a glimpse of a restored 1895 house and one of the last commercial bastions of hand-made cigars, where you can watch the cigar-making process and purchase stogies made the old-fashioned way.

Tampa's **Busch Gardens** combine a recreated African veldt where animals such as lions, tigers, hippos and elephants roam freely, with a diverse amusement park featuring waterslides and a roller coaster boasting an unforgettable 360-degree loop. The 300-acre property also offers live entertainment shows, tram tours, shops and games within seven theme areas that represent a Florida version of old-time Africa. You can easily spend a day here observing alligators and monkeys, belly-dancers and a brass band, and you may want to, to get your money's worth, considering the admission price, which runs around $30 daily.

A lower-priced stop for seeing exotic animals is **Noell's Ark Chimp Farm**, across the Bay in Tarpon Springs. The Noell Family once had a touring chimp show, including a gorilla that would box with all comers. In retirement, the family moved here and opened their doors to a variety of ex-performing primates who were past their primes and facing untimely death due to infirmities. Although

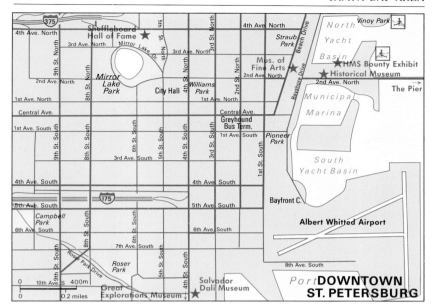

some of the residents have been bred here, others are blind or crippled. All are allowed to live out their days in the Florida sunshine, like so many others who find Florida appealing in retirement. The Chimp Farm charges only $2 for admission and is open every day of the year.

After a stop at the Chimp Farm, wander the nearby sponge docks and stop in at **Pappas Restaurant** for some *ouzo* and *baklava*. The enormous restaurant is a sight to see in itself, featuring the best of Greek foods.

Heading back down the Gulf Coast, in Clearwater, visit the **Boatyard Village**, a recreated 1890s fishing village nestling in a cove on Tampa Bay. Included are restaurants, shops, galleries and a playhouse.

Also in Clearwater, a **Marine Science Center** features live and model displays of indigenous marine life. This is a working research and rehabilitation center, which includes tanks containing numerous varieties of fish, as well as popular baby sea turtles. And **Yesterday's Air Force**, located adjacent to the St. Petersburg-Clearwater International Airport, features a display of post-World War II aircraft and aviation artifacts.

In the city of **Indian Shores** the Suncoast Seabird Sanctuary is perhaps the pre-eminent refuge and rehabilitation center for seabirds and waterfowl in the world. As many as 500 injured or crippled birds are cared for here by a non-profit-making corporation. The wild birds are brought here from all over the state with broken wings or embedded fish hooks and nursed back to health. Many are set free when they recover, while others which can no longer survive in the wild are kept on exhibit. These include brown pelicans, cormorants, white herons, birds of prey and songbirds among other species. There is no admission charge, although donations are gratefully accepted.

In **Largo, Heritage Park and Museum** is another collection of restored homes and buildings situated on 21 wooded acres. An historical museum

depicts pioneer life with exhibitions of frontier arts such as spinning and weaving. Nearby, also in Largo, the **Suncoast Botanical Gardens** is a 60-acre property landscaped in suncoast cactus, 85-foot tall Eucalyptus trees, palms, crepe myrtle and hundreds of flowering plants.

Madeira Beach is home to **John's Pass Village**, a shopping area overlooking the fertile fishing grounds of John's Pass. John's Pass Village is also home to a large commercial and charter fishing fleet. From the looks (and fine taste) of the seafood pouring onto these docks, this seems like a good place for fisherfolk to arrange seagoing excursions.

Out of the village, **The Southern Belle**, a 100-foot paddlewheeler, offers luncheon and sightseeing cruises of the Intracoastal Waterway, and the **Europa Sun** leaves here for six-hour lunch or dinner cruises into the Gulf of Mexico.

In **St. Petersburg** proper, the **Pier** is a

Above: A delight for the eyes and taste buds – Columbian Restaurant at Ybor City.

focal point for downtown visitors. The multi-storied structure jutting out into the bay includes a number of inexpensive restaurants, retail shops, a farmer's market, observation deck and aquarium.

St. Petersburg was one of Florida's first developed resort areas and the city's **Historical Museum** is also downtown, within walking distance of the Pier. It features artifacts and documents, as well as exhibits including china, glassware, coins, dolls, shells and pictures of early community life.

A **Planetarium** located at St. Petersburg Junior College runs shows during the school year, from September through May, in a sky theater beneath a 24-foot domed ceiling projection screen.

And **Sawgrass Lake park**, within the city limits, is a 360-acre learning center for schools and community groups. A mile of elevated boardwalks run through a maple swamp, while an observation tower provides a panoramic view of Sawgrass Lake. An **Environmental Education Center** houses a laboratory, classroom and displays.

St. Petersburg's Sunken Gardens offer an exotic collection of 50,000 tropical plants and flowers, which bloom year-round in this benign, if not sublime, climate. An **Orchard Arbor** contains rare orchids, and there is a walk-through aviary featuring tropical birds.

South of St. Petersburg, spanning Tampa Bay and connecting the city with neighboring Manatee County, is the impressive **Sunshine Skyway Bridge**. It was modeled after the Brotonne Bridge over the Seine, in France, and built to replace the previous bridge which was severed when it was rammed by a tanker ship.

Someday, if city planners have their way, the disconnected remains of the old bridge will be converted into the world's longest fishing pier. In the meantime, the new bridge is 4.1 miles long, with a roadway towering 183 feet over Tampa Bay.

TAMPA / ST. PETERSBURG / CLEARWATER
Accommodation

LUXURY: **Innisbrook Resort**, Box 1088, Tarpon Springs, 34689, 813/942-2000. A complete, deluxe resort on 1000 wooded acres. Saddlebrook, 100 Saddlebrook Way, Wesley Chapel 34249, 813/973-1111, 15 miles north of Tampa. Golf, tennis and variety of accommodation. **Don Cesar Beach Resort**, 3400 Gulf Blvd., St. Petersburg Beach 33706, 813/360-1881. **Belleview Biltmore Hotel & Spa**, 25 Belleview Blvd., Clearwater 34616, 813/442-6171.

EXPENSIVE: **Guest Quarters**, 555 N. Westshore Blvd., Tampa, 33069, 813/875-1555. All-suites. **Tradewinds**, 5500 Gulf Blvd., St. Petersburg Beach, 33706, 813/367-6461. Canal-laced property with a wide beachfront. **Sheraton Sand Key Resort**, 1160 Gulf Blvd., Clearwater Beach, 33515, 813/595-1611. Overlooks the gulf.

MODERATE TO BUDGET: **Holiday Inn** Busch Gardens, 2701 E. Fowler Ave., Tampa, 33612, 813/971-4710. **Sirata Beach Resort**, 5390 Gulf Blvd., St. Petersburg Beach, 33706, 813/367-2771. Centrally located.

Restaurants

LUXURY: **King Charles Room**, at the Don Cesar Hotel, 813/360-1881. Continental dining with harp music in the background. Reservations are suggested. **Bern's Steak House**, 1208 S. Howard Ave., Tampa, 813/251-2421. Steaks, wine and organically grown vegetables. Reservations suggested. **Palm Court** at Tradewinds Resort, 813/360-0061. Nouveau American menu: veal, shrimp, lamb, duck. *MODERATE:* Seafood & Sunsets at **Julie's**, 351 S. Gulfview Blvd, Clearwater Beach, 813/441-2548. Casual Key West-style dining across the street from the beach. **Hurricane Seafood Restaurant**, 809 Gulf Way, St. Petersburg Beach, 813/360-9558. Family-owned, dine inside or out on fresh seafood, with live jazz. **Leverock's Seafood House**, 10 Corey Ave., St. Petersburg Beach, 813/367-4588. Popular for seafood. **Pappas Riverside**, 10 W. Dodecanese Blvd., Tarpon Springs, 813/937-5101. Greek salad is a must, and so are reservations. *BUDGET:* **Harp and Thistle Pub**, 650 Corey Ave., St. Petersburg Beach, 813/360-4104. Scottish/Irish/English-style pub food.

Seasonal Events

Hall of Fame Bowl, football in Tampa Stadium, January. *Epiphany*, Tarpon Springs, a day-long Greek Orthodox celebration including diving for a cross in Spring Bayou, January. *Florida State Fair*, Tampa, February. *SPIFFS International Folk Fair*, St. Petersburg Beach, March. *Highland Games*, Dunedin, April. *Fun'n Sun Festival*, Clearwater, April. *Fiesta de la Riba*, St. Petersburg's annual Spanish Festival held at the Dali Museum, May. *Pirate Days Invasion*, Treasure Island, July. *Clearwater Jazz Holiday*, October. *John's Pass Seafood Festival*, one of the biggest seafood feeds in the state, October.

Access and Transportation

Tampa International Airport is served by Continental, British Airways, Pan Am, Transworld, Northwest and many other airlines. Car rentals, taxis and airport limousine services are available. Many hotels provide gratis airport transfers. **Amtrak** trains service Tampa; phone 813/229-2473 for information. **Greyhound** Lines/Trailways, provide bus service between Tampa Bay communities and other areas of the state and country. **Hillsborough Area Regional Transit** provides local service in Tampa.

Tourist Information

The Greater Tampa Area Chamber of Commerce, 801 E. Kennedy Blvd., 33602, 813/228-7777. **Ybor City Chamber**, 1800 E. 9th Ave., Tampa, 33605, 813/248-3712. **Tampa-Hillsborough Convention & Visitors Bureau**, 100 S. Ashley Drive, Suite 850, Tampa, 33602, 813/223-1111, or toll-free 800/826-8358. **Greater Clearwater Chamber of Commerce**, 128 N. Osceola Ave., 34615, 813/461-0011. St. Petersburg Beach Chamber of Commerce, 6990 Gulf Blvd., 33706, 813/360-6957. **St. Petersburg Area Chamber of Commerce**, 100 Second Ave., 33701, 813/821-4069. **Tarpon Springs Chamber of Commerce**, 210 South Pinellas Ave., 34689, 813/937-6109. **Pinellas Suncoast Tourist Development Council**, 4625 E. Bay Dr., Suite 109, Clearwater, 34624, 813/530-6452. **Greater Pinellas Park Chamber of Commerce**, 5851 Park Boulevard, Pinellas Park 34655, 813/544-4777. **Greater Dunedin Chamber of Commerce**, 434 Main Street, Dunedin 34698, 813/736-5066. **Gulf Beaches Chamber of Commerce**, PO Box 273, Indian Rocks Beach 34635, 813/595-4575.

Parks

Caladesi Island State Park, Number 1 Causeway Boulevard, Dunedin 33528, 813/443-5903. **Hillsborough River State Park**, 15402 US 301 North, Thonotosassa 33592, 813/986-1020. **Honeymoon Island State Recreation Area**, Number 1 Causeway Boulevard, Dunedin 33528, 813/734-4255. **Little Montanee River State Recreation Area**, 215 Lightfoot Road, Winauma 33598, 813/634-4781. **Weedon Island State Preserve**, 1500 Weedon Island Drive, St. Petersburg 33702, 813/577-0651.

NAPLES, FORT MYERS, SARA-SOTA

The far southwest coast of Florida, starting at the northern boundary of the Everglades and stretching past Fort Myers to Sarasota, is a popular area with urban Floridians seeking respite from big city ills. And now, with the opening of a Southwest Florida Regional Airport in Lee County, the area is more accessible than ever before.

Naples

This small, but very proper community has been a retirement haven for years, and only recently has it begun to enjoy a major tourism influx. With zoning restrictions galore, designed to preserve the city's long-cherished exclusivity, **Naples** is something of a haven of tranquility amidst the booming growth and congestion that characterizes so much of modern day Florida.

In past years, Naples has been a sort of Palm Beach west, a semi-exclusive preserve of the rich and powerful, dating back to its founding by a Civil War general from Kentucky named John S. Williams and his friend, Walter N. Haldeman, then owner and publisher of the *Louisville Journal*. The two men visited the area and Williams is credited with naming the city in honor of his friend, the King of Naples, Italy.

In the early part of this century the city and surrounding wilderness areas became known as a rich man's hunting and fishing grounds, even though a visit here required a strenuous 40-mile boat trip from Fort Myers. Today, although hunting opportunities are not what they once were – except when alligators are in season – the fishing is still outstanding along 41 miles of public beaches.

Left: Relaxing in Naples. Above: There's an ideal breeze most of the time.

The city is sandwiched between the **Big Cypress National Preserve**, a swamp that extends out of the Everglades, and the Gulf of Mexico. The National Audubon Society runs the **Corkscrew Swamp Sanctuary**, an 11,000 acre wildlife habitat 35 miles west of Naples. It is the site of the world's largest remaining stand of virgin bald cypress trees. Many of the trees are 500 years old and over 100 feet tall.

Along with flora, one can find endangered species of woodstorks nesting in the tall trees, as well as alligators lolling in the swampy lowlands. These sights are most readily visible from a 1 3/4-mile boardwalk.

In the same area, in the city of **Palmdale**, is one of Florida's more curious attractions, the **Cypress Knee Museum**. Run by an octogenarian named Gaskins who has appeared on TV on the Johnny Carson Show, the museum and adjacent cypress swamp (served by a 3/4 mile long boardwalk) are touted along rural Route 27 with crude roadside signs

saying "Lady, If He Won't Stop, Hit Him Over the Head With a Shoe."

The focus here is on cypress knees, which are gnarled stumps and shoots growing out of cypress trees. Gaskins not only gives names to these natural creations, such as "Lady With a Baby", or "Lady Hippo Wearing a Carmen Miranda Hat," he creates his own living art by shaping the growth of certain trees around empty bottles or other household items. This is definitely a strange place, and despite its unique appeal, somehow representative of the spirit of Florida.

For a commercial view of wildlife, **Jungle Larry's African Safari Park** features wildlife shows, animals and birds from all over the world, including a Tiglon, which is a cross-breed between a tiger and a lion.

In Naples, when not partaking of golf, tennis, swimming, sailing or other water sports, shoppers flock to Fifth Avenue South or Third Street South shops and boutiques featuring pricey goods. The **Old Marine Market Place** at **Tin City** is a cluster of art galleries, artist's studios and more trendy shops enclosed in old-time fisherman's shacks.

Fort Myers & Lee County

The Lee Island Coast is comprised of the communities of Sanibel/Captiva, Fort Myers Beach, Fort Myers, Cape Coral, Bonita Springs, North Fort Myers, Pine Island and Lehigh Acres.

Inland communities are residential or commercial enclaves, while coastal areas tend to house resorts. The region boasts the greatest number of golf courses per capita of any place in America, and there are none too few tennis courts, many of them open to the public for free.

Fort Myers is nicknamed the City of Palms, for the thousands of towering royal palms that were planted along McGregor Boulevard by an early winter

Above: The Pier of Naples has become a monument. Right: Over a thousand patents were registered by Thomas Alva Edison.

resident, **Thomas Alva Edison**. Edison's 14-acre riverfront property, including his Florida home, experimental gardens and laboratory, is now a tourist attraction. The gardens are maintained, including a banyan tree presented as a seedling to Edison as a gift by Harvey Firestone, a friend who made tires. Today, the tree's circumference is more than 30 feet. And the lab is left just the way it was in Edison's time. The royal palms Edison planted have become something of a local trademark. They can be seen, with their thick trunks and towering height, standing like sentinels along McGregor Boulevard.

The **Lee Island Coast** is also known for tarpon fishing and sea shells. Tarpon, a prized game fish known for its size and aerobatic abilities, come to spawn in the Gulf of Mexico from as far away as Nova Scotia or South America. Their season here, in the calm, warm waters of the gulf, is summer. Among anglers in the know, **Boca Grande Pass** is considered the tarpon capital of the world.

As for shells, this is the home of the "Sanibel stoop", that oddly crooked ritual step affected when scouring the coastal sands and tide pools for more than 400 varieties of seashells. Hundreds of prowling shell-seekers come out to Sanibel and Captiva beaches in the hazy hours before dawn. Many carry flashlights, but aficionados wear miners hats with lights, to scour for scallops, clams and coquinas, conchs, fluted tulips, and speckled junonia.

There are more varieties of shells found here than in any other North American beach area. But for those who would like to see a rare shell on the mantel without getting sand between their toes, the **Shell Factory**, in North Fort Myers, is an enormous retail store that resembles a museum.

The **Caloosahatchee River** passes through downtown Fort Myers, serving as a starting point for scenic day cruises or dining cruises which explore regions of the Everglades, as well as secluded gulf-side inlets and bays. The **City Yacht**

Basin is the home port for many of the tour boats.

A popular travel mode based at the Port **Sanibel Yacht Club**, is flotilla sailing. A string of sailboats captained by tourists follow the lead of a real captain who knows where he is going and what he is doing. Sailing instructions are available for beginners, then, after proficiency is established, the boats sail the gulf waters for as long as a week, docking at a different gulf port nightly.

Thoroughfares through Sanibel and Captiva are chock-a-block with resorts, and only recently have efforts been made to limit future construction.

On the north side of Sanibel Island, the **J.N. "Ding" Darling National Wildlife Refuge** is another effort to preserve elements of natural Florida against development. The refuge, administered by the US Forest Service, covers more than 5000 acres that may be explored by car, on foot, by bicycle or in a canoe. A 5-mile dirt road leads visitors past 290 species of birds and numerous varieties of reptiles. Bird watchers favor an observation tower off the side of the road.

Some call **Captiva Island**, connected to Sanibel via a causeway, "Florida's Tahiti". The barrier island is noted for its white sand beaches bordered by thick mangrove swamps. It is said that pirate Jose Gaspar kept prisoners on Captiva in the eighteenth century. Lime and coconuts have been commercially grown here, and these barrier islands were later a fishing retreat for winter tourists from up north.

Cayo Costa State Island Preserve is a another worth seeing site for shelling and naturalist-led tours. Across Pine Island Sound, on Pine Island, you can find an old-time-style Florida fishing village, and you can also see rare mango groves in one of theses few places in North America where the tropical fruits are able to grow.

Above: A popular souvenir. Right: Besides the Ringling Circus Museum there is also a Circus School.

Cabbage Key is accessible by boat only. It is the site of an ancient Calusa Indian shell mound and burial site, as well as an evocative country inn and restaurant built by American novelist Mary Roberts Rinehart in 1938.

Sarasota, Venice, Bradenton

The **Sarasota** area has been something of a cultural center in Florida ever since the circus came to town. The circus that came to spend winters in nearby **Venice** was run by a man named John Ringling. It was "The Greatest Show on Earth", the Ringling Brothers, Barnum and Bailey Circus. You can still see winter dress rehearsals here.

Ringling had been a long-time winter resident of Sarasota, and his home with his wife, Mabel, is now a tourist attraction as part of the **Ringling Museum of Art**, Florida's state art museum. Called Ca'D'Zan, the house is a 30-room Venetian-style palace which is filled with tapestries and works of art. More of Ring-

ling's fabulous art collection is on view at the two adjacent buildings, the **Art Gallery** and the **Circus Gallery**. Situated on 38 acres of manicured grounds, the Art Gallery contains one of the world's top collections of Rubens paintings, and the Circus Gallery houses one of the largest collections of circus memorabilia and artifacts. Also on the grounds is the **Asolo State Theatre**. The building was once an Italian castle. It was dismantled, then carefully reconstructed here in 1950. The much loved speciality of the theater are eigtheenth-century Italian plays.

Another wonderful museum for the ladies, gentleman and children of all ages who visit Sarasota is the **Lionel Train and Seashell Museum**. Model trains operate on elaborate set-ups of tracks winding through toy train villages. And along with the train collection, seashells and coral specimens from around the world are on display.

Sarasota Jungle Gardens are home to more indigenous Florida wildlife and flora. The jungle trails pass through 15

123

acres of fern and hibiscus gardens bordered by a banana grove, and a number of animal and reptile shows are performed daily. A **Kiddie Jungle Playground** is a must for young ones.

Another Sarasota garden spot is the **Marie Selby Botanical Gardens**, where you can stroll through 14 acres of garden with an incredible variety of orchids. Located near the **Island Park yacht basin**, the site stretches along Sarasota Bay.

Marine scientists display many species of ocean life at the **Mote Marine Science Center**. Sharks and manta rays are included in the sealife brought here for study out of local waters.

And on the south shore of the **Manatee River**, west of Bradenton, stands **Fort DeSoto National Memorial**. The best guess is that Hernando DeSoto and the conquistadors landed near here in 1539. The exact site between Fort Myers and St. Petersburg is unknown, but this is

Above: You can buy antiques in this out-of-service train.

where the first European landing in this area is commenmorated. A film shown in the visitors' center describes DeSoto's explorations, costumed guides give period weapons demonstrations, and in addition there are nature trails for your own exploring.

In **Ellenton**, across the Manatee River from Bradenton, you can visit the only surviving antebellum mansion still standing in South Florida. It was built in 1850 by Major Robert Gamble, from which he ran a 3500-acre sugar plantation. The plantation is one of the best standing examples of the peculiar Florida construction material called "tabby", which was a mortar compound mixed from crushed shells and molasses produced from the sugar works.

Sarasota County also contains ten beaches offering swimming, fishing, volleyball nets, playgrounds, horseshoe pits, nature trails and picnic grounds. Several beaches include boat ramps and tennis courts. And the shelling is nearly as good as farther south.

NAPLES / FORT MYERS / SARASOTA
Accommodation

LUXURY TO EXPENSIVE: **Ritz-Carlton Hotel**, 280 Vanderbilt Beach Rd., Naples, 33963, 813/598-3300. Mediterranean-style gulf-front resort. **Casa Ybel Resort**, 2255 W. Gulf Dr., Sanibel, 33957, 813/481-3636 or 800/472-3145. Condos and villas on the gulf. **South Seas Plantation**, South Sea Plantation Rd., Captiva, 33924, 813/472-5111. Cottages and villas on 330 secluded acres at the tip of the island. **Sanibel Sonesta Harbor Resort**, 7260 Harbor Point, Ft. Myers, 33908, 813/337-0300. On San Carlos Bay. **The Meadows Golf & Tennis Resort**, 3101 Longmeadow Dr., Sarasota, 34234, 813/378-6600. All suites, 54 golf holes, 16 tennis courts. *MODERATE:* **Best Western Robert E. Lee Motor Inn**, 6611 US 41 N., N. Ft. Myers, 33903, 813/997-5511. Balconies on the Caloosahatchee River. **Sandpiper Gulf Resort**, 5550 Estero Blvd., Ft. Myers Beach, 33931, 813/463-5721. Well-located apartment motel on the beach. **Days Inn Sarasota-Siesta Key**, 6600 S. Tamiani Trail, Sarasota, 34231, 813/924-4900. Save money by staying a mile from the beach.

Restaurants

EXPENSIVE: **The Chef's Garden**, 1300 3rd St., Naples, 813/262-5500. Award-winning Continental cuisine. Suit jackets required in winter. **LaTiers**, Sheraton Harbor Place Hotel, 2500 Edwards Dr., Ft. Myers, 813/337-0300. Formal Continental cuisine. **The Bubble Room**, Captiva Road, Captiva, 813/472-5558. 1940s music, art deco decor. **Cafe L'Europe**, 431 Harding Circle, Sarasota, 813/388-4155. Reservations suggested. *MODERATE:* **Truffles**, 1300 3rd St. S., Naples, 813/262-5500. Informal dining upstairs from the Chef's Garden. **The Prawnbroker**, 6535 McGregor Blvd., Ft. Myers, 813/489-2266. Freshest seafood. **The Mucky Duck**, 2500 Estero Blvd., Ft. Myers Beach, 813/462-5519. **McT's Shrimphouse and Tavern**, 1523 Periwinkle Way, Sanibel, 813/ 472-3161. All-you-can-eat shrimp or crab. **Thistle Lodge**, Casa Ybel Resort, 2255 W. Gulf Dr., Sanibel, 813/472-9200. Cajun, Creole and Continental cuisine in a New Orleans-style mansion. **Casa La Chaumiere** 8197 S. Tamiani Trail, Sarasota, 813/922-6400. Classic French cuisine. **The Attic** at Kissin' Cousins, 1775 S. Tamiani Trail, Venice, 813/493-3666. Pennsylvania Dutch-inspired foods. *BUDGET:* **Miami Connection**, 11506 S. Cleveland Ave., or 2112 2nd St. S., Fort Myers, 813/936-3811. Kosher-style deli. **Woody's Bar-B-Q**, 6701 N. Tamiani Trail, Ft. Myers, 813/997-

1424. **Chan's Hunan**, 4725 Del Prado Blvd., Cape Coral, 813/549-2119. Spicy Oriental food.

Seasonal Events

Edison Pageant of Light, Ft. Myers, February. *Pine Island Seafood Festival*, Pine Island, March. *Bonita Springs Tomato Snook Festival*, Bonita Springs, March. *Cracker Festival*, N. Ft. Myers, April. *Safe Boating Festival*, Ft. Myers, June. *Jazz on the Green*, Sanibel, Oct. *Munich in Cape Coral*, Cape Coral, October. *Sand Sculpture Competition*, Ft. Myers Beach, November.

Guided Tours

Florida Adventure Tours and Charters, 813/394-8870. Motorcoach and van tours to greyhound races, the Everglades, Edison home. **The Deliquesce**, 813/351-7839. 41-foot yacht tours of Sarasota Bay. **Everglades Jungle Cruise**, 813/334-7474. River trips of three hours to two days. **Wooten's Everglades**, 813/394-8080. Airboat and swamp buggy trips.

Access and Transportation

Southwest Florida Regional Airport serves the Ft. Myers Naples area, with connections on Continental, American, Delta, Eastern, Northwest, United. Sun Lines airport limousine service is the least costly of several companies carrying passengers to regional hotels and resorts. Rental cars are available. **Sarasota County Transit**, 813/951-5850, and the **Lee County Transit System**, 813/939-1303, provide local bus service.

Tourist Information

Lee County Tourist Development Council, 2180 W. 1st St., Ft. Myers, 33901, 813/335-2631, or 800/533-7433. **Naples Area Chamber of Commerce**, 1700 N. Tamiani Trail, Naples, 33940, 813/262-6141. **Sanibel-Captiva Islands Chamber of Commerce**, PO Box 166, Sanibel, 33957, 813/472-3232. **Sarasota Convention and Visitors Bureau**, 655 N. Tamiani Trail, Sarasota 34236, 813/957- 1877.

Parks

Cayo Costa State Preserve, PO Box 150, Boca Grande 33291, 813/964-0375. **Colier-Seminole State Park**, Route 4, Box 848, Naples 339621, 813/394-3397. **Delnor Wiggins Pass State Recreation Area**, 11100 Gulf Shore Drive, North Naples 33963, 813/597-6196. **Gasparilla Island State Recreation Area**, PO Box 1150, Boca Grande 33291, 813/964-0375. **Koreshan State Historic Site**, PO Box 7, Estero 33928, 813/922-0311. **Big Cypress National Preserve**, SR Box 110, Ochopee 33943, 813/695-2000. **Corkscrew Swamp Sanctuary**, Route 6, 1875 A., Naples 33964, 813/657-3771. **J.N. "Ding" Darling National Wildlife Refuge**, 1 Wildlife Drive, Sanibel 33957, 813/472-1100.

CENTRAL FLORIDA

ORLANDO
DISNEY WORLD
CAPE CANAVERAL
DAYTONA
GAINESVILLE

ORLANDO AND DISNEY WORLD

It all began as a campground for soldiers during one of the Seminole Wars. The settlement was Fort Gatlin in 1837, later Jernigan and finally, after 1875, was named **Orlando**, perhaps after Orlando Reeves who was killed fighting against the Seminoles.

Then, not so long ago, sleepy Orlando, a sultry country town surrounded by orange groves, was awakened by the sweet kiss of tourist dollars. Some would say success has turned Orlando into a harlot, hellbent for the big buck. Indisputably, the city's roads are packed to a standstill. The ecosystem is a shambles. Still, the City Beautiful sails on a shining sea of newness, and the growth goes on and on. Except for a few seedy pockets, everything has a washed, fresh look.

It looks as if the city is struggling to keep up with the high standards set by the ultra-scrubbed **Walt Disney World**, undoubtedly the biggest and most squeaky-clean show on earth.

Today more visitors come to Walt Disney World than to any other tourism

Preceding pages: The miraculous world of Mickey Mouse – industrial society's dream-come-true. Left: Walt Disney's creatures are still fun to children.

destination in the world. The formula works and for good reason.

The Worlds of Disney

Even for a visionary fellow like Walt Disney, buying 28,000 acres of Florida's bug-ridden, inland belly in 1964 was a bold, perhaps even cockeyed, step.

Yet today Walt Disney World still has many square miles untouched. Already, three theme parks exist, the **Magic Kingdom**, **Epcot** (Experimental Prototype Community of Tomorrow) **Center**, and the new **MGM-Disney Studios**. And there is a separate nightclub-restaurant complex, sort of an adult-theme park unto itself, called **Pleasure Island**.

Each park merits at least one full day from the serious visitor attempting to grasp the enormous complexity of it all in one trip. Most visitors need at least a week in Walt Disney World and wish it were longer. In various stages of completion at Walt Disney World are several new hotels, which will add a total of seven more by 1995. A fourth major theme park, whose design had not been decided at the time of writing, will be built during the 1990s. Two new Epcot pavilions, Russia and Switzerland are being built, and with Perestroika, others are sure to follow.

Besides the theme parks, WDW has three championship golf courses, countless tennis courts, a campground complete with its own restaurants and entertainment. Horseback riding trails wind through a 7500-acre wilderness preserve. Miles of white sand beaches surround mirrored lakes. The property boasts more boats than most navies of the world.

To enjoy WDW to the fullest is to spend entire days in the theme parks, broken up by days of fishing, canoeing, playing golf, water skiing, bird watching, paddleboating, sailing, lazing by the pool, swimming, and otherwise enjoying the wilderness, waterways, and miles of manicured WDW grounds.

Two Disney water theme parks have separate all-inclusive, all-day admission. **Typhoon Lagoon** has an enormous wave pool and a salt water reef where swimmers can snorkel among live fish. The quieter **Discovery Island/River Country** is an attraction for more contemplative aficionados of the Disney-brand of wilderness.

To make the most of every expensive minute of a WDW stay requires planning. Entire books are written on the park, including Stephen Birnbaum's official guide, and Prentice-Hall's unofficial one.

There are Disney-owned hotels, resorts and villas and a camp ground, plus a choice of fine independent hotels, within the **Walt Disney World Village**.

All WDW properties are connected to the excellent, frequent transportation system that operates for free, threading throughout WDW. Staying anywhere on the grounds, you can spend the morning in a theme park, hop a bus back to your room for a nap and a swim, then jump on the monorail or a boat back to the theme park for dinner and the fireworks.

Another perk for staying on the property is that WDW guests get priority reservations for shows and restaurants.

A second choice is to stay in the general area, preferably at a hotel which

ORLANDO & VICINITY

0   2   4   6 km

0   3 miles

offers a shuttle service to the theme parks. Some area hotels offer free WDW transportation, others offer it at a token price. In both instances, it is possible and preferable to get by without a car.

The third choice for the WDW portion of your Orlando visit is to stay at lodgings outside Walt Disney World and drive each day to the theme park of your choice, allowing a few extra dollars for parking. This takes longer, accounting for riding shuttles between the parking lots and park entrances. Staying on WDW property, either in an independent hotel in the WDW Hotel Plaza, or in a Disney-owned hotel, is a definite plus.

Children delight in the Magic Kingdom surrounding **Cinderella's Castle**. Divided into six areas, the park has sights, rides and giggles for everyone and especially for small fry. Space Mountain in **Tomorrowland** is a thrill ride for only

Above: In Cypress Gardens there is always time for a chat. Right: In EPCOT you are transported into the 21st century.

the most daring, but there are plenty of tame rides for toddlers, and dozens of adventures, like the **Haunted House** and the new Mickey Land, that the family can enjoy together. Even for those who have been here before, there are new attractions, special events and constant surprises making you wish to come back again.

Do not ever assume that once having visited any portion of WDW, you have "done" the World. On entering Epcot, you are in **Future World**. Exhibits are devoted to new technology in communication, transportation, oceanography, agriculture and health. Each show is a spectacle, well worth waits of as long as an hour on busy days. **Body Wars**, the newest thrill ride addition, takes passengers zooming crazily through the human body in a desperate attempt to keep infection from setting in after a sliver enters a finger. It is a bruising and heart-stopping ride, adored by thrill seekers but forbidden for pregnant women, children under the age of three and the unwell.

Every exhibit is outstanding. Try to see every show and ride every ride. It can take several days, so the multi-admission passports are a good buy. In the **Living Seas**, an ocean of fish are on view in a glass-walled 200-foot diameter, 27-foot deep tank that can be seen from a number of vantage points including one of WDW's best dining rooms.

The Land, covering six acres, is devoted to food exhibits and experiments. Some are pure fun, others show serious experiments in growing better food on less land using fewer chemicals. The 3-D film shown at **Journey into Imagination** will have you blinking your eyes in disbelief. Creatures leap off the screen at you. Sounds surround you all the time.

Across a lagoon lies a second section, the **World Showcase**, with pavilions from a dozen countries, each showing off its best foods, wares, and culture. China

shows a dazzling 360-degree movie on the Wonders of China.

The pavilion itself is a half-scale replica of Beijing's Temple of Heaven, set in a collection of shop fronts, ponds and street scenes that look for all the world like China.

You can shop for Chinese goods in all price ranges, from costly silks and jade to flimsy paper fans, which a calligrapher will inscribe with your name in Chinese. The fixed price dinner at the restaurant is excellent value, or there is fast food.

Norway greets you with an ancient Viking church and a thrilling spin through the Maelstrom, one of WDW's best rides. Eat *smorgasbrod*, or pick up a pastry in the fragrant bakery.

In Germany you find nonstop Oktoberfest in a charming Biergarten. The village is straight out of Bavaria, dominated by a traditional clock tower.

Above: Walk-in high-tech. Right: Commedia dell' arte at EPCOT – Venetian flair in Florida.

England has street performers and shops, but unlike the other pavilions, does not have a ride or show. It is spontaneous and fun in a hodgepodge of styles ranging from a London square to a thatched cottage. Snacks and cold drinks are available at the Rose and Crown Pub.

Morocco sells bright brasses and woodcraft in an exotic marketplace. The food in Marrakech is exotic and delicious, and a belly dancer entertains as you dine. You will not see long queues because there is no formal show, but be sure to see the building which is one of Epcot's best. Nine tons of mosaic tile were assembled here by artisans brought in from their homeland to recreate the landmark minaret of Marrakech. A nice museum features changing exhibits of all kinds of Moroccan art.

Enter Italy under a model of the bell tower that overlooks St. Mark's Square in Venice. There's a real feeling of Italy in the fountains, columns, and bridges. Grab a sweet snack or a pizza, or make reservations to dine nobly at Alfredo's

where the speciality is, of course, *fettucine Alfredo*, made with fresh pasta.

To enter Japan is to escape into a serene world fashioned after a seventh-century shrine, traditional pagodas, and artful gardens. Street performances include the ancient art of candy sculpting. The restaurant, of course, features table-side cooking.

The American Adventure, Epcot's American pavilion, captures so much that is American, in so brief a time, that even the most jaded hearts swell with patriotism. Scrubbed and talented young people give song and dance programs, a fast-moving summary of American history is given by lifelike animatronic figures, and the Liberty Inn is a good place to get a quick meal of fast-food standards. Then enter Canada through an Indian village with an enormous totem. The 360-degree France shows a soothingly beautiful wide-screen movie, and hosts a superb French restaurant and outdoor cafe. The setting is Paris at the turn of the century, La Belle Epoque.

Mexico has *mariachi* bands and *tacos*. A 7-minute boat ride through the River of Time takes you from Maya, Toltec and Aztec times to modern Mexico. Pavilions under construction at present are Russia and Switzerland.

Disney-MGM Studios are working studios where you might run into a famous star or sit in on the taping of a TV show. Three studios may be taping simultaneously and in a walk-through tour, you might see a game show, Siskel and Ebert, or the Mickey Mouse Club, being taped side by side. The park recreates the Hollywood of the 1940s. Here you can see Grauman's Chinese Theater, dine in the Brown Derby, star in a show, watch a stunning stunt demonstration, ride through Catastrophe Canyon, and tour the back-lot.

Walk through the animation studios, where new movies are being drawn. Ride through the work areas, to see costumes being designed and sewn. Strap on your seat-belt and fly through Star Tours, with audio and video made more

DISNEY WORLD

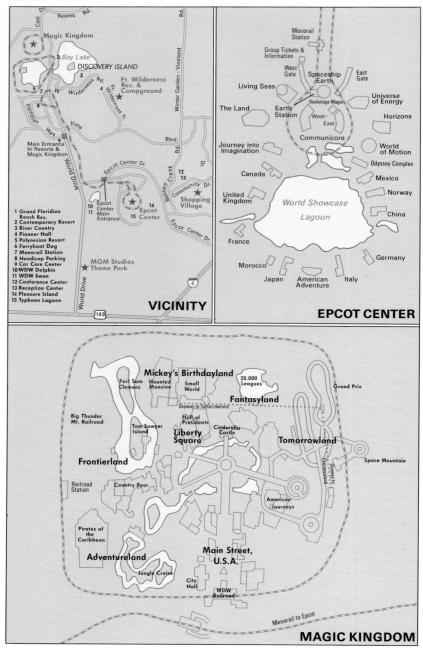

VICINITY

1 Grand Floridian Beach Res.
2 Contemporary Resort
3 River Country
4 Pioneer Hall
5 Polynesian Resort
6 Ferryboat Dog
7 Monorail Station
8 Handicap Parking
9 Car Care Center
10 WDW Dolphin
11 WDW Swan
12 Conference Center
13 Reception Center
14 Pleasure Island
15 Typhoon Lagoon

Magic Kingdom
Bay Lake
DISCOVERY ISLAND
Ft. Wilderness Res. & Campground
Reams Rd.
Cast Dr.
Winter Garden - Vineland Rd.
Wilderness Rd.
Ft. Wilderness Tr.
Floridian Way
Vista
Blvd.
Bonnet Creek Rd.
Community Dr.
Epcot Center Dr.
Shopping Village
Epcot Center Main Entrance
Epcot Center
Main Entrance to Resorts & Magic Kingdom
World Drive
MGM Studios Theme Park
192
4

EPCOT CENTER

Monorail Station
Group Tickets & Information
West Gate
East Gate
Spaceship Earth
Living Seas
The Land
Earth Station
Backstage Magic
Universe of Energy
Horizons
West-East
Communicore
Journey into Imagination
World of Motion
Odyssey Complex
Canada
Mexico
United Kingdom
Norway
China
France
World Showcase Lagoon
Germany
Morocco
Japan
American Adventure
Italy

MAGIC KINGDOM

Mickey's Birthdayland
Fort Sam Clemens
Haunted Mansion
Small World
20,000 Leagues
Grand Prix
Fantasyland
Skyway to Tomorrowland
Big Thunder Mt. Railroad
Tom Sawyer Island
Hall of Presidents
Cinderella Castle
Liberty Square
Tomorrowland
Skyway to Fantasyland
Space Mountain
Frontierland
Railroad Station
Country Bear
American Journeys
Pirates of the Caribbean
Adventureland
Jungle Cruise
Main Street, U.S.A.
City Hall
WDW Railroad
Monorail to Epcot

dazzling and scary by seats that seem to send you hurtling through the black holes of outer space. Again, this is a ride for the strong of heart. It is closed to pregnant women, children under the age of three and anyone with heart problems. Hollywood characters roam the streets. You may be approached by a starlet who hopes you will put her in your next movie, or by an autograph hunter, or by a director who tells you to hurry over to make-up and do something about your hair before the next take. It is all in good fun, and a whale of a show.

The studio restaurants are Hollywood themed. One is the **Brown Derby**, elegant and requiring early reservations. Another is the **Prime Time Cafe**, where each seat faces a black and white TV screen which is showing 1950s sitcoms. The waitress treats you like an American mom is supposed to treat the kids. She sits down at your table, asks what you would like to eat, and then fusses if you do not finish your vegetables.

The **Indiana Jones stunt exhibit** is a shocker, as breathtaking scenes from the movie are recreated by live actors on stage. Keep your camera ready for a non-stop spectacle of explosions, narrow escapes, fights, frights, and surprises.

An agreement has been made between Disney and the Muppeteers, which will result in new movies and shows, and perhaps a theme park section based on the Muppets. While Mickey Mouse is the symbol of Walt Disney World, Bacchus has not been forgotten.

Nightlife at WDW can be romantic, sophisticated, even a bit racy. Many of the Disney hotels house gourmet restaurants, glittery supper-clubs, and lounges with dancing or listening to live entertainers. Evenings at Pleasure Island are to adults what a candy store is to a kid. The nightclubs cover all bases, from jazz to blaring disco. There is a roller rink, a

comedy club, shopping, and no end of restaurants to suit any taste or budget.

Walt Disney World is indeed a world in itself, bigger, lustier, busier and more impressive than visitors are prepared for. It will take more time, money, film and energy than you expected in your wildest imaginings. Bring comfortable shoes, cool clothing and a high credit limit.

Hours at all Orlando's theme parks and other major attractions are open every day, but vary slightly with the seasons. It is always wise to call ahead. Arrive early, before the park opens, and plan to stay late because much of the fun takes place after dark. Admissions are high, averaging $20-$40 daily, but if you make the most of each day, the value is excellent because admissions include all rides and shows. Except for a few special instances, there are no extras except for meals and shopping.

Package deals are almost always the best value, wrapping up airfare, accommodation, admissions, and no end of extras. Disney has enlisted Premier as its of-

Above: Out for a stroll in Disneyland.

ficial cruise line, offering a package that includes a Bahamas cruise out of Port Canaveral.

Although Premier's ships rank with the best of the love boats, in fact, one of them is the original ship used in the TV show, the cruises are more family oriented than most. Chip or Dale may stop by the table to give you a hug. Donald Duck may waddle up to pose for a picture with you, or Goofy may come galloping along at any time. Complete, day-long children's programs are offered for four age groups, from tykes to teens, at no added cost. For adults, there is gambling in the casino, lounges with live music and dancing, and moonlit strolls under an ocean moon.

Ports of call, depending on the cruise, may include Bahamian villages or a private island complete with beaches, watersports, snorkeling in gin-clear waters, and duty free shopping.

Above: Orlando's entertainment center, Church Street Station.Right: A must at recreation parks are the dolphin-shows.

Other theme parks have appeared in the area and with Walt Disney setting the pace, Orlando has attracted only the best. **Sea World** is a sprawling, 150-acre spread devoted to marine life including its famous killer whales. It is superb entertainment, but is also a center for serious research. The first killer whale born in captivity was born here. Walk a transparent tunnel through a shark-filled aquarium. Feed the dolphins. Laugh at the sea otters' antics.

The **Penguin Encounter** gives you a look at an entire penguin community, feeding and scolding, strutting and slithering. Each night there's a Polynesian dinner show. Give Sea World a day, perhaps two.

The new 444-acre **Universal Studios Florida** theme park gives MGM-Disney a run for its money. Rides and shows are based on such blockbuster movies as *Jaws, King Kong, E.T., Back to the Future,* and *Earthquake*. This, too, is a working studio where such movies as *Psycho IV* and *Parenthood* were made, and TV shows including *Double Dare*, *The New Leave It To Beaver*, and *Kid's Court* are produced. More than 50 locales, from San Francisco to New York, are reproduced on the back-lot. Dominating the park is the stark, shadowy Bates Motel, looking for all the world as scary as it was in the *Psycho* movies.

Within Universal Studios are 40 restaurants and shops including Mel's Diner from *American Graffiti*, Schwab's Drug Store (where many starlets were discovered) and the Studio Commissary. Plan to spend at least two days here.

Although it began as a simple garden in the l930s, **Cypress Gardens**, between Orlando and Tampa, ranks with the best theme parks and continues to burst forth year-round with well-tended botanical pleasures.

In addition to acres of groomed pathways and millions of blooms during all seasons, there are bird shows, a pet zoo,

restaurants, shops, and stupendous water-ski and ice skating productions. Cypress Gardens is not the spot for scream rides and roller coasters, but its Island in the Sky ride is quietly awesome. Slowly and smoothly, an entire island filled with people is lifted high into the air for a bird's eye view of the park. Sea World and Cypress Gardens are owned by the Busch Gardens people, so look for packages and combination tickets that save money on admissions to all three. **Wet 'n Wild** is one of the nation's best water parks, filled with screamers, shockers, and splashers. Rocket down a water slide and through a tunnel, then dance in the wave pool. It is a very popular all-day attraction that is open from mid-February through December. In summer buy a late-admission discount ticket and come for the evening.

Other Orlando Attractions

Orlando itself is a vibrant community with a love of the arts and the outdoors. Countless parks, tennis courts and golf courses are found in the area, and you are never more than a few minutes from a lake leaping with bass.

The city has been settled for more than a century, so there are at least a few historic points. Unrivaled chief among them is **Church Street Station**, a downtown complex of boutiques, arcades, restaurants and shows set in turn-of-the century buildings. After dark, it's one of the city's best centers for dining, pub hopping, noshing, and hobnobbing in clubs where you will find a wide choice of music, from easy listening, to folk, country and Dixieland.

Leu Botanical Gardens are a showplace of native and imported flowers and shrubs. Come any time, but especially in January for the camellias and in February for the azaleas. The original Leu home has been restored to the period 1910-1930. The city is dotted with lakes and parks for your recreation.

A favorite is **Eola Park**, which is the scene of many special events and band

shell concerts. Its fountain is lit at night. During the day, you can rent a paddleboat that looks like a swan.

Fun 'n Wheels, in the heart of the International Drive bustle, is an old-fashioned amusement park featuring go-karts, miniature golf, and traditional rides. Because there is no admission charge, and you pay only for those rides and attractions you want to use, it is a change of pace from the all-inclusive parks. Another Fun 'n Wheels is found on U.S. 192 in Kissimmee. The **Mystery Fun House** on Major Blvd. is a 15-room, walk-through mansion where you encounter no end of scares and surprises.

Afterwards, play the 18 holes of miniature golf. It is touristy and not inexpensive, but combination and discount tickets ease the bite.

Within **Loch Haven Park** is the **Orlando Science Center** which includes a

planetarium named after local astronaut John Young, the **Orange County Historical Museum**, and the **Orlando Museum of Art**, which has a mixed collection from the Americas and overseas.

Also in the park is **Fire Station No. 3.** It is the city's oldest, built in 1926. Antique fire fighting pieces are on display.

Winter Park

Winter Park, now a part of the Orlando megalopolis, still has its original college town, artist colony flavor. **Rollins College** has a beautiful campus to explore on pleasant days, and is the scene of frequent concerts and plays. Come to stroll the **Walk of Fame** with its 800 stones from the homes and home-towns of famous people.

Or see the college with its stunning **Spanish Mediterranean chapel**, and some of the area's mansions, from a boat tour that begins at Lake Osceola and from there glides through a series of lakes and canals.

Above: Orlando – one of Florida's business and cultural centers. Right: Some like it hot – Marilyn at Church Street Station.

Downtown Winter Park is lined with chic shops, coffee houses and restaurants, and is a favored Sunday strolling spot. The park from which the city takes its name is bordered by Park Avenue. It is the scene of art and cultural events. The **Charles Hosmer Morse Museum of American Art** is best known for its collection of Tiffany glass. When the Tiffany home burned on Long Island, much of the surviving glasswork found its way here.

One of the best free shows in Orlando is held every Friday at 0945, Navy time. It is the **US Navy Training Center** graduation ceremony in which 600 snappy sailors pass in review. The one-hour ritual includes the drill team, band and chorus, flags, salutes, and heart-swelling patriotism.

The **Recruit Training Command**, home to 16,000 sailors, is on General Rees Rd. Phone 407/646-4474.

Admission is also free to Places of Learning, on Academic Drive, in the International Drive area. On display are children's books and games.

A few minutes south of Orlando on U.S. 441, find the world headquarters of the giant **Tupperware** organization. Plant tours are interesting, fun and free. The museum houses food containers dating from 4000 BC Tours, which last 25 minutes, leave every 15 minutes, Monday- Friday, 9 am to 5 pm.

The largest collection of Presley-ana outside Memphis is housed in the **Elvis Presley Museum** on International Drive. On display are Elvis' clothes, his 1976 Harley, and assorted guns, badges, awards, furniture and photos.

For a look at the old Florida, which still nibbles at fringes of the skyscrapers, take the river ship *Romance* on a dinner cruise of the **St. Johns River**. Based in **Sanford**, the ship also makes two- and three-day trips to **St. Augustine** or **Palatka**.

Along the route are forgotten old homesteads, abandoned piers and wildly

overgrown banks where rice and indigo once grew, and where a nonstop panorama of wildlife can now be seen. The mood aboard is casual yet elegant, with lavish meals. For a closer look at central Florida au naturel, rent a canoe to explore the spring-fed **Wekiva River**, walk the nature trails in **Turkey Lake Park**, or drive to nearby **Mount Dora** where the state's longest boardwalk probes deep into teeming marshlands surrounding sparkling **Lake Dora**.

Walk quietly, wait a bit and listen, for a nonstop show of shorebirds, predators, songbirds, fish, raccoon and the occasional alligator.

Another boardwalk perches over the 19-acre **Reedy Creek swamp** at the **Osceola School's Experimental Center** on Poinciana Rd. Alligators bask on logs, ospreys circle overhead waiting to pounce on their prey, and leggy water birds stalk the waters in search of a fish dinner. It is open only on weekends.

With the building of Walt Disney World, Orlando replaced Miami as the

state's vacation hub. Today, every bro-
chure in the state lists a destination's distance from WDW, even though it may be
hundreds of miles away!

In planning your trip, turn over the
pages to the map and look at city names.
While Orlando International is the airport, and Lake Buena Vista is the mailing
address of Walt Disney World, Kissimmee is the community which is actually closest to WDW.

Kissimmee-St.Cloud

Within the Kissimmee-St. Cloud area
alone, there are 18,000 hotel rooms, many
of them priced at half WDW rates.

Don't miss Kissimmee's attractions,
which include **Old Town** with its brick-
paved streets. **Xanadu** is a computerized
home of the future. **Gatorland Zoo** is

home to numerous Florida natives. **Alligatorland** is home of the incredible 1500-
pound Big Boy. **Water Mania** is a popular water park. **Reptile World Serpentarium** is where venomous snakes are
milked three times a day for venoms used
in laboratories.

Kissimmee is the winter home of the
Houston Astros, whose spring training
games are played at the county stadium.

One of the loveliest of side trips is to
the **Bok Tower Gardens**, where the singing tower peals out a carillon concert
every half-hour. Special concerts are held
during the full moon, on Easter Sunday,
and on the birthday of **Edward Bok** who
built the 205-foot tower in the 1920s as
his way of thanking the American people
for his success. Bok had arrived an immigrant and died as a well-known and
wealthy Pulitzer prize winning author.

Around the pink and gray marble
tower are 128 acres of gardens which
glow red and pink with camellias in
winter and with mountains of azaleas in
February and March. Walk the self-

*Above: In some parts of the world luxury is
an every-day thing. Right: Architectural accent – Kress-store at Orlando.*

guided nature trail, or just sit in the shade of a giant oak and listen to the carillon.

Since the 1930s, a Lenten tradition in Lake Wales has been the performance of **Josef Meier's Black Hills Passion Play** in which the life of Christ is acted out. Headquartered in South Dakota where the play is given in summer, the 250-member cast comes each spring to the amphitheater here.

Aviation History

Aviation buffs flock to Florida for its fine flying weather, the abundance of good, small airports, and the comradeship of like-minded souls.

One of the finest collections of old planes in the United States is at the **Flying Tigers Warbird Air Museum**, 231 Hoagland in Kissimmee.

Several companies offer hot air balloon flights over the area, and at Kissimmee Airport you can also sign up for a glider ride or a champagne flight to Key West aboard a venerable DC-3.

Beaches and Shopping

Beaches and shopping in the whole area are worth some time to even the most devoted WDW visitor. Most people usually spend at least a day outside the World enjoying Orlando's festival shopping areas such as **Mercado** and **Church Street Station**, as well as discount malls, conventional malls, factory outlets, and flea markets equal to the size of Rhode Island.

Orlando resorts have become skilled at landscaping, including hauling tons of sand to create artificial beaches around pools and ponds.

Many visitors do not bother to go to the coast at all. Still, if you long for the whisper of surf, salt air and long stretches of sugar sands, the nearest beaches are those to the east, adjacent to Ormond, Daytona, New Smyrna and Cape Canaveral, which has a National Seashore. Equally tempting are St. Petersburg and Clearwater beaches on the Gulf of Mexico, two and a half hours west.

ORLANDO AND DISNEY WORLD
Accommodation

LUXURY: **Disney Grand Floridian Beach Resort**, in Walt Disney World, 407/824-3000. 2000 rooms and suites, in the grandest of Victorian style. **Hyatt Regency Grand Cypress**, 1 Grand Cypress Blvd, Orlando 32819, 407/239-1234. 1604 rooms and suites, pool with waterfalls, all part of an enormous hotel/resort complex. **Disney Village**, 1901 Buena Vista Dr., Lake Buena Vista 32830, 407/827-1100. Wooded 450-acre resort, includes units with kitchens and specialized children's programs. **Buena Vista Palace**, **WDW Hotel Plaza**, Lake Buena Vista 32819, 407/ 827-3333; FL 800/432-2920; U.S. 800/ 327-2990. 841 units. **Grenelefe**, 3200 S.R. 546, Grenelefe, FL 33844, 813/ 422-7511, 800/237-9549 U.S.; 800/282-7875 FL. Clubby, 1000-acre golf resort. **The Peabody**, 9801 International Dr. Orlando 32819, 407/352-4000, FL 800/221-0496. **Radisson Plaza**, 60 S. Ivanhoe Blvd., Orlando 32804, 407/843-0262. Efficient, courteous business person's hotel downtown. **Stouffer Orlando Resort**, 6677 Sea Harbor Dr., Orlando 32821, 800/ HOTELS-1, local 407/351-5555. World's largest atrium encloses a magnificent aviary.

MODERATE: **Harley Hotel**, 151 E. Washington St., Orlando 32801, 407/841-3220. **Sonesta Village Resort**, 10000 Turkey Lake Rd., Orlando 32819, 407/352-8051. **Holiday Inn Main Gate East**, 5678 U.S. 192, Kissimmee 32741, 407/396-4488. 800/523-2309 U.S. **Orange Lake Country Club**, 8505 W. Spacecoast Pkwy., Kissimmee 32742, 800/ 432-8888 FL, (800) 327-4444 elsewhere.

BUDGET: **Comfort Inn Maingate**, 7571 Irlo Bronson Hwy. (U.S. 192), Kissim mee 32741, 407/396-7500. **Economy Inns of America**, 5367 Irlo Bronson Hwy., Kissimmee 32741, 507/396-4020; FL 800/423-3018; US 800/826-0778. **Sevilla Inn**, 4640 W. Irlo Bronson Hwy., Kissimmee 32741, 407/396- 4135.

BED & BREAKFAST: **Beaumont House**, 206 S. Beaumont Ave., Kissimmee, FL 32741. 407/846-7916. Shared bath. Home built early in 20th century, amidst oaks and pecan trees, overlooking Lake Toho. Excellent breakfasts cooked by the owner.

Restaurants

LUXURY: **American Vineyards**, in the Hilton. Reservations required, 407/ 827-4000, ext 3092. Brunch daily 10-2, dinner nightly until 10:30. Jackets required for men. **Arthur's 27**, in the Buena Vista Palace, Reservations necessary, 407/827-3450. Dinner until 10:30 nightly. Men's jacket and tie required. **Atlantis**, in the Stouffer Orlando Resort. Reservations recommended, 407/ 351-5555. **Bob Ruby's Great Steaks**, 999 Douglas Ave., Longwood, 407/682-7828. **Christini's**, 7600 Dr. Phillips Blvd., 407/345-8770. Open Monday-Saturday, 6 P.M.-midnight. Haifeng, Stouffer Orlando Resort. Reserv. required, 407/ 351-5555. Open for dinner except Sun. **La Normandie**, 20211 E. Colonial Dr., 407/896-9976. Reservations are essential.

MODERATE: **Bubble Room**, 1351 S. Orlando Ave., Maitland, 407/628- 3331. **Freddie's Steak and Seafood House**, 7355 S. U.S. 17-92, Fern Park, 407/ 339-3655. Open daily for lunch and dinner. **La Cantina**, 4721 E. Colonial Dr., 407/894-4491. Open for dinner, except Sunday and Monday. **Maison des Crepes**, 348 Park Ave., N. Winter Park, 407/647-4469. Creperie, specializing in seafood. Lunch, Monday to Saturday; dinner Tuesday or Saturday. **The Outback**, Buena Vista Palace, 407/827-3430. Aussie setting. **Straub's**, 5101 E. Colonial Dr., 407/273-9330 and 512 E. Altamonte Dr., Altamonte Springs, 407/831- 2205. Seafood. Open daily for lunch and dinner.

BUDGET: **Bavarian Schnitzel House**, three locations: 6159 Westwood Blvd., 407/352-8484; 1185 Spring Center S., S.R. 434 West, Altamonte Springs-Longwood, 407/774-9989. **Old Munich**, 61 Church St., 407/425-4060. Lunch and dinner daily. **Enclave Beach Cafe**, 6165 Carrier Dr., 407/352-5740. Open Sunday to Thursday, 7 A.M.-midnight, Friday and Saturday to 1 A.M. German beer garden atmosphere. **Numero Uno**, 2499 S. Orange Ave., Orlando, 407/841-3840. Seedy setting for authentic Cuban kitchen. Daily except Wednesday, 11:30 A.M.-9:30 P.M. **Ming Garden**, 6432 International Dr., 407/352-8044. Hunan, Szechuan, Cantonese, Mandarin menu or lunch buffet. Open daily from 11 a.m. **O'Scarlett's**, 6308 International Dr. (next to Wet N Wild), 407/345-0727. Fried chicken, cornbread, black-eyed peas and other Dixie specialties. Dinner daily. **Shells**, 852 Lee Rd., 407/628-3968. Lobster, oysters, shrimp, crab, scallops. **Aunt Polly's**, 2030 W. Colonial Dr., 407/422-6336. Breakfast, lunch and dinner daily. **Ferrari**, 6932 S. Kirkman Rd., 407/352- 2711. **Goomba Joe's**, 6515 International Dr., 407/351-3500. **Good Old Days Emporium**, Loomis Drugs Marketplace, 7600 Dr. Phillips Dr., 407/352-1177. **Cheap eats**. Daily 8:30 a.m.-8 P.M. **Vegetarian Cafeteria**, Florida Hospital, 601 E. Rollins St., 407/ 896- 6611. Meatless cuisine for those on a budget. Excellent breakfast bar. Open 7:30 A.M.-midnight.

Dinner Theater

Arabian Nights, 6225 E. Irlo Bronson Hwy. Kissimmee, 407/239- 9223. Popular, elaborate production. Reservations essential. **King Henry's Feast**, 8984 International Dr., Orlando, 407/351-5151. **Mardi Gras**, 8445 International Dr., Orlando, 407/351-5151. Beef and hearty fare. **Medieval Times**, U.S. 192, 8 miles west of I-4, 407/239-0214. Reservations required for popular show featuring actors on horseback. **Plantation Dinner Theater**, Heritage Inn, 9861 International Dr. Thursday through Saturday at 7. Reservations, 407/ 352-0008.

Jazz Clubs

Class Act Lounge, Winter Park. **Coconuts** or **Hubb's Pub**, Altamonte Springs. **Danielle's**, in the Park Suite Hotel. **Sparkles** in the Radisson Plaza; **Fibber McGee's**, Kissimmee. **Valentyne's**, downtown. the **Village Lounge**, Walt Disney World Village.

Reggae

Try the **Enclave Beach Cafe** or the **No Name Oyster Bar.**

Dancing

To live music at **Arthur's**, Buena Vista Palace. **Cheek to Cheek**, Winter Park. The **Giraffe Lounge**, Hotel Royal Plaza.

Tourist Information

Convention & Visitors Bureau, 7108 Sand Lake Road, Orlando, FL 32819. Visitor Information line, 407/363-5871. Address all Walt Disney World hotels at P.O. Box 10000, Lake Buena Vista, FL 32830. Other hotels including independent hotels in Walt Disney World Village, have their own addresses. For general information about WDW, write P.O. Box 10040, Lake Buena Vista FL 32830. WDW packages are available through travel agents or **Walt Disney Travel Co.**, P.O. Box 22094, Lake Buena Vista, FL 32820. Most economical accommodation in the area are in Kissimmee. Write Convention & Visitors Bureau, 1925 E. Irlo Bronson Hwy., Kissim mee FL 32741, 800/327-9159 in FL; 800/432-9199 U.S.

Emergencies

Dial 911 to summon fire department, ambulance, or police.

Major Sports Events

The Kansas City Royals and Minnesota Twins take spring training in Orlando. The Orlando Juice play in the Senior Professional Baseball League, with games scheduled from November through January. The Orlando Magic play professional basketball. The Citrus Bowl Football Classic is a yearly Orlando event, every January 1. Golf events include October's Walt Disney World Golf Classic, and the Nestle Invitational PGA tournament, in March.

Annual Events

Scottish Highland Games, January; Central Florida Fair, February; *Silver Spurs Rodeo*, Kissimmee, February and July; *Bluegrass Festival*, Kissimmee, March; *Bach Festival*, Winter Park, March; *Pioneer Days Folk Festival*, October; *Florida State Air Fair*, late Fall, Kissimmee; Florida Symphony Orchestra performs concerts September through May.

Museums and Galleries

Places of Learning, 6825 Academic Dr. Free. Daily 10 A.M.-7 P.M. An acre-size map of the U.S., life-size books and chessmen. 3800 educational books for sale. 407/ 351-5544.

Elvis Presley Museum, 5931 American Way, Orlando, 407/345-8860. Elvis' car, guns, guitars. Admission.

The **Maitland Art Center**, 321 W. Packwood. Monday-Friday 9 A.M.-4 P.M., Saturday and Sunday 1-4 P.M. Free.

Tavares and Gulf Railroad Depot, 101 S. Boyd St., Winter Garden. Free. Call to make arrangements. 407/656-5056 or 644-6777.

Orlando Science Center, 810 E. Rollins St., 407/896- 7151.

Beal Maltbie Shell Museum, Rollins College, Holt Ave., Winter Park. 2 million shells. Mon-Thu 10 A.M.- noon and 1-4 P.M., Friday 10 A.M.-noon. 407/646-2364. Also on Rollins campus is **Cornell Fine Arts Center**, free, Tue-Fri 1-5 P.M., and 1-5 P.M. Sat. 1200 watch keys. 407/ 646-2526.

The Orange County Historical Museum, 812 E. Rollins St., Orlando, 407/898-8320. Closed Monday. Free.

Fire Station No. 3. Old-time fire equipment. Open Tuesday-Friday 10 A.M.-4 P.M., Satur day and Sunday 2-5 P.M., 407/898-8320.

Zoos

Alligatorland Safari Zoo, 4580 W. Hwy. 192, Kissimmee, 407/396- 1012. One acre, but home 2000 alligators, plus other reptiles and animals. Admission. **Central Florida Zoological Park**, Lake Monroe, FL, 407/323-4450. More than 500 creatures including monkeys, lions, elephants, tigers, birds, snakes. Open daily. Admission. East of St. Cloud on U.S. 192 is **Reptile World Serpentarium**, which offers half-hour programs at 11 A.M., 2 or 5 P.M. Experts "milk" venomous snakes for venoms which are used for treatment and research around the world. More than 60 species can be seen. Daily except Monday, 9 A.M.-5:30 P.M. Admission. **Gatorland Zoo**, 14501 S. Orange Blossom Trail, Orlando, 407/855-5496.

CAPE CANAVERAL

Cape Canaveral is located at the midpoint of Florida's east (Atlantic) coast between Miami and Jacksonville. The distinctive shape of the cape sticking out into the Atlantic makes it easy to identify on a map or from the air.

Some evidence exists of migratory Indians having visited the area from time to time, and the Spanish explored this general vicinity about 450 years ago, but the cape's history was not worthy of much comment until July 8, 1947, when the US government picked this isolated spot as the launch site for its Atlantic Missile Test Range. It was from here that American and German rocketry pioneers tested and perfected the forerunners of today's rockets.

However, the Cape still received little notice until the USSR launched its Sputnik spacecraft. Once the race to explore space began, it grew rapidly until too little space remained at the Cape Canaveral site for the moon mission facilities. In 1964, the space center was relocated to adjacent **Merritt Island** and the current NASA **Kennedy Space Center** was opened, from which the Apollo missions were staged and the Space Shuttle is launched. The early launch facilities and some military installations remain at Cape Canaveral, however public access is only allowed via bus tours from the Kennedy Space Center.

John F. Kennedy Space Center

Kennedy Space Center encompasses 84,000 acres of land including over 25 miles of beach area. Much of this land is open to the public as a National Wildlife Refuge. In 1975, 16,600 acres were designated as part of the **Canaveral National Seashore**. The resulting dichotomy of space-age technology and wildlife refuge may seem strange at first, but it appears to work very well.

The space center includes the launch facilities for the Saturn V moon missions, the two Space Shuttle launch pads, the **Vehicle Assembly Building**, the **Shuttle Landing Facility** and the **Spaceport USA Visitors Facility**.

All visitors to Kennedy Space Center start at the Visitors Facility. Bus tours can be taken from here to the old facilities at Cape Canaveral or the new ones at the Kennedy Space Center. In addition to the bus tours, the **Visitors Center** offers a number of free and pay attractions. The free attractions include a simulated space station which focuses on the many types of satellites, and an outdoor display of rockets, lunar vehicles, capsules and other large space hardware. A children's **Exploration Station** where children are shown demonstrations and hands-on displays related to space (this facility may need to be scheduled in advance depending on the number of children at the Visitors Center).

The Boy From Mars is a fiction film about a 10-year-old boy who is born on Mars and is to visit Earth for the first time. The **NASA Art Gallery and Space Shuttle Exhibits** include over 250 paintings by some of America's greatest artists. A series of short (15-30 minute) movies are being shown almost continuously in the various theaters.

The pay exhibits include the bus tours of the Kennedy Space Center and Cape Canaveral Air Force Base and the IMAX giant screen motion picture *The Dream is Alive*, which is a history of the space program presented on a screen more than five stories high.

Canaveral National Seashore

In 1963 NASA turned over to the US Fish and Wildlife Service the management of all non-operational areas of the

Left: Perfect illusion of having met a real-life astronaut.

Canaveral Nat'l. Cape Seashore
Beach
Rd. Playalinda Beach

Parrish
Park
405
402
Wildlife Refuge Hdqrs.
Gate 4
Gates closed to public
Gate 5
Launch Complex

406
Merritt Island Nat'l.
Wildlife Refuge
Shuttle Landing Facility

95
Titusville
Green Bush Pt.
Banana
False Cape

405
1
South Titusville
Vehicle Assembly Building

NASA CAUSEWAY
John F. Space Center (N.A. S.A)

WEST
405
NASA PARKWAY WEST
405
Complex 37
Complex 34
Complex 19

407
Gate 3
Visitor Information Center
East Nasa
ICBM
Complex 14
Complex 13
Complex 12
Complex 36

Bellwood
Kennedy Space Center Hdqrs.
Causeway Rd.
Space Flight Control

Delespine
Gate 2
River
Space Mus.
Cape Canaveral

Port St. John
3
Courtenay
Home Pt.
Cape Canaveral Air Force Base Station
Cape
Canaveral Bight
Complex 5,6

528
Sharpes
Hall
Rd.
Kars Park
Gate 1 closed to public
401
Pier

BENNETT
KENNEDY
CAUSEWAY
Port Canaveral
Mus. of Sunken Treasure

Canaveral Acres
524
528
Jetty Park
Cape Canaveral

520
Merritt Island
501
OLD DIXIE
520
Canaveral Pier
Sheppard Park
ATLANTIC

Cocoa
Sykes Cr.
Banana
Sidney Fischer Park

Rockledge
Thousand Islands
Cocoa Beach

West Rockledge
502
Buck Pt.
OCEAN

Bona-venture
1
Georgiana
Banana River Aquatic Presurve
Patrick A.F.B. Missle Test Center

Pineda
509
Lotus

Palm Shores
404
PINEDA CSWY.
A1A

95
Satellite Beach
Pelican Beach Park

9
511
518
Indian Harbor Beach

West Eau Gallie
Eau Gallie
Paradise Beach Park

CAPE CANAVERAL

0 _____ 6km
0 _____ 3 miles

space center. More endangered and threatened species reside at America's Spaceport than at any other refuge in the continental United States.

Merritt Island National Wildlife Refuge

On the 7-mile Blackpoint Wildlife Drive through the Kennedy Space Center's **Merritt Island Wildlife Refuge**, visitors can observe many of these animals. The best times for viewing are early morning or late afternoon between October and March. See wood storks, bald eagles, hawks, owls, brown pelicans, herons, spoonbills, ibis, cormorants and egrets. Land animals include deer, wild pigs, bobcats, foxes, armadillos and a variety of reptiles including the Eastern Diamondback Rattlesnake. Otters and turtles also abound in the refuge as do alligators and manatees.

Spaceport USA

Access to the Kennedy Space Center is strictly controlled. All visitors must enter through the public access at Spaceport USA. This facility offers free parking, a multilingual staff and guide books, a number of free displays, ticketing for bus tours of the space center and a large theater and museum facility.

Bus tours are available for both the older Cape Canaveral Air Force Station and the Kennedy Space Center. Tours are conducted in English with the exception of pre-scheduled groups of 53 or more people. The exact tour schedule and what can be seen on any particular day are governed by flight operations.

The Kennedy Space Center tour normally includes visits to the Vehicle Assembly Building (no tourists are allowed inside the VAB) where the Space

Above: One of the most important harbors on the East Coast: Port Canaveral.

Shuttle's various parts are checked out and assembled, the Headquarters Building and the Operations and Checkout Building where the payloads are assembled and checked out prior to launch.

If your visit coincides with one of the launch dates, you may get a chance to see the launch vehicle being transported from the Assembly Building to the Launch Pad aboard the Crawler Transporter. This gigantic vehicle is the size of half a soccer field and weighs over 2,722 metric tonnes. It is designed to move at a sedate 1.6 kilometers per hour and attain a top speed of 3.2 kilometers per hour if it is unloaded. The Crawler can carry a fully assembled Space Shuttle with payload, a weight of 6,577,200 kg.

The Space Shuttle is a truly multinational undertaking. While the United States developed the Shuttle, ten nations of the European Space Agency designed, funded and built "Spacelab", which is a versatile and re-usable flight unit carried in the Shuttle's cargo bay. Austria, Belgium, Denmark, France, Germany,

149

Italy, Holland, Spain, Switzerland and the United Kingdom all share in the operations of Spacelab.

The Spaceport facilities are open from 9:00 am to dusk daily except on Christmas Day. The smallest crowds occur on weekends and it is strongly suggested that visitors arrive early and purchase tickets for the bus tours and movies immediately upon arrival. The various tour departures are announced throughout the facility shortly before they are ready to load. A minimal visit of five to six hours is recommended.

Space Coast Area

The three largest towns in the area of the space center are **Titusville, Melbourne** and **Cocoa Beach**.

Cocoa Beach is a beach community with modest resort trade which offers traditional beach activities, sailing and a

Above: Pride and public relations instead of secrecy: Cape Canaveral.

wealth of restaurants and hotels. Historically, Cocoa Beach is where the astronauts lived and played during the heyday of the space program. Today they are housed at the Space Center during training and pre-launch.

While nowhere in Central Florida it is inexpensive, one can expect to find better room and food buys in the Space Coast area than in Orlando.

Port Canaveral is completely independent of the Space Center. It is the home port for Premier and SeaEscape Cruise Lines and is the second largest passenger cruise terminal in Florida. From here SeaEscape Cruise Lines offers daily cruises to nowhere that allow the visitor to experience the luxury and relaxation of a cruise ship. The ship carries passengers into open seas, where, among other activities, they are free to gamble upon reaching international waters. After three typically enormous meals, the ship heads back to port. Premier Cruise Line offers three- and four-day cruises to the Bahamas.

CAPE CANAVERAL
Accommodation

No accommodation exists at the Spaceport. However, over 8000 rooms are available in the surrounding communities and many visitors stay in Orlando, taking a bus from their hotel directly to the space center.

Titusville is 10 miles west of the space center. In Titusville one can find comfortable, moderate-priced accommodation at Ramada Inn, Best Western, Rodeway and Quality Inn, all chain motels with toll-free 800 phone numbers listed in the guidelines at the back of the book. Cocoa Beach is 25 miles south of the space center on U.S. Highway A1A. One can find a Holiday Inn, Hilton and Howard Johnson's Lodge on the beach in Cocoa Beach, also with listed 800 numbers in the guidelines. The Space Coast has no truly luxury properties. Economy accommodation can be found at any number of camp grounds, RV parks or economy chain hotels such as Motel Six or Econo Lodge.

Restaurants

EXPENSIVE: **Mango Tree Restaurant**, 118 N. Atlantic Ave., Cocoa Beach, 407/799-0513.
MODERATE: **Aunt Catfish's**, 550 Halifax Dr., Port Orange, 904/767-4768.
BUDGET: **The Oyster Bar**, 225 N. US 19, Crystal River, 904/985-3949, a top local spot for fresh seafood, low on ambience, high quality, low-cost food. The primary food outlet at the Space Center is the **Orbit Cafeteria**. It serves mostly fast food items such as hamburgers and hotdogs. During the summer months **The Launch Pad Restaurant** is open. It serves a wider variety of foods such as fish, Bar-B-Q and chicken. The Space Center also has two snack bars, the **Snack Port** and **North Food**.

Access and Transportation

AIR: Melbourne Regional Airport is serviced by American, Continental, Delta, Eastern, U.S. Air and United Express. **SEA**: Port Canaveral for ocean-going vessels and a number of private marinas on the Inland Waterway for smaller vessels. **LAND:** There are two primary entrances to the Kennedy Space Center, state Route 405 runs east from the mainland and state Route 3 runs north along Merritt Island. Follow the signs for Kennedy Space Center, not those for Cape Canaveral. For visitors staying in Orlando, follow the Beeline East from Orlando to state Route 407. Proceed north on state Route 407 to state Route 405 and take state Route 405 east to the space center. Tour bus service is available from most of Orlando's larger hotels but not from Titusville or Cocoa Beach.

Hospitals

A nurse is on duty at all times at the space center. The **Jess Parish Memorial Hospital** in Titusville, 10 miles from the facility 407/268-6111.

Museums and Art Galleries

The Gallery of Spaceflight, NASA Art Exhibit, **Rocket Garden**, and the **Galaxy Theater** are all located at the space center. The surrounding communities enjoy a wealth of theaters, art galleries and museums.

In Titusville is the **Titusville Playhouse**; in Melbourne, the **Maxwell C. King Center for the Performing Arts**, **The Space Coast Science Center**, **The Melbourne Civic Theater**, the **Ensemble Theater** and the **Brevard Art Center and Museum**. Cocoa and Cocoa Beach are home to the **Porcher House**, **The Astronaut Memorial Space Science Center**, **Brevard Museum of History and Natural Science**, **Cocoa Village Playhouse** and the **Surfside Playhouse**.

Post Office / Telegraph

The space port has its own post office, where letters can be postmarked Kennedy Space Center.

Shopping

The **Gift Gantry** at the space center sells space-related gift items, film, batteries and a mind-boggling variety of other souvenir items.

Tourist Information

Brevard County Tourist Development Council, 2235 North Courtenay Parkway, Merritt Island, 407/453-2211, or 800/USA-1969. **Spaceport USA**, Visitors Center, Kennedy Space Center, 32899, 407/452-2121. **Brevard Cultural Alliance**, 407/636-ARTS. **Titusville Area Chamber of Commerce**, 2000 South Washington Ave., Titusville, 32780-4752, 407/267-3036. **Cocoa Beach Area Chamber of Commerce**, 400 Fortenberry Road, Merritt Island, 407/459-2200. **Greater South Brevard Area Chamber of Commerce**, 1005 E. Strawbridge Ave., Melbourne, 32901, 407/724-5400.

PARKS: **Canaveral National Seashore and Merritt Island National Wildlife Refuge**, Titusville 33090, 407/267-1110. **Flagler Beach State Recreation Area**, 3100 South A1A, Flagler Beach 32036, 904/439-2474. **Fort Pierce Inlet State Park**, 2200 Atlantic Avenue, Fort Pierce 33449, 407/468-3985. **New Smyrna Sugar Mills Ruins State Historic Site**, PO Box 861, New Smyrna Beach 32069, 904/428-2126. **St. Lucie Inlet State Park**, PO Box 8, Hobe Sound 33455, 407/744-7603. **Sebastian Inlet State Recreation Area**, 9700 South A1A, Melbourne Beach 32951, 407/727-1752. Tosohatchee, **William Beardsall State Reserve**, 3365 Taylor Creek Road, Christmas 32709, 407/568-5893.

DAYTONA BEACH

The World's Most Famous Beach, as **Daytona** likes to bill itself, enjoys fame for its scrubbed surf and sands and its many fine resorts. The area also draws unwanted notoriety for its high crime rate, sleazy spring-break crowds, and long rows of little look-alike motels – some of them sparkling and others on the dog-eared side.

Inexorably, the rising price of irreplaceable beachfront land is forcing out the smaller hotels and the occasional lone, single family dwelling. Taking their place are taller, grander hotels now offering more than 16,000 rooms at rates which are among the state's lowest.

Daytona Beach has one irrefutable claim to fame. You can drive on the beaches. This is a boon to some, but a

Above: Killing time. Right: Even space for parking: huge beaches. Far right: An "insider-view" from a Daytona racers' cockpit.

bother to others. The line seems to be drawn between those who do not mind having to watch for traffic while they sunbathe, and those who prefer beaches free of internal combustion engines.

The beaches themselves stretch for 23 miles; 18 miles are open to cars during daylight hours and until an hour after sunset. Speed limit is 10 mph; beach toll is $3. Although there are long, quiet stretches of beach, attention focuses on **The Boardwalk**, with its band shell, fishing pier, amusements, hot dog vendors, and rides – including a Ferris wheel. For years it has been **Coney Island South**, alight with daily sunshine and nighttime neon, but the honky tonk is giving way to a bright, new, family oriented image as part of a city-wide renovation. For visitors in search of more tony settings, the city has luxury hotels and resorts as well, and it is the headquarters of the renowned Ladies Professional Golf Association.

The late 1980s saw the opening of the **Ocean Center**, a 225,000 square foot

convention center that is often the scene of blockbuster attractions, from boat shows to ice shows, rock concerts to the circus.

Nearby, **Peabody Auditorium** hosts concerts, opera and dance. New in the 1990s, in the band-shell area across from Ocean Center and Peabody Auditorium, is the soaring **Marriott** resort complex, which is being joined by another, equally upscale, convention hotel. Together, they will provide 1000 hotel rooms for visiting conventioneers.

The city's colorful **Halifax Harbor Marina** bristles with 440 new yacht slips, in the center of what will become a waterfront complex rivaling Jacksonville's Riverwalk and Miami's Bayside Marketplace. About 100,000 square feet of speciality shops, restaurants and offices will set off a 10-acre park and river garden.

Ever since the days when speed records were set on the hard-packed sands of Daytona Beach by the automotive greats of the early twentieth century,

Daytona's destiny has been tied to speed. It was here that Arthur McDonald roared to a 34.04 mph record in 1905, and Sir Malcolm Campbell set a land speed record of 276.820 mph in 1935, breaking his own existing record for the fifth time.

Well into the 1940s, speed trials continued as technology was developed for the aircraft engines used in World War II. In 1990, the Tom Cruise movie *Days of Thunder* was filmed here. A special permit was issued, allowing racing scenes to be filmed on the beach.

In 1959, races were moved from the beach to an inland, 2.5-mile oval known to racing fans around the world. Best known races include the Daytona 500, the Sunbank 24 for sports cars, and the Daytona 200 for motorcycles.

The track is busiest during Speed Weeks in February, when formula and stock cars race, but equally exciting are major motorcycle races in March and October, stock car racing in July, and go-kart races just after Christmas. Call 904/253-6711 for information on all of these.

153

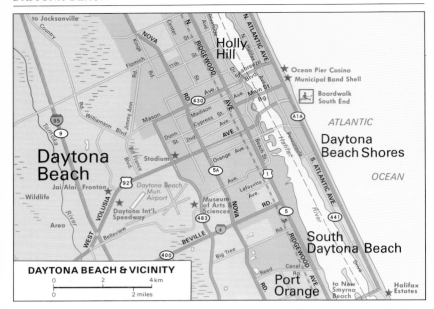

DAYTONA BEACH & VICINITY

Multi-millionaire John D. Rockefeller built a winter home in Ormond Beach and for years he was known as Neighbor John. Now a cultural center and museum, his home, **The Casements**, hosted some of the great names of Florida and United States racing history: Henry Ford, Harvey Firestone, Sir Malcolm Campbell.

All received a Rockefeller souvenir, a shiny dime. To the rich it was a lucky piece. To ordinary folks of the l930s, a dime was substantial walking-around money. Call 904/673-470l for news of art shows, exhibits, concerts, dance recitals at The Casements. Upstairs is a small **Boy Scout museum**.

Daytona is thrice blessed with watersports, in the ocean, the **Intracoastal Waterway**, and a wealth of fresh water, including the **St. Johns River** system. Fishing in all its forms is superb. All types of watersports gear, from jet skis to boats to board sailors, are available for rent in the area. To fish the famous bass waters of the St. Johns, call guide Bob Stonewater, 904/736-7120. To fish salt

water, check the Yellow Pages for long lists of charter skippers, boats of all sizes from individual sport-fishermen to party boats, and guides who specialize in billfish, drift fishing, Gulf Stream game fish or fresh water angling.

The **flea market**, held west of town, Friday through Sunday, is enormous. Give it an entire day. The city also has a discount mall, west of town, on Rt. 44. At the Volusia County Fairgrounds, the **Farmer's Market** held every Wednesday is a folk event not to be missed. Everything from food to flea market items is on sale. On Saturdays, an equally colorful, but smaller Farmer's Market gathers downtown at the riverfront.

As the "affordable" Florida, the Daytona area attracts large numbers of retirees and bargain seekers. As the Spring Break capital, it draws young fun seekers. As a motorcycle mecca, it is a magnetic attraction to thousands of leather-clad, tattooed bikers. As the beach nearest to Walt Disney World, it reaches out to a family audience.

DAYTONA BEACH
Accommodation

LUXURY: **Daytona Beach Hilton**, 2637 S. Atlantic Ave., 32018, 904/767-7350. **Daytona Beach Marriott**, 1401 N. Atlantic Ave., 32018, 904/254-8200 or 800/228-9290. **Inn at Indigo**, 2620 Volusia Ave., 32014, 904/258-6333, 800/223-4161, in Florida, 800/874-9918 elsewhere.

MODERATE: **Aku Tiki Best Western**, 2225 S. Atlantic, DAB Shores, 32018. 800/528-1234 or 904/252-9631. Motel rooms, efficiencies. Ocean beach, heated pool. Kiddie pool, pool bar. **Captain's Quarters**, 3711 S. Atlantic Ave. DAB Shores, 32018. 904/767-3119. Family-operated, New England look, all-suites hotel. On beach. Rates include newspaper and breakfast for two, other plans available. Balconies with rockers. Rooms sleep four and six. Pool. **DeLand Hilton**, 350 International Speedway Dr., DeLand, FL 32724, 904/738-5200. Inland on east edge of quiet, quaint college town. Rooms, suites, nightclub, bar, restaurant, pool.

BUDGET: **Best Western Airport Inn**, U.S. 92 at I-95, Daytona Beach, 32014, 904/253-0643. **Esquire Beach Motel**, 422 N. Atlantic Ave., 904/255-3601. **Holiday Inn Speedway**, 1798 Volusia Ave., 32014. 800/HOLIDAY, 904/255-2422. **Sun and Surf**, 726. N. Atlantic Ave., 32018, 904/252-8412. *BED & BREAKFAST:* **DeLand Country Inn**, 228 W. Howry Ave., DeLand, FL 32720, 904/ 736-4244.

Tourist Information

Destination Daytona, 126 E. Orange Ave., Daytona Beach, FL 32015, 800/854-1234, local 904/255-5478. **Daytona Beach/Halifax Area Chamber of Commerce**, PO Box 2775, Daytona Beach 32015, 904/255-0981. **Daytona Beach Shores Chamber of Commerce**, 3048 South Atlantic Avenue, Daytona Beach 32018-6102, 904/7163. **Daytona Beach / Volusia County Chamber of Commerce**, PO Box 871, Daytona Beach 32015, 904/257-1127.

PARKS: **Bulow Creek State Park**, 3351 Old Dixie Highway, Ormond Beach 32074,904/677-3931. **Bulow Plantation Ruins State Historic Site**, PO Box 655, Bunnell 32010, 904/439-2219. **De Leon Springs State Recreation Area**, PO Box 1338, De Leon Springs 32028, 904/985-4212. **Tomoka State Park**, 2099 North Beach Streat, Ormond 32074,904/677-3931.

Transportation

Daytona Beach Airport is served by American, Continental, Delta and Eastern. The city is served by **Greyhound** buses. **Amtrak** stops at DeLand, 30 miles west. Airport shuttle vans also serve Daytona from Orlando International.

Annual Events

Daytona Speedway events for automobiles and motorcycles attract an international audience. Contact the Speedway at P.O. Drawer S, Daytona Beach, FL 32015. Ask for a yearly schedule. An *Azalea Festival* is held in Palatka, in March. A Central *Florida Balloon Classic* is held in DeLand, in May. An *Antique Car Meet* is held in Ormond Beach, Thanksgiving weekend.

Restaurants

LUXURY: **Karling's Inn**, west on U.S. 92, then north on U.S. 17 to DeLeon Springs. 904/985-5535. Owner-chef, German kitchen. Reservations essential. Closed Sunday, Monday. **La Crepe en Haute**, 142 E. Granada, Ormond Beach, 904/673-1999. Open Tuesday-Friday for lunch; Tuesday-Sunday for dinner. Reservations. **Pondo's**, 1915 Old West New York Ave., DeLand, 904/734-1995. A hideaway on a lonely road. Reservations recommended.

MODERATE: **Anchorage**, 607 Dunlawton, Port Orange. 904/756-8102. Longtime landmark. Open for dinner Monday-Friday, lunch weekends. Reservations recommended. **Aunt Catfish's**, 550 Halifax Dr., at the Port Orange Bridge. 904/767-4768. Locals flock here. Sunday brunch. Full bar. Open daily.

BUDGET: **Asian Inn**, 2516 S. Atlantic Ave., DAB Shores, 904/788-6269. **Cantonese**, Japanese, Szechuan, Mongolian. Dinner daily except Tue until 2 am. **Blackbeard's Inn**, 2 miles S. of Port Orange Bridge, 904/788-9640 and 701 N. Dixie Highway, New Smyrna Beach, offer fried fresh fish with chowder, salad bar, hush puppies, raw bar, lounge, children's menu. Hours vary. Call.

Nightlife

J.J.'s Hideaway at 288 N. Nova Rd. is open Mon-Sat 11 am to 2 am Dining, drinking, dancing. Tropical setting around a pool fountain. **The Boulevard** at 542 Seabreeze Blvd. Disco,two dance floors, four bars, three levels, special events. Open 7:30 pm to 3 am

Museums

Birthplace of Speed Museum, 160 E. Granada, Ormond Beach, 904/672-5657. Stanley Steamer, Model T, Model A, Glenn Curtiss memorabilia. **DeLand Museum**, 449 E. New York Ave., DeLand, 904/734-4371. Local history and Southeastern artists. Indian collection. Admission. **Museum of Arts and Sciences,** 1040 Museum Blvd., 904/255-0285. A Giant Ground Sloth, which roamed the earth 15,000 years ago, is on display, the largest skeleton ever found in North America. Cuban art from the pre-Castro period is featured.

GAINESVILLE

Most people come to **Gainesville** on University of Florida business, which could mean anything from Gators games to treatment at the university's famed teaching hospital, Shands. In all respects it is a college town, with the typical American college amenities, fast foods and inexpensive motels, all geared to a college student's budget.

Tourism has touched little Gainesville – population about l00,000 – less than almost any other Florida city, yet the area has some surprising bonuses to offer the motivated traveler.

To take a look at the old Gainesville, drive the streets of the historic district in the northeast part of town, where almost 300 historic buildings show time-warp **Americana**, erected in the years between 1890 and l910, a time of wooden spacious homes and sprawling green spaces.

This is **Alachua County**, one of Florida's oldest. Some say the name is an Indian word for jug, describing the deep chasm south of town which is so uncharacteristic of flat Florida. The original land grant goes back to l817 when the King of Spain gave 289,000 acres to Don Fernando de la Maza Arredondo and his sons. Even today, thousands of Florida homeowners find that their deeds go back to the Arredondo Grant.

Buffalo were abundant here until they were hunted to extinction. The Spanish once ran enormous herds of cattle on these fertile plains. Now buffalo have been reintroduced, and are thriving here. Two of Gainesville's tourism treasures are natural phenomena.

Payne's Prairie is an 18,000-acre preserve best known for its flocks of sandhill cranes and its herds of buffalo. Climb the observation tower, look out over this vast, sere, featureless prairie, and im-

agine it as the large lake which it was until a century ago. Suddenly, it drained – so abruptly that fish, and even a large passenger boat, were stranded.

Today a wildlife preserve, Payne's Prairie offers swimming, picnicking, horseback riding, camping, hiking, and ranger-guided tours. The **Devil's Millhopper** is an enormous sinkhole, so deep and wide that it has its own cool, damp, unique ecosystem which allows hundreds of plant species – some of them rare in Florida – to flourish here. The visitor will not find any facilities except for some of the state's most interesting hiking trails.

Also included is the **San Felasco Hammock State Preserve**, which has hiking trails but no other amenities. In town, the **Florida Museum of Natural History** is the southeast's largest and one of the nation's top ten natural science museums. Of special interest are a faithful replica of a **Mayan palace** and a Timocuan Indian household typical of those found here when the first Spanish explorers arrived. Amble through the

Left: Like an abstract painting: diver. Above: Stop when the school bus stops.

Kanapaha Botanical Gardens at 4625 S.W. 63rd Blvd. Its collections include lovely butterfly gardens, bamboos, and a palm garden. Also in the city, off S.W. 13th St., is the **Lake Alice Wildlife Preserve**, a quiet place to picnic and birdwatch. And a hammock preserve, out post Main St., has a boardwalk and nature trails.

The **Living History Farm at Morningside Nature Center** is a good place to take children. Familiar farm animals roam pleasant pastures. It is not touristy or flashy, but is simply an inside look at timeless picturebook farm scenes. Marjorie Kinnan Rawlings, whose book *The Yearling* won a Pulitzer prize, fled the city of New York to find inspiration in country life and a simple home at **Cross Creek**, and her tough, earthy presence can still be felt when visiting her house. The typewriter sits on a table on the ramshackle porch. Some of her home-

Above: Children at the gathering: "non-smokers of the year 2000".

canned foods remain in the kitchen, and park rangers continue to tend her gardens. Her scrapbooks are filled with clips about her public and private battles, and her liquor closet still yawns open to reveal where she kept her bottles during the time of Prohibition.

The home is open to the public Thursday through Monday. Rawlings' grave can be seen nearby, at **Island Grove**, south of Gainesville off I-75. Have a look at the historic hamlet of Micanopy (Mick-an-OH-pee) which is making a comeback as a haven for quaint shops and a bed and breakfast inn. One of the state's oldest communities, it was once a popular winter resort.

Ichetucknee Springs State Park, not far away, is best known for its clear, spring-fed stream. Rent a tube and float the spring run, which takes three or four hours. The waters empty into the Sante Fé, which is a tributary of the Suwannee. The park also has swimming, scuba diving, nature trails, snorkeling, and picnicking.

GAINESVILLE
Accommodation
Everyone thinks of the high prices of accommodation in Florida, yet here is another area lacking the costly tourist facilities found elsewhere. You will not find lavish Disney-style hotels, and Goofy will not be here to shake your hand when you register, but then you will not have to pay for them, either. What you will find are modest prices, clean, comfortable accommodation, and a quiet break from the tourist congestion.
MODERATE: The **Hilton**, 2900 S.W. 13th St. 32608, phone 904/377-4000. Each room has its own balcony overlooking a small lake. **Holiday Inn University Center**, 1250 W. University Ave., 3260l, phone local 904/376-1661 or 800/HOLIDAY elsewhere. Downtown hotel with jogging paths, rooftop pool. **Marriott's Residence Inn**, 400l S.W. 13th St., 32602, phone 904/37l-2101 or (800) 331-3131. Suites with cooking facilities, microwave, fireplace. Cocktail hour, continental breakfast, newspaper included in rates. Lounge, pool, spa, guest laundry. Free airport, bus pick-up. **University Centre**, 1535 Archer Rd., 32608, phone 904/371-3333. Special rates for Shands Hospital patients. Suites have refrigerators. Free airport or bus transportation. Restaurant, bar, beauty salon, famous Fiddler's rooftop restaurant.
BUDGET: **Cabot Lodge**, 3726 S.W. 40th Blvd., phone 800/843-8735 from out of state, 800/331-8215 from within in FL, or 904/375- 2400. Rates include cocktail hour, continental breakfast. **Super 8 Motel**, 4202 S.W. 40th Blvd., phone 904/378-3888 or 800/843-1991. Basic motel amenities at rock bottom price. Restaurants nearby. **University Inn**, l901 S.E. l3th St., 32608, phone 904/376-2222. Large swimming pool, local shuttle, free continental breakfast.
BED & BREAKFAST: **Herlong Mansion**, Micanopy, phone 904/466-3322. Elegant home atmosphere with complete and personal pampering from live-in hosts. Some rooms have private baths.

Restaurants
LUXURY: **Ironwood**, 2100 N.E. 39th Ave., phone 904/378-5111 for reservations. Continental dining in elegant room. Business or cocktail dress. Open weekdays for lunch. Dinner daily except Sunday. **Sovereign**, 12 S.E. Second Ave., phone 904/378-6307. Reservations are recommended for this dressy, celebration room. Duckling, veal, prime beef.
MODERATE: **Iron Horse**, 1120 E. University Ave., phone 904/376-9999. Hefty servings of hearty fare. Raw bar, casual ambience. Open for

lunch Tue-Fri, dinner daily except Mon. **The Yearling**, Rt. 3, Hawthorne, Tel: 904/366-3033. Country fare in the spirit of early Florida pioneers who ate quail, alligator, turtle and the like. Closed Mon. Reservations accepted except for Sundays, which can be busy because visitors combine a meal here with a visit to the Rawlings home.

Sightseeing
The Gainesville Northeast Historic District contains 290 historic buildings from the late nineteenth century. Many of the structures have been restored and include large public lawns and cool, leafy gardens that were popular in that era. A self-guided walking tour can be made with the aid of a map supplied by the Visitors and Convention Bureau.

Annual Events
The Gatornationals stock car races are held in Gainesville every March.
Museums and Galleries
Florida Museum of Natural History, Museum Rd. at Newell Dr., phone 904/392-1721. The collection comprises the largest natural history museum in the southeast. Objects Gallery contains thousands of specimens, dating back to prehistoric times. Open daily except Christmas. Free. **Fred Bear Museum**, Fred Bear Dr. at Archer Rd., phone 904/376-2411. A museum devoted to archery, from earliest man to present day. Open every day except Christmas. Admission. **University Art Gallery**, on campus, phone 904/392-020l. Changing exhibits. Hours vary with the school year. Free admission.
Access and Transportation
Gainesville Airport is served by Eastern, Delta, and US Air. The city is also served by Amtrak trains and Greyhound bus.
Tourist Information
Gainesville Visitors and Convention Bureau, 10 S.W. Second Ave., Gainesville FL 3260l, phone 904/374-5210. Among other services that can be arranged through this office, a multilingual staff is available on request for those who speak French, German, Dutch, Italian or Spanish. Parks: **Devil's Millhopper State Geological Site**, 4732 NW 53rd Avenue, Gainesville 32601, 904/377-5935. **San Felasco State Preserve**, c/o **Devil's Millhopper State Geological Site**, 4732 NW 53rd Avenue, Gainesville 32601, 904/336-2008. **Paynes Prairie State Preserve**, Route 2, Box 41, Micanopy 32667, 904/836-4281. **Marjorie Kinnan Rawlings State Historic Site**, County Road 335, Route 3, Box 92, Hawthorne 32640, 904/466-3672. **Ravine State Ornamental Garden**, PO Box 1096, Palatka 32077, 904/328-4366.

NORTHEAST FLORIDA

ST. AUGUSTINE
JACKSONVILLE
SUWANNEE COUNTRY

ST. AUGUSTINE

Four hundred years of local history are recorded here, much of it in entire neighborhoods that have been faithfully restored to their origins in one century or another. The first known landing by a European explorer was by Ponce de Leon in 1513, making this America's oldest city.

St. Augustine has been settled since 1565 when Pedro de Menendez rowed ashore and took possession in the name of Spain. A 208-foot stainless steel cross, the tallest in the nation, rises from a quiet field a few blocks north of downtown to mark this memorable place. Also on the site is the oldest Marian shrine in the country, **Our Lady of LaLeche**. Each September, the founding of the city is re-enacted on this spot.

The time warp is total in **San Augustin Antiguo** (Old St. Augustine), and its **Spanish Quarter**. When restoration was first discussed in 1936, nothing remained of the Spanish period. Researchers went back to original inventories and architectural drawings, many of them in Spain,

Preceding pages: Jacksonville is considered the city with the largest surface area in the U.S. Left: More than one building bears Henry Flagler's name at St. Augustine.

while archaeologists dug for foundations, wells, relics, and roadbeds. Almost two hundred years ago when England took over from Spain, the city was already in sad repair. Then a yellow fever epidemic killed many of the newly arrived Britons. Those who survived were kept busy by the Seminole Wars, then the Civil War.

Prosperity did not return to St. Augustine until the 1880s when Henry Flagler arrived with his railroad, but for the old city that only meant more destruction to make room for the hotels, homes and offices of a brash new era. The final blows were fires that raged through the old Spanish Quarter in 1887 and 1914. Little was left of the old town. Restoration began in earnest in the 1960s, with the goal of recreating the St. Augustine of the period from 1565 to 1821. The years included the First Spanish Period, the English occupation, and the Second Spanish Period. Today the restoration area is alive with people who are working, playing, eating and laughing – in short, living everyday lives in the seventeenth to nineteenth centuries. Stop in a bodega for a meal, buy freshly made candles, baked goods or a newly rolled cigar, or just stroll the streets to bask in the feeling of unhurried yesterdays.

Clusters of costumed characters can be seen here and there; fragments of guitar

music steal out from hidden courtyards; on feast days there may be a sudden mustering of men in armor or a parade. At Christmas, carolers roam cobblestone streets by candle light.

It is rare to find so faithful and complete a seventeenth century streetscape, with authentic smells and sounds, and without cars or other modern intrusions. Except for the tourists clad in shorts and sunglasses, this could well be the St. Augustine of 1760 or 1850. In the restoration area you will see dozens of shops and homes including the grand **Ribera House**, built by a prominent family, the humble **Gomez House**, and the **Gonzalez de Hita House** where weaving, dyeing and other textile skills are practiced and taught. Oldest of the houses is the **Gonzalez-Alvarez House** built in the eighteenth century on a site that had been

Above: America's oldest city sports its ancient cannons. Right: Nearly all of Florida's lighthouses have become monuments.

occupied since the 1600s. Today it is a National Historic Landmark, furnished to show how it looked under Spanish, British, and American ownership.

In the late 1700s, the wealthy Ribera family lived at 22 St. George St. Today restored to the style of that period, their home serves as an office and starting point for tours of the restoration area.

In the **Gallegos House**, a Spanish soldier lived simply with his family in the 1750s. It is that period that has been recreated here. The **DeMesa-Sanchez House** is one of only 33 colonial homes which survived. It is restored to its appearance in the early nineteenth century.

The blacksmith shop, where a "Spanish" smithy of the 1700s can be found at work on most days, is made of tabby – a building material used widely in early Florida dwellings.

Tabby is a mixture of oyster shells and lime, bound with molasses. Other homes were built of coquina, a hard coral rock which was cut from quarries. Wood was available; brick was introduced later; any stone had to be imported. Cobblestones for the streets arrived from Europe as ballast in trading ships. Guidebooks, which describe the homes and their inhabitants in detail, are a good investment for history lovers.

A tour can take an entire day; tickets which buy admissions to seven homes and the blacksmith shop are good value. Many other restored buildings contain shops or restaurants, and charge no admission.

Still others, including the Old Wooden **Schoolhouse, Dr. Peck's House** and the **Oldest Store Museum**, have their own admissions. Admission to the **Ximenez-Fatio House** (1798) and the **Sanchez House** (1816) is free. Most notable of St. Augustine's landmarks is the great **Castillo de San Marcos**, a powerful symbol of the strength that was Spain in the New World. Now a national monument, it has walls 13 feet thick and the distinction of never having surrendered, despite many days of siege.

On a guided tour, you will hear the fort's fascinating and swashbuckling history, starting with its building in the seventeenth century when it was the northernmost defender of Spain's vast, gold-hungry Caribbean empire. The fort endured battles between the Spanish and English, then the Civil and the Seminole wars, in following years it was used as a prison for soldiers who deserted during the Spanish-American War.

Even though the mothballed fort had been a national monument since 1924, it was still very close to action as late as World War II. Only a few miles north of the Castillo, on **Ponte Vedra Beach**, eight German saboteurs came ashore from a submarine and were promptly rounded up. Six were hanged.

Start your visit at the Visitor Information Center, 10 Castillo Drive, one of the few places where adequate parking can be found. An excellent orientation movie is shown continuously.

In addition to its famous history, the St. Augustine area has everything from deep sea fishing to camping, bass fishing to golf. Parking spaces are almost impossible to find in the inner city, so leave the Visitor Center on foot. Better still, start with a guided tour because the city's professional guides are entertaining and well informed. On a tour, you can get oriented, and decide where to go later. Sightseeing trains, which include admission to some points of interest, are an excellent buy. So are one-hour tours by horse and carriage, because you have the driver and his narratives all to yourself. For a change of pace, and a look at St. Augustine and **Matanzas Bay** as seen by the earliest explorers, take a sightseeing cruise or a day fishing excursion.

Surviving from the Flagler railroad era at the turn of the century are the ornate, Moorish minarets of **Flagler College** – originally a hotel built in 1888 when the equally flamboyant Alcazar Hotel, now the **Lightner Museum**, was also thrown up in the frenzy of building that hit the

165

city that decade. When Flagler's granddaughter and her baby were lost at sea, Flagler brought in hundreds more construction workers and set them to work around the clock for a year to build an elaborate monument.

Also remaining from this extravagant period are neighborhoods of Victorian mansions – some of them incorporating parts of even older structures from the Spanish or English periods. Many of them are now cozy bed and breakfast inns. Modern hotels line St. Augustine Beach. Resorts and sightseeing attractions pepper the entire area.

In and around St. Augustine there are many other layers of local social and natural history that should not be missed. In the city itself, commercial attractions include **Ripley's Believe It Or Not Museum**, a wax museum, and the Lightner Museum with a hodgepodge of collections: toys, musical instruments, dolls,

Above: St. Augustine has become some kind of a pleasant open-air-museum.

paintings, and other Victoriana. There is even a **Fountain of Youth Museum**, dedicated to Ponce de Leon. For a small fee you get to drink a cup of water said to be drawn from the original spring discovered by the explorer. Of course, everyone knows de Leon failed to find a real Fountain of Youth, so take this attraction with a grain of salt.

There is an alligator farm outside town on AIA. Farther south on AIA, **Marineland** is the nation's oldest marine attraction and still one of the best. Aquatic shows are continuous, and the shell museum is one of Florida's most complete. Plan an entire day here. Marineland has its own hotel, campground, and restaurants. Continuing south on AIA, you will find Washington **Oaks State Gardens**. The gardens themselves are a quiet place to hike and picnic among reedy waterways and towering live oaks. On the beach side is a dramatically rocky shore, thundering and swirling with surf in contrast to the flat, sandy beaches to the north and south.

ST. AUGUSTINE
Accommodation

LUXURY: **Ponce de Leon Resort**, 4000 N. U.S. l, St. Augustine, 32085, 904/824-2821. Golf, tennis. **Sheraton Palm Coast**, 300 Club House Dr., Palm Coast, 32037, 904/445-3000. Golf courses. *MODERATE:* **Holiday Inn Oceanfront**, 3250 AIA S., St. Augustine Beach, 32084, 904/471-2555. Beach. **Topaz Hotel**, 1224 S. AIA, Flagler Beach, 32136, 904/439-3301. Antiques. Some units have kitchens. *BUDGET:* **Days Inn Downtown**, 2800 Ponce de Leon Blvd., St. Augustine, 32084, Tel: 904/829-6581. Pool, playground, cafe. **Lantern Lodge**, 3654 N. Ponce de Leon Blvd., St. Augustine, 32084, 904/824- 3321. Free bus station pick-up. *BED & BREAKFAST:* **Carriage Way**, 70 Cuna St., St. Augustine, 32084, 904/829-2467. Victorian vernacular mansion. Private baths. **Casa Solana**, 21 Aviles St., St. Augustine, 32084, 904/824-3555. 225-years old, in historic district. **St. Francis Inn**, 279 St. George St., St. Augustine, 32085, 904/824-6068. Built 1791. Private baths. **Southern Wind**, 18 Cordova St., St. Augustine, 32084, 904/825-3623. Victorian antiques. Private baths.

Restaurants

EXPENSIVE: **Raintree**, 102 San Marco Ave., 904/824-7211. Lobster, rack of lamb outdoors on the balcony of this old home. Free pick-up at your hotel in city. Lunch, dinner. **Le Pavillon**, 45 San Marcos Ave., 904/824-6202. Continental dining. *MODERATE:* **Columbia**, 98 St. George St., 904/824-3341. Spanish paella, black beans, filet salteado. Lunch, dinner, Sunday brunch. **Palermo's Fisherman**, 2085 S. AIA, St. Augustine Beach, 904/471-2811. Seafood with Italian accent. **Topaz Cafe**, 1224 S. Ocean Shore Blvd., Flagler Beach, 904/439- 3275. Menu includes vegetarian dishes. Reservations.

Annual Events

Blessing of the Fleet, Palm Sunday; *Spanish Night Watch*, June; *Greek Festival*, June; *Days in Spain*, mid-August, three nights of entertainment, sword fights, dancing, food, and games in the Plaza area. Founding Day, September 8, at the Mission of Nombre de Dios to re-create the scene when Menendez landed here and claimed the land for Spain. *British Night Watch, Tour of Homes, Christmas Boat Parade* and other events add up to a busy, bright December. The official Florida State Play, Cross and Sword, tells the story of early St. Augustine. It plays in an outdoor amphitheater south of town on AIA, from mid-June to the end of August. Closed Sunday. 904/471-1965.

Sightseeing

Administered by the **Historic St. Augustine Preservation Board**, the Spanish Quarter is open every day except Christmas, 9 am-5 pm. Tickets buy admission to a number of restored homes, exhibits, and museums. 904/925-5033. Starting point is the Ribera House at 22 St. George St., which serves as an information center for the restoration area. **The Castillo de San Marcos National Monument** on Rt. AIA is open daily except Christmas for a small admission charge. 904/829-6506. The oldest Marian shrine in the US is **Our Lady of La Leche** at the Mission of Nombre de Dios, the site where this land was first claimed for Spain. It is free, but donations are requested. 904/824-3045. **The Gonzales-Alvarez House**, built in the eighteenth century on a site that had already been occupied for a century, is a National Historic Landmark. Open daily except Christmas. Admission. **Sanchez House**, 105 St. George St. **The Lightner Museum** was built in the Gaslight Era as a grand hotel, the Alcazar. Collections are chiefly Victoriana. Take time to stroll the grounds. Admission. 904/824-2874. **Zorayda Castle**, built in 1883, was patterned after the Alhambra, complete with seraglio. Admission. 904/824-3097. The **St. Augustine Alligator Farm** is the state's oldest, founded a century ago. Animals, reptiles, shows, on AIA, 2 miles south of the Bridge of Lions. **Anastasia State Recreation Area**, camping, swimming, picnicking, mountainous dunes, forests, beaches. Admission. Scenic cruise, 904/824-1806. Sightseeing trains, 904/829-6545. Carriage tours, 904/829-0818. **Fountain of Youth**, 155 Magnolia.

Access and Transportation

Closest airport is **Jacksonville**, where rental cars are available. Some lodgings offer airport pick-up.

Tourist Information

St.Augustine-St. John's Chamber of Commerce, 52 Castillo Drive, St. Augustine, FL 32085, 904/829-5681.
PARKS: **Anastasia State Recreation Area**, 5 Anastasia Park Dr., St. Augustine, 32085, 904/471-3033. **Faver-Dykes State Park**, Route 4, Box 213-J-1, St. Augustine 32086, 904/794-0097. **Washington Oaks State Gardens**, Route 1, Box 128-A, St. Augustine 32086, 904/445-3161. **Castillo de San Marcos National Monument**, 1 Castillo Dr., St. Augustine 32084, 904/829-6506. **Fort Matanzas National Monument**, c/o Castillo de San Marcos National Monument, 1 Castillo Dr., St. Augustine 32084, 904/471-0116.

JACKSONVILLE

Visitors usually breeze right through **Jacksonville** with its heavy traffic and eye-smarting smell. Those who stay to discover this many-faceted city will be surprised, and amply rewarded. One of the most culturally rich cities in the South, it is abuzz with business travelers, conferences and energy.

Yet Jacksonville is surrounded by forests, streams and sea – so much of a center of sailing, hunting, fishing and camping that the local newspaper, the *Florida Times-Union* has one of the largest and most comprehensive outdoors sections in the nation. When the prevailing winds carry away the sulphurous paper mill smells, Jacksonville shines.

The **River of May** was claimed by French Huguenots in 1562. Under the English years later, the community was named **Cowford** and the Spanish name for the San Juan was changed to the **St.**

Above: Crossing St. Johns River by car.

Johns River. The city was finally named for Andrew Jackson.

Today the river remains not just an important commercial artery (barges travel deep inland to Sanford) but the silvery ribbon on which much of the city's recreation is strung. Stroll the riverfront with its shops, sculptures and fountains; schedule a sightseeing dinner or lunch cruise aboard a paddlewheeler; rent a boat. And if you are here in October, do not miss the jazz festival on the river at **Metropolitan Park**. It is one of the nation's best.

After the Civil War, balmy Jacksonville was drawing 75,000 tourists each winter. Then in 1888 came yellow fever and quarantine. Tourism cringed, then died completely in the Great Fire of l901.

Yet Jacksonville's location, with its deep port and benign climate, made up in industry what it could not win in tourism. By the 1920s, 30 movie studios had moved here, abandoning cold and cloudy New York for Florida's blue skies. Jacksonville was America's first Hollywood.

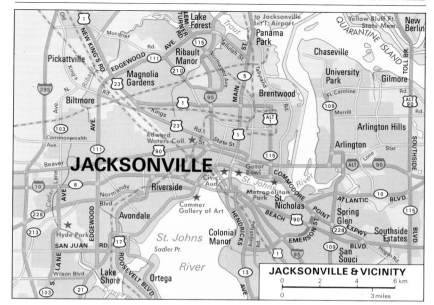

Lumber, citrus, pulp products and cigars made the city an import-export hub. Today it is a major paper producer, medical and corporation headquarters, coffee and banana importer, and the insurance capitol of the South.

Savor Jacksonville on many levels. First is the smart, modern city itself, with its quaint neighborhoods – **San Marco,** developed during the 1930s, **Riverside, Avondale,** the old area of downtown and Springfield. Historic homes from the period 1870-1930 are opened to public tours just once a year, in mid-May.

Next are the outdoor sports - fishing in all its forms from ponds to offshore sportfishing, boating and sailing, and miles of pristine, tide-washed beaches.

Last is the area's rich and exciting history, beginning with Timocuan Indians 2000 years before Columbus. Pack a picnic and drive the **Buccaneer Trail,** starting at Eastport and stopping at historical markers along the way. **Fort Caroline National Monument** replicates the fort built by the French.

Kingsley Plantation, built in 1791, is the oldest surviving plantation in Florida. Tour the home and slave cabins with a guide and learn the sordid story of eccentric slave trader Zephaniah Kingsley. Trees that line the long entry drive to the plantation, planted by slaves long ago, still stand. **Fort Clinch** is a big brick fort, surrounded by a beachside sprawling park where you can fish, swim, camp, or picnic. It was one of a chain of brick forts built around the Atlantic and Gulf coasts to defend against further British advances after the war of 1812. The masonry is a fine example of the bricklayer's art, and the endless tunnels and dungeons of the fort make for interesting exploring on a hot day. Climb the ramparts for a superb view of **Cumberland Sound** and the mouths of the **St. Marys** and **Amelia rivers.**

Route A I A leads into **Fernandina Beach,** which for years was the center of intrigues under eight flags including Spanish, Mexican, British, and Confederate. Building boomed here during Vic-

169

torian times, and many of the showplace mansions remain. On Center Street, find the **Palace Saloon**, oldest in the state and then push through the swinging doors into what could well be a Dodge City movie set.

The main street ends at the colorful docks, packed with working shrimp boats and transient yachts. Stop at the old railroad depot, which is now the Chamber of Commerce, and ask for free brochures which describe a walking tour.

Although most of the homes are privately owned and are not open to the public, the tour is a trip through the architectural history of the period from just before the Civil War into the early twentieth century, Fernandina's heyday.

Downtown points of interest include the depot, which served Florida's first cross-state railroad, **The Swann Building**, circa 1890, the red brick Victorian courthouse with its cast iron Corinthian

Above: A peculiar Santa Claus during the holy season.

columns, and the **Florida House**, once a posh hotel where guests included the wealthy Rockefellers and Carnegies.

The mansions along south 7th, 8th, and 9th streets are among Florida's finest Victoriana. The **Bailey House** at the corner of 7th and Ash is a fine Queen Anne; on another corner stands a house built of tabby, an early Florida building material, made of crushed seashells and molasses. On South 7th between Beech and Cedar is the **Fairbanks home**, a superb Italianate house built in 1885 for a major in the Confederate army.

One of the best gingerbread homes, with its elaborate Chinese Chippendale porch, is on the northeast corner of Beech and South 8th. The **Williams house**, at 103 S. 9th, was where the personal belongings of Jefferson Davis, president of the Confederacy, were stored during the Civil War.

Some of the churches may be open; try the doors. **St. Peter's Parish Episcopal Church**, which dates to 1859, has handmade carved furnishings of Florida cedar and pine and a Tiffany window honoring two doctors who served during a yellow fever epidemic.

The **Presbyterian Church** was a garrison during the Civil War. It is one of the state's oldest churches. Even the old cemetery, Bosque Bello, is worth a visit because it so poignantly records city history – sailors drowned at sea, the many victims of yellow fever epidemics and wars, and names changing from Spanish and English to Portuguese and Greek as waves of immigrants came and went in Fernandina's turbulent history.

Although **Cumberland Island** is just across the Georgia border, it can be reached from Fernandina by ferry.

Dungeness, a 30-room Carnegie mansion burned here in 1959 but its stark ruins stands in a wilderness that is alive with raccoons, deer, birds and beach life, and feral horses. It is well worth a day's hike or an overnight camping trip.

JACKSONVILLE
Accommodation

LUXURY: **Jacksonville**, 565 Main St., 32207, 904/398-8800, 800/327-0131 from within Florida, 800/332-9001 from other US. Overlooks river, Riverwalk. Free garage. Pool, free buffet breakfast. **Marriott**, 4670 Salisbury Rd. at I-4, 32216, 904/739- 5800. Indoor, outdoor pools, tennis and golf privileges, exercise equipment, restaurant, lounge with entertainment. **Omni**, 245 Water St., 32202, 904/355-6664. 354 rooms, suites, heated pool, concierge level, restaurant, lounge with dancing. Garage, valet parking extra. Located downtown.

MODERATE: **Airport Plaza**, 14000 Dixie Clipper Dr. at Airport Rd. and I-95, 904/757-1741. Free airport transportation. Pool, restaurant, bars, exercise room. **Compri**, 4700 Salisbury Rd., 32256, 904/281-9700. I-95 at Turner, Southpoint area. Heated pool, exercise room. Club area is cozy public room with big-screen TV, library. Free breakfast, night snacks, van to restaurants.

BUDGET: **Economy Inns of America**, 5959 Youngman Circle East, 32244, 904/777-0160. No-frills 100-room hotel with 24-hour restaurant next door. Also at Salisbury Rd., off Butler Rd. exit I-95, 904/281-0198. **Red Roof Inn**, 14701 Duval Rd., 32218, 904/751-4110. Free airport transportation, coffee.

Beach Accommodation

LUXURY: **Lodge** at Ponte Vedra Beach, 607 Ponte Vedra Blvd., 32082, 904/273-0210. Home of Professional Golf Association. Beach resort, 54 holes of golf. Best rooms have fireplace, private whirlpool. Casual or gourmet dining. **Marriott** at Sawgrass, 1000 TPC Blvd., Ponte Vedra Beach 32082, 904/285-7777. Hotel rooms, suites, villas with kitchen. Concierge, golf, tennis.

MODERATE: **Howard Johnson on the Beach**, 1515 N. First St., Jacksonville Beach 32250, 904/249-3711. Pool, room service.

BUDGET: **Comfort Inn**, 2401 Mayport Rd., Atlantic Beach 32233, 904/249-0313. Free breakfast. Near fishing charters, Mayo Clinic. One mile to beach park.

Restaurants

LUXURY: **Admiralty Room**, in the Sheraton on St. John's Place, 904/396-5100. Elegant. Closed Monday. **Augustine Room**, Marriott at Sawgrass, Ponte Vedra Beach, 904/285-7777. Continental cuisine. Open daily. Reservations. **Mediterranean Room** at the Lodge, Ponte Vedra Beach, 904/273- 0210. Reservations. Upscale dining. *MODERATE:* **Cafe Carmon**, 1986 San Marco Blvd., 904/398-3377. Al fresco dining in historic district. Closed Sunday.

Cafe on the Square, 1974 San Marco Blvd., 904/399-4422. Open daily except Christmas, New Years. **Crustaceans**, 2321 Beach Blvd., Jacksonville Beach, 904/241-8238. **Ragtime**, 207 Atlantic Blvd., Atlantic Beach, 904/241-7877. Cajun seafood, Sunday brunch. Reservations.

BUDGET: **Beach Road Chicken**, 4132 Atlantic Blvd., 904/398-7980. No credit cards, no reservations, no dress code, just great chicken at a great price. Local hangout.

Annual Events

Pilot Club Antique Show, worldwide dealers, January; *Civil War battle reenactment*, February; *Delius Festival*, March; *Taste of Jacksonville*, April; *Bluegrass Festival*, Art Festival, Sept; *Florida National Jazz Festival*, October; *Gator Bowl festival* and football game, December.

Museums / Galleries / Theater

Cummer Gallery of Art, 829 Riverside Dr., 904/356-6857. Meissen porcelain, Grecian through modern art. Donation requested. **Firehouse Museum**, Catherine St., 904/630-0844. **Jacksonville Art Museum**, 4160 Boulevard Center Dr., 904/398-8336. Oriental arts. Closed Monday. **Lighthouse Museum**, Jacksonville Beach, 904/241-8845. **Museum of Science and Industry**, on the Riverwalk downtown, 904/396-7062. Hands-on programs, science theater, planetarium programs, cosmic concerts. Admission. **Museum of Southern History**, Ortega, 904/388-3574. **Dinner Theater**, Alhambra, 12000 Beach Blvd., 904/641-1212. Matinees Sat and Sun. Nightly except Mon. Dinner menu, lively musical performed by professional cast.

Access and Transportation

Jacksonville International Airport is served by American, Continental, Delta, Eastern, Pan American, Trans World, United, and US Air. Amtrak, Greyhound bus. Water taxis. Bus system.

Tourist Information

Jacksonville and Its **Beaches Convention & Visitors Bureau**, 6 East Bay St., Suite 200, Jacksonville, FL 32202, 904/353-9736. Arts hotline information, 904/353-5100. **Amelia Island Chamber of Commerce**, PO Box 472, Fernandina Beach 32034, 904/259-6433. The Beaches of **Jacksonville Chamber of Commerce**, A Dept. of the Jacksonville Chamber, 413 Pablo Ave., Jacksonville Beach 32250, 904/249-3868. **PARKS: Fort Clinch State Park**, 2601 Atlantic Avenue, Fernandina Beach 32024, 904/261-4212. **Fort Caroline National Monument**, 12713 Fort Caroline Road, Jacksonville 32225, 904/641-7155. **Little Talbot Island State Park**, 12157 Heckscher Drive, Fort George 32226, 904/251-3231.

SUWANNEE COUNTRY

Suwannee, the river made famous by Stephen Foster, oozes out of the warm muck of the Okefenokee Swamp in Georgia, rambling through Florida where it is fed by other springs and rivers before emptying into the Gulf of Mexico near Cedar Key. A long time before the white man came, the river formed a natural boundary between the lands of the powerful Apalachee, and the less well organized Timucuan Indians.

All along its sunlit, 250-mile length, the Suwannee boasts uncrowded parks, villages, viewpints, and picnic sites inescapably blessed by the imagined strains of *Old Folks at Home*, perhaps better known from its first lyric, *Way down upon the S'wannee River*. It is Florida's official state song, written by the immortal composer, Stephen Foster. The irony is that Foster never saw the river. He needed a two-syllable name, and he liked the sibilant sound of this one. So he changed the spelling to S'wannee to eliminate one syllable, and a legend was born.

The stately **Stephen Foster State Folk Culture Center Memorial**, overlooking the river at **White Springs**, is a repository of Florida music and culture. On display are several dioramas depicting Foster's short, unhappy life. Born in 1826, he was an early music success. His talent surfaced at age four, and his *Tioga Waltz* was written at the age of 15. An alcoholic, and unable to make a go of his marriage or his career, he died alone in New York City at the age of 37, with only 38 cents in his pocket. Yet his legacy of more than 200 songs, including *Oh! Susanna, Camptown Races, Old Dog Trey* and *My Old Kentucky Home*, are a treasury of Americana known to every American school child, as well as throughout the world.

In the Foster Cultural Center is a 200-foot, 97-bell carillon tower which is open

Above: Relaxing or just being plain lazy?
Right: Watching an alligator-show.

to guided tours. Also on display are Foster's desk and piano, sheet music and other memorabilia. Hauntingly lovely concerts are played every half-hour. As his music steals out across the surrounding park and picnic grounds, it is easy to imagine that Foster's blessing lies over a spot he never saw.

The Center is also the scene each May of the Florida Folk Festival in which native craftsmen display their wares. Storytellers entertain the crowds with folk tales. Folk singers and musicians perform. Old-fashioned Florida foods are served. The Center's other annual event is the Jeanie Auditions and Ball, in which women vie for music scholarships. It is held in early October.

White Springs was a posh spa during Victorian times. Sulphur springs here were held sacred by Indians and as late as Civil War times, the injured from both sides could come here safely to nurse their wounds. The ruins of the bathhouse have been turned into a pleasant gazebo and viewpoints. The village of White Springs is a page out of pioneer times, with shops, general stores, and rustic restaurants.

Nearby, **Suwannee Springs** was also a thriving spa during the l9th century, when "taking the waters" was considered the chic, as well as the healthful, thing to do. Today nothing remains but a ghost town of homes, an old gas station, and the ruins of the bathing pool. Gospel singing, three days and nights of it, are celebrated in Live Oak's Suwannee River Jubilee, held each June on the banks of the river.

The Battle of Olustee was a major Confederate victory fought at Olustee, 15 miles east of Lake City, in l864. The site, strategically located between Jacksonville and Tallahassee, is now a quiet corner of the Osceola National Forest.

Each year in February, "soldiers" in authentic uniforms reenact this Civil War battle, which involved l0,000 soldiers of whom more than l00 died and 800 were wounded. Come any time, to see the site and hike its nature trails including the battlefield trail, and tour the museum.

173

North of **Lake City**, the 157,000-acre **Osceola National Forest**, with its cypress swamps, woods and ponds, offers camping, hiking, boating, swimming and fishing. The park is named for Osceola, the greatest Seminole leader and the last to make an effective stand against Washington. Most park activities center around **Ocean Pond**, which lies just inside the park's main entrance east of Lake City.

One of the best spots to enjoy the river is **Suwannee State Park**, near **Live Oak**, which has camping, fishing and hiking.

County-operated **Dowling Park** also has campsites. Nearby at **Falmouth Spring**, 125 gallons of clear, 70-degree, water boils out of the earth every second and begins its route into the Suwannee.

At **Hart Springs Park** and **Manatee Springs State Park**, both down-river, the Suwannee gets wider. You can swim all year in the 72-degree waters, or "spring boils," which are pools where water appears to be boiling up out of the earth. Canoes for exploring the river are rented by outfitters including the Spirit of Suwannee Campground, north of Live Oak.

The canoeing is fairly easy, without whitewater, but it is best to rent from an outfitter who provides drop-off and retrieval service so you can enjoy a one-way trip with the current. When water levels allow, a paddle-wheel boat offers pleasant sightseeing rides out of White Springs.

Only a century ago, steamboats plied these same waters, bringing travelers and cargo deep into countryside that had no other highways. Another riverfront state park is **O'Leno**, south of Lake City, on the Sante Fé, a river which flows into the Suwannee. Like many other rivers in this region, it's fed by springs which have formed enormous labyrinths of caves.

Scuba divers dote on the dark and dangerous sport of underwater cave exploration. Even if you are an experienced diver, do not try cave diving without special instruction and adequate equipment. Suwannee County alone has a dozen of major springs. **Peacock** and **Ginnie Springs** are among the most popular with divers.

This is a forgotten corner of Florida, untouched by razzle-dazzle theme parks. Tobacco barns and turpentine stills remain from another era. Sap buckets still cling to pine trees. Tobacco is still grown here and the state's only remaining tobacco auction is held in Lake City.

Roaming country roads, you'll see some driveways which are separated from the road by a length of pipe laid across ditches. Cars can drive across them easily, hooves cannot. This rural Florida area consists of homes with barriers against loose cattle!

Suwannee country is an ideal area for hiking, bicycling, camping and picnicking along the river with the name that sounds like a melody.

Above: Ospreys – the "national birds" of Florida.

SUWANNEE RIVER AREA
Accommodation

Far from the high prices of modern Florida, you will not find costly or luxurious accommodation in these parts. What you will find are homier, more personalized places to stay, family-style motels and housekeeping cabins that retain a flavor of rural Florida.

MODERATE: **Holiday Inn**, U.S. 90 at I-75, Lake City, phone 904/752-3901. Spacious grounds, restaurant, bar, pools, playground, guest laundry, lighted tennis courts, golf privileges.

BUDGET: **Howard Johnson**, U.S. 90 at I-75, phone 904/752-6262 or toll-free 800/654- 2000. Golf privileges, pool, playground. Restaurant. **Quality Inn**, U.S. 90 at I-75, phone 904/752-7550 or toll-free 800/228-5151. Pool, whirlpool, playground, restaurant, bar. **Colonial House Inn**, I-75 at S.R. 136, White Springs 32096, phone 904/963-2401. Bare essentials, nice hosts, swimming pool, playground.

Restaurants

Nell's Steak and Bar BQ, Branford, west of Ichetucknee Springs, phone 904/935-1415. Down-home comfort, food like Mom used to make – that is if she favored Dixie specialities, including chicken gizzards, deep-fried mullet, greens, cornbread and breaded catfish, all offered as part of a bounteous buffet. Open for three meals every day. **Wayside Restaurant**, U.S. 90 at I-75, phone 904/752-1581, opens for a fisherman's breakfast at 6 am, closes at 11 pm More hearty southern fare.

Museums and Galleries

Stephen Foster State Folk Culture Center, U.S. 41 North, PO Drawer G, White Springs 32096, phone 904/397-2733. The museum is set amidst a lush, 250-acre park. Open every day. Admission. A new museum, opened in late 1989, the **Florida Sports Hall of Fame**, honors the achievements of more than 100 athletes who live in Florida or participated in sports in the state. Located on Hall of Fame Drive, off US 90-W. for information contact PO Box 1847, Lake City, 32056-1847, 904/755-5666.

Sightseeing

The **Osceola National Forest** is one of the primary remaining wilderness areas in the southeastern US. Camping sites are available at the Ocean Pond area and the river swimming and boating are idyllic. In addition, the park includes a Civil War battlefield. Route 7, Box 95, Lake City 32055, 904/752-2577. **Olustee Battlefield Historic Site** has hiking trails through another Civil War battlefield. PO Box 40, Olustee 32072, 904/752-3866. **Suwannee River State Park**, Route 8, Box 297, Live Oak, FL 32060, 904/362-2746, offers camping fishing and hiking along the scenic river. **Ichetucknee Springs State Park**, Route 2, Box108, Fort White, 32038, 904/497-2511, is a great place for river tubing, which is simply floating in an inflated automobile or truck tire tube. Canoeing is also fine, and there are hiking trails which lead to secluded swimming spots. **O'Leno State Park**, Route 2, Box 307, High Springs 32643, 904/454-1853, is another fine site for river activities, camping,fishing, hiking and swimming.

Guided Tours

Suwannee Country Tours offers numerous active tours including canoeing on the Suwanee River, bicycle riding and historic tours. Some of the tours combine walking and biking and include an overnight stay in a small country inn. Phone 904/397-2349 for information and rates.

Tourist Information

Chiefland Area Chamber of Commerce, P.O. Box 1397, Chiefland, FL 32626. **Hamilton County Chamber of Commerce**, P.O. Drawer P, Jasper, FL 32052, 904/792-1300. **Suwannee County Chamber of Commerce**, P.O. Box C, Live Oak, FL 32060, 904/362-3071. **Lake City-Columbia County Chamber of Commerce**, 15 East Orange Street, PO Box 566, Lake City, FL 32056, 904/752-3690.

Annual Events

Battle of Olustee Reenactment, near Lake City, is held in February. Hundreds of elaborately costumed participants clothed in authentic-looking blue and gray uniforms, complete with period weaponry, act out maneuvers of Confederate and Union forces on the now tranquil spot where the real battle was held. They put on a realistic show for fans of this sort of thing, who come from far and wide to participate or watch. And since this is one battle the Confederacy won, this deeply southern part of the United States carries on with other localized celebrations and special events at this time of year. Florida Folk Festival, White Springs, features traditional music and crafts, held in late May. Jeanie Auditions and Ball are held in October. North Florida Air Show, Lake City, October. This is a big air show with stunt and aerobatic flying, parachuting contests, antique and special interest aircraft, and so forth.

Transportation and Access

Nearest airports are Jacksonville, Gainesville, and Tallahassee. Many towns and cities throughout the region are served by Greyhound bus service, but this area is not highly developed for tourism, as compared with other Florida locales, so a rental car would be an excellent idea for touring.

NORTHWEST FLORIDA

TALLAHASSEE
PENSACOLA GULF COAST
NORTHERN PANHANDLE
MIRACLE STRIP

TALLAHASSEE

Tallahassee, the state capital, is located between the foothills of the **Appalachian Mountains** and the juncture of the panhandle and peninsula.

The first inhabitants were native Americans of the Paleolithic Age – 12,000 years ago. Their remains and those of a mastodon found in the area are displayed at the Museum of Florida History. The oldest evidence of a permanent settlement is that of Mississippian Indians who settled by Lake Jackson between 1250 and 1500.

In 1539, the Spanish conquistador, Hernando de Soto, set up his winter encampment on the site of present-day Tallahassee. It was here that the first Christmas celebration in North America occurred that December. Artifacts from the encampment are on display at the site, less than a mile from Florida's Capitol complex, which hosts an annual re-enactment of the first Christmas.

In 1823, William Pope DuVal, the first civilian governor of the Territory of Florida – just acquired by the United

Preceding pages: Shrimp boats at anchor in the evening. Left: Florida's capital demonstrates its loyalty to the Federation.

States – decided to pick a location for the territorial capital by sending one person west on horseback from St. Augustine and another east by boat from Pensacola. Where they met was to be the new capital. They rendezvoused near a waterfall – a place the Indians called *tallahassee.*

Three log cabins served as the territory's first government buildings. A two-storey masonry capitol was erected in 1826 with periodic expansions coinciding with attempts to remove the capital from Tallahassee. With the completion of the **New Capitol** in 1977, the **Old Capitol** – erected in 1845 – has been restored to its 1902 appearance, complete with red-and-white candy-striped awnings and a gracious dome adorned with stained glass.

A unique aspect of the area, as compared with the rest of the state, is Tallahassee's terrain. Rolling hills and vegetation resemble the countryside of Pennsylvania or New York rather than the lowlands and swamps of Florida. This may have induced the Marquis de Lafayette to plant grapes on land he was given by the government for his role in the American Revolutionary War. Wine produced from those grapes won gold and silver wine medals at the 1900 Paris Exposition. Today, 38 acres of the original land grant are the home of the Lafayette

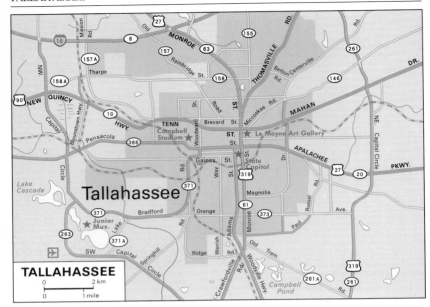

Vineyards and Winery – one of only five wineries in Florida. It is open for tours.

Tallahassee's oldest remaining residence, known as **The Columns**, is a white-columned brick home, built in the 1830s on land purchased for $5 by William "Money" Williams. Rumored to have a nickel embedded in every brick, it now houses the **Tallahassee Area Chamber of Commerce**.

On Adams Street Commons the **Governor's Club**, a 1900s Masonic lodge, and **Gallie's Hall**, built in 1874, are situated in a southern town square setting. Adjacent to the Governor's Mansion is **The Grove**, the home of "The Tallahassee Girl", Ellen Call Long, the first white child born in town. Nearby **Goodwood Plantation** features a number of underground passages.

One of the last plantations built is the 307-acre masterpiece of floral architecture known as **Alfred B. Maclay State**

Right: Tranquility and cosiness are typical of capitals.

Park. It features graceful landscaping fashioned around reflecting pools, fountains and a natural lake. The **Killearn Country Club**, located on original Maclay land hosts the Ladies Professional Golf Central Classic Tournament. Golf is a favorite sport of the outdoors-minded Tallahassee residents. The area offers 99 holes of golf on six public and private courses. **Golden Eagle Country Club** takes advantage of the Tallahassee hillsides, boasting the highest slope rating in the entire pancake flat state of Florida with its new Fazio course.

Off the greens and back in the downtown area, on Bronough Street, visitors who want to delve deeper into their own Florida research can begin at the **Convention and Visitors Bureau**, where scads of information are available for free, then move on to the various offices of the Department of Commerce, including the Division of Tourism, as well as other goverment agencies. The Florida State Archives are administered by the Departement of State and are located in

the **Capitol Building**. They have the most complete collection of historic photography and maps of historic Florida at the present day, with files expanding daily. Digging ever deeper into Florida's past, some may want to visit **St. John's Cemetery**. Located at Call and Boulevard Streets, this is where the Napoleon's nephew is buried along with his wife, a relative of George Washington.

For antsy children who are not impressed with name-dropping at gravesites, a visit to the **Tallahassee Junior Museum** may be in order. The large outdoor site at 3945 Museum Drive encloses a turn-of-the-century farm, a plantation house, log cabin, wagon and farm equipment exhibits, picnic areas, a snake house, and indigenous Florida wildlife, as well as several nature trails.

Highly cultured children may prefer the **Le Moyne Art Gallery**, 125 North Gadsden Street. Admission is free to this 1853 house displaying Florida and Georgia artists, and in a special children's section the paintings are hung lower.

Surrounding Area

St. Marks Wildlife Refuge and the **Apalachicola National Forest** are only some minutes away from downtown, easily accessed via the **Historic Railroad State Trail** or the **St. Marks Trail** – which features an 18-mile path laid over one of Florida's oldest abandoned railroads. It starts in **Leon County** and ends by the majestic lighthouse at St. Marks Wildlife Refuge.

Natural Bridge State Historic Site is located south of the city, on Natural Bridge Road, in Woodville. Open daily, admission is free to this place where a depleted Confederate battalion made up of old men and youngsters held off advancing Union troops in 1865. These Civil War heroics, that allowed Tallahassee to remain the only Confederate capital east of the Mississippi River to stay out of Union hands, are commemorated here, and remembered yearly with a vividly authentic re-enactment every March.

TALLAHASSEE
Accommodation

EXPENSIVE: **Governor's Inn**, 40 units one-half block from the State Capitol in the Adams Street Commons area. Very tastefully decorated, first quality restaurant. 209 S. Adams Street, 32301, 904/681-6855. **Las Casas Motor Inn**, 2801 N. Monroe Street, 32301, 904/386-8286. **Killearn Country Club & Inn**, resort motor inn on the Killearn Country Club grounds, pool, saunaand golf, 100 Tyron Circle, 904/893-2186.

MODERATE: **Ramada Inn North**, very quaint and good value, 2900 North Monroe Street, 32303, 904/386-1027. **Holiday Inn-University Center**, 316 W. Tennessee Street, 904/222- 8000. **Holiday Inn-Parkway**, 1302 Apalachee Parkway, 904/ 877- 3141. **Courtyard by Marriott**, 1018 Apalachee Parkway, 904/222- 8822.

BUDGET: **Wakulla Springs Lodge**, Rte 61 and Rte. 267, Wakulla Springs, 32305, 904/224-5950. Simple rooms in a converted Spanish-style lodge, set amidst state park lands and a wildlife refuge. **La Quinta Motor Inn-North**, 2905 North Monroe Street, 904/385-7172. **Cabot Lodge**, 2735 North Monroe Street, 904/386-8880. **Days Inn Airport South**, 3100 Apalachee Parkway, 904/877- 6121.

Restaurants

EXPENSIVE: There are three five-star restaurants in Tallahassee – **Andrew's Second Act**, the **Golden Pheasant** and the **Silver Slipper**. Andrew's serves continental cuisine, their tournedos St. Laurent is excellent. The Golden Pheasant serves classical French cuisine and offers a unique dish of braised South African lion. The Silver Slipper is the oldest family-run restaurant in the state and is a favorite of the political crowd – five presidents of the US have eaten there.

MODERATE TO BUDGET: For Apalachicola oysters and Panacea blue crab, try **Spring Creek** or **JV's On The Coast**. **Barnacle Bill's** is a rustic restaurant where almost anything goes. Their unique offerings of smoked dolphin and cobia are a rare experience. For a good ole' Southern home-cooked meal complete with beef grown on the farm and fresh baked bread try the **Nicholson's Farmhouse**. This is an actual family plantation home built in 1820. Another unique dining experience is **Rooster's**. This boot-stomping local hangout allows guests to personally grill their own 32-ounce sirloin.

Access and Local Transportation

AIR: Delta/ASA and Eastern. Flight time to Atlanta is less than one hour; to Miami is just over one hour.

LAND: On I-10 166 miles west of Jacksonville and 244 miles east of Pensacola.
The Old Town Trolley, a replica turn-of-the-century street car, provides free downtown transportation.

Hospitals

Apalachee Center for Human Services 904/487-0300, **Capital Rehabilitation Hospital** 904/656-4800, **Tallahassee Community Hospital** 904/757-5000 and **Tallahassee Memorial Regional Medical Center** 904/681-1155.

Festivals / Seasonal Events

Springtime Tallahassee is a week-long festival in late March or early April. It includes concerts, home and garden tours and art shows. *The Blue Crab Festival* in May at nearby Panacea attracts 20,000 crab lovers annually. The *Native American Heritage Festival* in September honors the various Indian tribes. It features Indian foods, as well as craft and culture exhibits.

Museums / Art Galleries

The Museum of Florida History in the R.A. Gray Building at Bronough and Pensacola Streets 904/488-1484, the **Black Archives Research Center and Museum** at Gallie's Hall and the **Tallahassee Junior Museum** at Lake Bradford are three of the best in the state. The Black Archives displays objects which chronicle the entry of blacks into the United States and traces their history in Florida.

Tourist Information

Leon County Tourist Development Council, Leon County Courthouse, Tallahassee, 32301, 904/488-3990; **Tallahassee Chamber of Commerce**, PO Box 1639, Tallahassee, 32302, 904/244-8116; **Tallahassee Area Convention & Visitors Bureau**, 100 N. Duval St., Tallahassee, 32301, 904/681-9200.

Parks

Alfred B. Maclay State Gardens, 3540 Thomasville Road, Talahassee 32308, 904/893-4232.
Lake Jakson Mounds State Archaeological Site, 1313 Crowder Road, Talahassee 3208, 904/562-0042.
Lake Talquin State Recreation Area, Star Route 1, Box 2222, Talahassee 3204, 904/576-8233.

Guided Tours

Capitol Town Tours, PO Box 1372, Tallahassee, 3202, 904/681-8687, employs multi-lingual guides who speak English, French, German or Spanish. Private guides are available, or group rates offer a discount for eight or more people, reservations required. Minimum rate is $55 for a two-hour tour.

GULF COAST – MIRACLE STRIP

0   10   20   30   40   50 km

0   15   30 miles

PENSACOLA GULF COAST

The Panhandle area can be divided into a northern and southern portion. In the south are the beaches and Gulf Coast cities. In the north are the rivers and springs, caverns, parks and antebellum homes. The Gulf Coast area boasts 343 sunny days a year with mild winters and summer heat tempered by winds off the Gulf of Mexico. The coastline is protected by a series of barrier islands with white quartz sand beaches. Behind the barrier islands are a series of deep bays which form natural harbors that attracted

Preceding page: An attractive and artificial town – Seaside.

early settlers. In 1559, Tristan de Luna settled a colony of about 1,500 people at **Pensacola Bay** and reported to King Philip II that it was "the best port in the Indies". Two years later it was devastated by a hurricane. The area belonged to Spain, France, and England at various times until 1821 when it became a part of the United States who built three forts to protect the bay area, **Fort Barrancas**, **Fort Pickens** and **Fort McRae**. Fort Barrancas has been restored and can be visited today at the Pensacola Naval Air Station. Fort Pickens can be visited daily on **Santa Rosa Island**, but Fort McRae has sunk into the bay and can only be glimpsed beneath the water on clear days.

After the Civil War, the vast forests of

Cape San Blas

oak, cedar, cypress and pine led to the timber boom of the 1880s and 1890s – probably the Panhandle's most prosperous period. The shipping and railroad industries also benefited enormously from the great harvesting of timber.

The **Museum of Industry** in Pensacola is dedicated to depicting this period of the Florida Panhandle's history. It not only shows the booming lumber industry, but also the importance of the shipping business to the area. Pensacola was an early naval store supplier, selling tar, pitch and durable woods. The Museum of Industry is located in the **Seville Historic District** – one of three historic preservation districts here.

More recently 150 miles of barrier is-

lands along the coastline have been declared the **Gulf Islands National Seashore**, set aside for public recreation and wildlife preservation.

Pensacola

The largest city along the Gulf Coast is Pensacola. It boasts three historical districts and the Pensacola **Naval Air Station**, training grounds for most of the US Navy's pilots. The Naval Air Station is the home of the **National Museum of Naval Aviation** where an authentic collection of Naval, Marine and Coast Guard memorabilia is displayed. It is also the home base for the Blue Angels precision flying group who perform regularly. Aviation history is traced from Kittyhawk to the Space Age at the museum.

Just a few miles away from the beaches is much of Pensacola's rich history. The town has three historic districts – **North Hill Preservation District**, **Palafox** and Seville Historic District.

The Seville District includes the **Historic Pensacola Village**. It was the center of the young town as well as being the fashionable neighborhood where wealthy merchants built their bay-front homes. The area shows a mixture of Scottish, French, Spanish and English influence. This is a rare concentration of Frame Vernacular, Folk Victorian and Creole homes, which date from the early to late nineteenth century, including some of the oldest homes in Florida. The simplicity of the buildings represents the tradition of Florida's early years.

The **Museum of Commerce** offers an old-time Pensacola streetscape, reconstructed within this masonry warehouse and containing representations of many businesses common to the Victorian era. Included are a fully outfitted print shop, a pharmacy, a toy store, and a hardware store. Some are open for business. It also includes horse-drawn buggies and an early twentieth-century gas station.

Another popular attraction in the Seville area is **Julee Cottage**. This "to the side-walk" cottage has a long association with the free black population of Pensacola. It was bought in 1805 by Julee (JEW-lee) Panton, a "free woman of color", and was later owned by a succession of free black women. The cottage was reconstructed as a **Black History Museum**.

The Palafox District was the commercial heart of Old Pensacola. While a number of the old wooden buildings have been lost to fire, hurricane and urban renewal, many still remain and have been restored to their original beauty. Noteworthy in this area is the old city hall, circa 1908, which is now the **T.T. Wentworth Jr. Florida State Museum**.

This Renaissance Revival-style building, now a part of the Historic Pensacola Village, was constructed in 1907-8. Visitors can see galleries and exhibits featur-

ing the collection of T.T. Wentworth – the largest ever given to the State of Florida by an individual. The third floor contains Discovery – a hands-on museum experience for children, sponsored by the Junior League of Pensacola.

Another interesting adaptation of a former government building is the **Pensacola Museum of Art**. This two-story Mission Revival building once housed the Pensacola City Jail and City Court.

The North Hill District developed as a residential area between 1870 and 1930. It contains examples of Queen Anne, Neoclassical, Tudor Revival, Craftsman Bungalow, Art Moderne and Mediterranean Revival architecture.

One of the many interesting attractions in this area is the **Christ Episcopal Church**. It was unusual for an Episcopal Church to build in a style based on the lines of a Spanish Colonial Church.

The **Zoo**, located in nearby **Gulf Breeze**, has over 500 animals, with its main attraction, Colossus, the world's largest lowland gorilla.

Above: In Pensacola the victims of World War II are not forgotten.

PENSACOLA / GULF COAST
Accommodation

LUXURY: **The Pensacola Hilton**, 200 E. Gregory Street, Pensacola, 32590, 904/433-3336. This unique hotel uses as its lobby and public area a restored 1912 railroad station. The hotel itself is completely modern. **The Homestead Inn**, 7830 Pine Forest Road, Pensacola, is an old-fashioned country inn. The property serves a full country breakfast every morning included in the price of the room. Phone 904/944-4816.

SUPERIOR: **Best Western Village Inn**, 8240 N. Davis Highway. Most units are one-bedroom suites. Phone 904/479-1099. **Hampton Inn**, 7330 Plantation Road. Phone 904/477-3333. **Holiday Inn-North**, 6501 Pensacola Blvd. 904/476-7200. **Holiday Inn-University Mall**, 7200 Plantation Road, Phone 904/474-0100. **The Residence Inn**, 7230 Plantation Road, is a 64-unit all-suite motor hotel. Phone 904/479-1000.

MODERATE: **Red Roof Inn**, 7340 Plantation Road, Phone 904/477-7155. **Econo Lodge**, 7226 Plantation Road, Phone 904/474-1060.

PENSACOLA BEACH
Accommodation

EXPENSIVE: **Holiday Inn-Pensacola Beach**, 165 Fort Pickens Road, 150 units of typical Holiday Inn quality, the beachfront location is what makes this property outstanding. Pool, beach, rental boats, lighted tennis courts racquetball courts. Phone 904/932-5361.

MODERATE: **Sunset Motor Lodge**, 14 Via De Luna. This former Howard Johnson's offers beach, pool, lighted tennis courts, playground and suites. Phone 904/932-5331.

Restaurants

Pensacola offers a plethora of good eating at mostly moderate to inexpensive prices. At the top of the list has to be its fresh seafood caught daily by local fishermen. **Captain Jim's Seafood**, 905 E. Gregory is a family-owned and operated bay-front eatery favored by the locals. Seafood and steaks are the house specialties. Phone 904/433-3562. For a bit of variety try **Marchelo's Italian Restaurant**, 620 S. Navy Blvd. The veal and pasta are outstanding but don't pass up the seafood prepared with an Italian flair. Phone 904/456-5200. For an Irish night including fine food, entertainment and locally produced beer try **McGuire's Irish Pub and Brewery** located on Gregory Street between Bay Bridge and the Civic Center. The steak and ribs are superb and the nightly Irish entertainment is the best south of Boston. Phone 904/433-67689. The **1912 Restaurant** at the Pensacola Hilton serves steak,

prime rib and fresh seafood. Dress is informal, the servings are generous. Phone 904/433-3336. Pensacola Beach is a great place to go for fresh seafood and a relaxed atmosphere. The **Casino Restaurant** in the Holiday Inn Pensacola Beach at 165 Fort Pickens Road serves a seafood buffet from Easter through Labor Day that is an excellent value. The Sunday champagne brunch is a local favorite. Phone 904/932-5361. For fresh seafood broiled over hickory fires try **Flounder's Chowder and Ale House** at the traffic light in Pensacola Beach. Flounder's is open nightly with servings of some of the area's best seafood and reggae music. Phone 904/932-2003. **Jubilee Restaurant and Oyster Bar/Captain Fun's** at 400 Quietwater Beach Road is the place to go on the beach for oysters. Items range from hamburgers to oysters on the half shell. Open for lunch and dinner, we feel that this is the place to come for fresh seafood. Phone 904/934-3108.

Museums / Art Galleries
Pensacola Museum of Art, T.T. Wentworth, Jr. Florida State Museum, **Museum of Industry and the Museum of Commerce** are all located in Pensacola's Historical District. The **National Museum of Naval Aviation** is located at the Naval Air Station.

Tourist Information
Pensacola Area Chamber of Commerce, PO Box 550, Pensacola, 32593, 904/438-4081; **Pensacola Convention and Visitor Center**, 1401 East Gregory St., Pensacola 32501, 904/434-1234, 800/343-4321 from within Florida, 800/874-1234 from elsewhere in the US. **Greater Gulf Breeze Chamber of Commerce**, 913 Gulf Breeze Parkway, Suite 17, Gulf Breeze 32561, 904/932-7888. **Sant Rosa Country Chamber of Commerce**, 501 Stewart St. SW, Milton 32570, 904/623-2339. **South Walton Tourist Development Council**, PO Box 1248, Santa Rosa Beach 32459, 904/267-1216, or 800/822-6877. **Walton County Chamber of Commerce**, Chatauqua Bldg, Circle Drive, Defuniak Springs, 32422, 904/267-3511.
PARKS: Big Lagoon State Recreation Area, 12301 Gulf Beach Highway, Pensacola 32507, 904/492-1595. **Blackwater River State Park**, Route 1, Box 57-C, Holt 32564, 904/623-2363. **Grayton Beach State Recreation Area**, Box 2, Route 790-1, Santa Rosa Beach 32459, 904/231-4210. **Gulf Island National Seashore**, PO Box 100, Gulf Breeze 32561, 904/932-5302.

Access and Local Transport
LAND: I-10 runs east-west the length of the panhandle. **AIR:** There are local airports at Tallahassee, Panama City and Pensacola.

NORTHERN PANHANDLE

The Panhandle area can be divided into a northern and southern portion. The southland beaches and Gulf Coast cities cater to a growing tourist trade with resort and golf course developments sprouting faster than palm trees. The north meanders slowly through rivers and springs, fishing lakes, trails, caverns, parks and antebellum homes.

Florida Caverns State Park

Just north of Tallahassee, in **Marianna**, this unexpected attraction offers the beach-goer Florida's only publicly accessible limestone caverns.

The caverns were first reported by the Spanish in 1693. Indian artifacts have been found in the area that date back as far as 1100 years with the most populous Indian settlements found to have been

Above: Paddling through untamed nature.
Right: Unexpected – the Marianna Caverns.

living here as recently as within 450 years. The park's "natural bridge" across the **Chipola River** was used by Andrew Jackson in 1818 during his second expedition into Spanish Florida to subdue the raiding Indians.

In addition to the caverns, the park offers swimming in the **Blue Hole Spring**. The spring's clear waters maintain a constant temperature of 71.6 degrees F. year round. The spring discharges 36.6 million gallons of water per day. The park also offers extensive nature trails, camping, hiking, canoeing and picnicking. Ranger-guided spelunking (caving) tours can be arranged as well.

Plantations

Before the Civil War, the Panhandle area owed much of its success to cotton. Large plantations stretched north from Tallahassee into Georgia. Even today 71 plantations on 300,000 acres exist between Tallahassee and Thomasville, Georgia, 28 miles away. Some are open to interested visitors.

Wakulla Springs

Just north of Tallahassee is **Wakulla Springs**, a sink hole formed from the eroded bed of ancient limestone and natural springs. The Museum of Florida History's mastodon skeleton came from this spring. Tour the spring in glass-bottomed boats or swim and dive. Because of Wakulla Springs' clear water and tropical vegetation many of the early Tarzan movies were made here, as well as other early films that featured underwater photography.

Eden Mansion and State Park

Thirty minutes north of Panama City Beach, this stately 1895 mansion stands among moss-draped live oak trees. This post-Civil War plantation was built by

lumber baron William Henry Wesley. The house has a porch that completely surrounds it, floor-to-ceiling windows and seven columns along each side. The house has been furnished with period antiques and is the epitome of what one would imagine a Southern plantation home should be.

Torreya State Park

About half way between Tallahassee and Panama City, the **Torreya State Park** features a restored antebellum mansion and nature preserve that is unique. The house has been nicely restored and affords a pleasurable visit, but it is the unique vegetation that makes this place worth a visit. During the last Ice Age, as the glaciers moved slowly south, the cold weather flora and fauna moved south ahead of them. As the ice receded, that same flora and fauna usually retreated with it. Not so at Torreya.

Here one finds a collection of rare vegetation that is not known anywhere else in the South and, in some cases, anywhere else in the world. Torreya is a little isolated island of northern and ancient vegetation that, by all rights, should not be there. In the autumn it boasts the best colors in the South. The park offers many walking trails and picnic spots for the visitor to enjoy.

Falling Waters State Park

An hour north of Panama City, **Falling Waters State Park** features a spectacular 63-foot waterfall that empties into a 100-foot deep, 15-foot diameter sink hole. The water then exits the sink hole via an underground river through a series of caverns. The park also includes 945 feet of boardwalks traversing dry sink holes, swimming and picnic areas.

DeFuniak Springs

About 25 miles north of the Fort Walton Beach area is **DeFuniak Springs**. In the late 1800s and early 1900s this area

189

hosted a winter Chautauqua, an educational and cultural movement that migrated to DeFuniak from western New York State. Activities such as concerts, symposiums, plays, elocution lessons and Bible study were held each summer around Lake Chautauqua in western New York. In the winter they were held around Lake DeFuniak.

The original Chautauqua building still stands, and Chautauqua events still are held in DeFuniak each spring, culminating in the **Chautauqua Day Festival** in the latter part of May. In addition to the Chautauqua building, many of the homes built by Chautauqua attendees are available for viewing.

Cypress Springs

This popular area offers swimming, tubing and canoe trips. Fed by 90 million gallons of water per day from **Cypress**

Above: In Junior Park pristine nature is still alive.

Springs, Holmes Creek is one of the state's 36 canoe trails. This trail is 16 miles long and offers the first-time canoeist gently flowing water, lush swamplands and some high sandy banks. The trail is rated easy. Cypress Springs also offers cave diving to those holding the proper certification. Various tube and canoe outfitters offer rentals and return buses in the area.

Econfina and other Canoe Trails

Econfina Creek is also one of the state's canoe trails. It offers up to 22 miles of canoeing streams rated moderate to strenuous. In addition to Econfina and Cypress Springs there are 13 more canoe trails in the Florida Panhandle area. They range from as little as 4 miles long to 56 miles. Most are rated easy or moderate. Econfina is the only canoe trail in the Panhandle which has a strenuous rating.

Outfitters are available at most of the areas with canoe rentals and return transportation.

Accommodation at:
CREST VIEW
EXPENSIVE: **Holiday Inn**, 1/2 mile south of I-10 exit 10, P.O. Box 1355, Phone 904/ 682-6111.
BUDGET: **Econo Lodge**, 1/4 mile north of I-10 exit 10, P.O. Box 1466, Phone 904/682-6255.

DEFUNIAK SPRINGS
MODERATE: Best **Western Crossroads Inn**, at the junction of I-10 and US 331, P.O. Box 852, Phone 904/892-5111.

LIVE OAK
BUDGET: **Econo Lodge**, at the junction of I-10 and US 129, P.O. Box 820, Phone 904/362-7459.

MARIANNA
EXPENSIVE: **Holiday Inn**, 3/4 of a mile northwest of I-10 exit 21 on Hwy 90E, P.O. Box 979, Phone 904/526-3251.
MODERATE: Best **Western Marianna Inn**, south of the junction of I- 10 and SR 71 P.O. Box 980, Phone 904/526-5666.
BUDGET: **Econo Lodge**, 1 1/2 miles northeast on US 90 from I- 10 exit 20, 1119 W. Lafayette Street, Phone 904/526-3710.
Travelodge, 1 1 miles northeast on US 90 from I-10 exit 20, 1114 W. Lafayette Street, Phone 904/526-4311.

NICEVILLE
EXPENSIVE: **Bluewater Bay Resort**, 1950 Bluewater Blvd., P.O. Box 247, three pools, tennis, golf, racquetball, saunas, beach, rental boats and marina. Phone 904/897-3616.
MODERATE: **Comfort Inn**, 101 Highway 85N, Phone 904/678-8077.

WAKULLA SPRINGS
Wakulla Springs Lodge & Conference Center, on the grounds of Wakulla Springs State Park, 1 Springs Drive, is surrounded by nature trails, offering peace and tranquil beauty. Phone 904/224-5950.
The above named motels are the only accommodation in the north Panhandle area other than camp grounds and RV parks. Therefore we recommend that visitors stay in Tallahassee, Panama City Beach, Destin, Ft. Walton Beach, one of the myriad small beach communities or in Pensacola; then visit the inland area from there. The panhandle is only 50 miles across from border to Gulf.

Restaurants
The only good restaurants we can recommend in the northern Panhandle area are the La Fontana and Nichols Seafood Restaurant and Marina.
EXPENSIVE: The **La Fontana** is in Niceville at the Bluewater Bay Resort. The setting overlooking the marina is restful and the Italian cuisine is filling. Phone 904/ 897-2186.
BUDGET: **Nichols Restaurant** is in Milton - just off I-10 exit 8 on Robinson Point Road. This is an informal family seafood restaurant where the seafood is always fresh. This is not a fancy eatery but the value is excellent. Phone 904/623- 3410.
Because of the proximity of the beach, with its abundance of excellent restaurants, we again recommend that travelers stay in one of the larger beach communities and enjoy the fresh seafood.

Access and Local Transport
LAND: About the only way to see this area is by private car. There are no regularly scheduled bus tours and the sights are too spread out to fly into a central point and use a taxi. I-10 runs east-west the length of the Panhandle from Tallahassee to Pensacola, various state routes run north and south at regular intervals.
AIR: There are local airports at Tallahassee, Panama City and Pensacola served by Eastern Metro and Delta/ASA Airlines.

Museums / Art Galleries
The various state parks have small museums but none worth comment.

Tourist Information
Write to the **Florida Department of Commerce/Division of Tourism**, Tallahassee, Florida 32399-2000 for the Florida Vacation Guide. It is a free publication.
For information about Canoe Trails and State Parks contact the **Department of Natural Resources**, Division of Recreation and Parks 904/487-4784.
For boating regulations and safety information contact **Florida Game and Fresh Water Fish Commission**, Division of Law Enforcement, 904/488-6523.
STATE PARKS: **Eden State Gardens**, PO Box 26 (North of US 98 on CR 395), Point Washington 32454-0026, 904/231-4214.
Falling Waters State Recreation Area, Route 5, Box 660, Chipley 32428, 904/638-4030;
Florida Caverns State Park, 2701 Caverns Rd., Marinna 32466, 904/482-3632.
Natural Bridge Battlefield, c/o Wakulla Springs, Walkulla Springs Rd., Wakulla Springs 32305, 904/925-6216.
Torreya State Park, Route 2, Box 70, Bristol 32321, 904/643-2674. Wakulla Springs,
Edward Ball State Park, Wakulla Springs Rd., Wakulla Springs 32305, 904/576-7630.

MIRACLE STRIP COAST

The gulf coast beaches of the Panhandle are sometimes referred to collectively as the **Miracle Strip**, and indeed, this 100-mile stretch of beaches, clubs, hotels, amusement parks, restaurants, miniature golf courses and stores is dedicated to having fun in the sun.

And the name Miracle Strip does sound a wee bit better than the old, unofficial name for the area – the "Redneck Riviera". As colorful as was that name for this popular coast with bargain-conscious vacationers from America's southeast, the new name derives from **Miracle Strip Amusement Park** in **Panama City Beach**. For the purposes of this guide we will refer to the entire coastal area from **Apalachicola** to **Fort Walton Beach** – approximately 100 miles of shoreline – as the Miracle Strip Coast.

Panama City Beach

Panama City and Panama Beach typify the communities in the area. Combined they are the most developed area along the coast with all the good and bad that implies. It is the primary tourist area along all of Miracle Strip.

Located on the Gulf Coast midway between Tallahassee and Pensacola, the area's most unusual feature is the extremely fine, almost blindingly white sand found packed along its 23 miles of Gulf of Mexico beaches.

The sand originates in the distant north, in the deep underground quartz deposits beneath the Appalachian Mountains. As the quartz breaks down over eons, it is washed into the gulf. Eventually what is left behind is a fine white powder-like sand. Over the centuries these fine sand beaches have also built up

Left: A hundred miles of white beaches – enough to forget the Caribbean! Above: Phantasy brings the world to the peninsula.

as a series of barrier islands. These barrier islands have existed as a single island or as a changing series of many islands, sculpted sand coming and going with the wind and waves. This is probably why so many of the various bays and inlets along the North Florida coast lay officially undiscovered for so many years, while yielding a treasure trove of local pirating or rum- running or modern smuggling stories and myths. Today channels have been unromantically dredged to allow unobstructed commercial passage from the bay to the ocean.

World War II attracted many Americans to the area's military facilities. At the end of the war, the beach communities experienced a growth boom that continues today as more and more people are attracted by the exceptional beaches and the mild climate.

The Gulf Current

Another important growth factor is the warm current that flows north out of the

Gulf of Mexico providing a year-round mild climate. The average water temperature is 70 degrees and the average air temperature is 74 degrees F. This warm current also brings some of the world's best deep sea fishing close to shore.

In 1974 the **Panama City Marine Institute** was formed which has established or augmented nine artificial reef sites off the coast. These artificial reefs have become the habitat of a wide variety of fish and a delight to fishermen and divers. Divers of all levels of expertise find a great variety of diving opportunities. The area includes shallow reef and wreck diving in very sheltered areas close to shore, deep wreck and reef diving in open water, far off-shore and even cave diving at **Florida Cavern State Park**.

Some of the more noteworthy dive sites are: the **Empire Mica**, a 465-foot British tanker torpedoed on her maiden

Above: One man and the open sea. Right: Plea and warning at the same time: dunes are an important ecological factor.

voyage in 1942. **The Grey Ghost**, a 105-foot tugboat that was sunk in 103 feet of water by the Panama City Marine Institute's Artificial Reef Program in 1974 as their first project.

The **Vamar**, a small cargo vessel used by Admiral Byrd during his Antarctic explorations during the 1920s. The Vamar capsized and sank in 25 feet of water during a storm in 1942. The **Tarpon**, one of the oldest surviving wrecks on the coast, was built in the late 1800s. She served as a shuttle between Mobile and Carrabelle until 1937, when she sank in the heavy seas. Other favorite dive spots include six more shipwreck sites, numerous artificial reefs and hundreds of natural reefs.

Boating

Sailors of all ability levels and preferences find challenges in the area. Everything from a windsurfer or sunfish to an ocean-going yacht is available. Along the beach, small sailboats, windsurfers, surf

boards and jet skis can be rented by the hour. On the bay side, charters and/or rentals are available in all sizes and capacities from canoes to yachts that sleep 10 or more.

Wildlife

Bird lovers will enjoy a never-ending variety of water fowl because the locals have dedicated a small artificial island, **Audubon Island**, formed when the channel into St. Andrew's bay was last dredged, to the preservation of some of the coast's more fragile species. Pelicans, seagulls, skimmers and the great grey heron, egrets and sand darters thrive and entertain visitors.

The mild temperatures produce a wide variety of lush tropical and sub-tropical vegetation. Palms, ferns, live oaks and scrub oak abound. Pampas grass, philodendron and flowering plants thrive. The most important, however, are sea oats. This tough grass covers the dunes closest to the beach and offers the first threshold for vegetation as well as the primary barrier to erosion. Sea oats are so important in preventing beach erosion that they are protected by law from being cut. Their root system holds the sand in place, stabilizing the soil against both the permanent wind and the ocean.

Barrier Islands

One of Panama City's barrier islands called Shell or Hurricane has at one time or another been one single island or as many as four independent islands. An uninhabited natural preserve, the island was named **Shell Island** because of the variety and number of shells. Tourists can visit it by boat any day of the week.

The most popular time to visit the Miracle Strip coastline is from late February through the end of October. All of the attractions are open from Memorial Day through Labor Day. However some, such as the Miracle Strip Amusement Park, are closed from the end of August until late May.

Thousands of American and Canadian college students visit the strip from late February to the middle of April depending on when their spring break occurs.

Some travelers find visiting the area in the early fall while the water and sun are still warm and the crowds have dispersed is ideal. Others, mostly visitors from northern climates, prefer mid-winter, from December through March. It is cooler here than in faster-paced South Florida, but these visitors are still affectionately known as "snowbirds".

The primary attraction, the **Miracle Strip Amusement Park**, features one of the world's foremost roller coasters – at 2,000 feet – plus an assortment of 60 rides, 13 arcade games, carnival pastimes and live entertainment. The 40-foot high "Sea Dragon", shaped like a Viking ship, rocks passengers up to 70 feet in the air. Nine acres of attractions include rides

Above: Having a rest at a beach gallery.
Right: Thousands (!) of greyhounds are out during the racing-season.

such as a log flume, Abominable Snowman-Scrambler and ferris wheel, continuous entertainment, contests, games and various special events.

Adjacent to the Miracle Strip extends **Ship Wreck Island**, a 6-acre water park complete with water slides, white water rapid rides, wave machines, lazy river floats and rope swings. The park offers a junior version of its exciting attractions for younger children, too.

The strip also includes arcades, shops, carnivals and miniature golf courses. Miniature golf, a craze of the 1920s, is enjoying a resurgence in popularity nationwide. Panama City Beach has six major courses. One mini-golf course has an adjacent giant maze spanning the length of a football field. Following a safari theme, this is actually a race against time.

Another of Florida's Top Ten attractions is **Gulf World**, not far from the City Pier. The park's accomplished marine performers – bottle-nosed dolphins, sea lions and colorful tropical parrots – enter-

tain visitors daily. Set in tropical gardens, the facility includes the **Coral Reef Theater** and a tide pool where visitors can pet a wild stingray. Constant entertainment includes shark feeding and a scuba demonstration and underwater show.

Panama City is also the home of the unique **Museum of Man and the Sea**. The museum tells the story of man's struggle to live, work and play underwater. Marine life sciences, underwater exploration, marine salvage and construction, oceanography and underwater archaeology are only a few of the many underwater activities regularly demonstrated by highly trained divers.

Dogs and Discos

Night time activities also abound in Panama City Beach. From discos to the amusement park to the dog races, there is something for everyone. Dog racing started in the United States in 1919 and has been growing ever since. The grey-

hounds chase a mechanical rabbit around a circular track. There is one track just outside of Panama City Beach where you can have an excellent meal, a few drinks, watch the races and maybe even win a few dollars.

If the dog races are not to your taste there is a romantic evening dinner cruise around the bay or a day-long cruise to nowhere aboard the *Southern Elegance* cruise ship. The Southern Elegance offers a chance to just relax and unwind while sampling the elegant life aboard ship.

For the younger at heart who are looking for a little more energetic entertainment Panama City Beach has a number of discos. The major ones are **La Vela** and **Spinnaker** – located next door to each other on the beach – they include multi-level sun decks, pools, stage areas for shows, male and female dancers, and spacious dance floors. Both book name acts at times. In addition to these two super clubs there are a number of other night spots such as **Pineapple Willie's** with its comedy acts and name bands and the

Ocean Opry Show with a country and western program.

St. Andrew's State Park

St. Andrew's State Park, on the eastern tip of Panama City Beach, is the most-visited park in Florida. Encompassing 1063 acres of beaches, forests and marshes, and particularly noted for its pristine beaches and unusually clear waters, the park offers RV travelers and camping devotees waterfront sites on attractive **Grand Lagoon**.

Distinctly identified nature trails cross the dunes and woodlands. Alligators, wading birds, deer, raccoons and many small animals may be seen. The extensive shoreline and rock jetties offer an excellent place to study marine life. All plant and animal life is protected in state parks. Campfire programs and guided walks are provided seasonally.

Above: Modern raised houses like these skirt the beaches.

Fort Walton / Destin

Between Pensacola and Panama City Beach is an area of residential beach communities. The largest of these are **Destin** and **Fort Walton Beach**. They offer a number of private homes and condominiums for long-term visitors.

While they do not have the activities of Panama City Beach or the history of Pensacola, they are ideal for rest and relaxation and some of the area's most beautiful beaches can be found here.

Apalachicola

An hour east of Panama City Beach is the historic town of **Apalachicola**. One of the South's important ports during the Civil War, the town has seen extensive restoration in recent years. The area also offers some of the best oyster beds in the state. The **John Gorrie Museum** is a must. Gorrie, a country doctor, was the inventor of the country's ice making machines and the first air conditioner.

MIRACLE STRIP
Accommodation

LUXURY: **Marriott Bay Point Resort**, Magnolia Beach Road, Panama City Beach, 904/234-3307. **Edgewater Beach Resort**, 11212 Highway 98E, **Panama City Beach**, 904/235-4044. **Sandestin Beach Hilton**, 5540 Highway 98E, Sandestin, 904/267-9500.

MODERATE: **Tops'l Beach and Racquet Club**, 5550 Highway 98E, Destin, 904/267-9222. **The Inn at St. Thomas Square**, 8600 Thomas Drive, Panama City Beach, 904/234-0349. **Sheraton Coronado Beach Resort**, 1325 Miracle Strip Parkway, 904/243-8166. **The Gibson Inn**, Market St. and Ave. C, Apalachicola, 904/653-2191.

BUDGET: Numerous campgrounds, RV parks, church camps and most of the economy motel chains, as well as a number of independent properties exist. For information regarding accommodation throughout the area call the Panama City Beach Visitors Bureau at 1-800-PCBEACH.

Restaurants

If you like seafood you cannot go wrong along the Miracle Strip. Fresh oysters, shrimp, scallops, grouper, snapper, amberjack, scamp, flounder and blue shell crabs are readily available at most moderate-priced restaurants.

The Sound Restaurant and Lounge in Fort Walton Beach (904) 243-7772 and the **Treasure Ship** in Panama City Beach (904) 234-8881 are both on the waterfront and serve fantastic fresh seafood. A rare treat is scamp, a member of the grouper family that is little known outside northwest Florida's Gulf Coast. The succulent, white, flaky meat of the scamp is considered a delicacy by local fishermen and can be prepared in a variety of ways - broiled, char-grilled, pan sauteed with fresh lemon and butter, or baked with fresh lump crab meat topping. For those who cannot make up their minds, we recommend one of the local buffets early in your stay so that you can try a little of everything. For a change of pace from all that healthy seafood, the **Boer's Head** at 17290 West Highway 98A in Panama City Beach, 904/234-6628 serves excellent beef and the **Melting Pot** at 11053 Middle Beach Road, Panama City Beach, 904/233-6633 specializes in fondue.

Access and Local Transportation

AIR: Just under one hour flying time from Atlanta or one and a half hours from Miami via Eastern Metro and Delta/ASA Airlines – the airport is 15 minutes from the beach area.

LAND: Follow I-10 either east or west to State Highway 231 South. Turn west on State Highway 98 which goes through downtown Panama City, across the bridge to Panama City Beach, follows the beach along the length of the islands.

Hospitals

Gulf Coast Hospital, 904/769-8341, **Bay Medical**, 904/769-1511 - both in Panama City.

Local Festivals

The *Snowbird Golf Tournament* in late January and early February matches the local golfers against the winter visitors, a.k.a., snowbirds. *Spring Break* in late February and early April is not an official festival. It does, however, attract thousands of US and Canadian college students to the beach area during their spring class break for relaxation and play. Panama City Beach has become one of the primary destinations for the spring breakers. The *Offshore Classic Power Boat Races* in April features ocean racing at well over 100 miles per hour in powerful ocean-going speed boats. The boats compete on a course that parallels the beach. The *Indian Summer Seafood Festival* in October features many of the area's best seafood chefs and southern cooking.

Museums / Art Galleries / Theater

The Museum of Man and the Sea, 17314 Hutchinson Road, Panama City Beach, Phone 904/235-4101. **Bay County Junior Museum**, 1731 Jenks Ave, Panama City, 904/769-6128. **John Gorrie State Museum**, 6th St. and Ave., D, Apalachicola, 904/653- 9347. **Gulf World**, 15412 West Highway 98A; Panama City Beach 32407, 904/234-5271. **Indian Temple Mound Museum**, 139 Miracle Strip Parkway, Fort Walton Beach 32548, 904/243-6521. **Institute of Diving**, 17314 Hutchinson Rd (Highway 98), Panama City 32413, 904/235-4101. **Museum of the Sea and Indian**, 4801 Beach Highway, Destin 32541, 904/837-7625. **Snake-A-Torium**, 9008 West Highway 98A, Panama City Beach 32407, 904/234-3311.

Tourist Information

Panama City Beach Visitors Bureau, PO Box 9473, Panama City Beach, 32407, 904/234-6575. **Bay County Chamber of Commerce**, P.O. Box 1850, Panama City, 32402, 904/785-5206. **South Walton Tourist Development Council**, PO Box 1248, Santa Rosa Beach, 32459, 904/267-1216. **Apalachicola County Chamber of Commerce**, 314 East Central Ave., Blountstown, 32424, 904/674-4519. **Greater Fort Walton Beach Chamber of Commerce**, PO Drawer 640, Fort Walton Beach, 32549, 904/244-8191. **Apalachicola Bay Chamber of Commerce**, 128 Market St., Apilachicola, 32320, 904/653-9419. **Port St. Joe-Gulf County Chamber of Commerce**, PO Box 964, Port St. Joe 32456, 904/227-123.

NATURAL AREAS / CAMPING / UNDERWATER PARKS

First impressions to the contrary, Florida is not all man-made entertainment like Walt Disney World, concrete canyons like Miami Beach, or never-ending sub-divisions throughout the state. With 900 new residents arriving every day and millions of visitors a year, it is sometimes hard to get away from all these people, their houses and shopping centers.

Still, Florida-the-Natural exists, the *raison d' etre* for coming here: coral reefs, barrier islands and mangroves, pinelands and hardwood hammocks, cypress swamps, fresh and salt water marshes, and the Everglades, unique in the world.

Seasonal changes are subtle, with an annual average temperature range between 65 and 85 degrees F. Generally,

Preceding pages: Typical scene at Ding Darling nature reserve. Right: This diver seems to be listening to an underwater sermon.

summers are humid and wet, winters cool and dry with possible night frost in the north and central sections and one or two freezing days in the southern regions.

Spring through fall is the optimal time for camping in North Florida. In the south, from late fall to the first rains of summer in June is the best time to pitch your tent and explore the territory. Fishing is outstanding year-round.

For diving we prefer the glass-calm mornings of summer with warm water temperatures and almost unlimited visibility. Summertime, too, brings violent and potentially dangerous thunderstorms, and in densely foliated woods and mangroves, more mosquitoes, the vital link in our food chain. Mosquitos, like sand flies, are most active in the early evening hours, so it is easy to schedule activities around them.

Almost without exception, all natural areas have adequate lodging facilities nearby. A plethora of private camp grounds, geared mainly toward recreational vehicle campers, can be found

throughout the state. For many away-from-it-all places though you need a tent and accompanying paraphernalia. Once you have set up camp, a canoe is an enjoyable way to explore nearby scenic rivers and waterways. Outfitters throughout the state will provide rentals, drop-off and pick-up.

Almost without exception, the best tent and RV sites are found in the public domain: the national and state parks, forests and recreational areas. Camping in wilderness areas generally requires a back country permit, available at no cost at the park office, and you should be well versed in wilderness skills and etiquette. With hundreds of possible wilderness areas to choose from, we picked a number of well-loved sites for a sampling. Since most first-time visitors choose Miami, Orlando or Tampa as gateways, our choices are concentrated around those areas. To do so, we have had to neglect some very scenic but harder to reach natural lands like the Blackwater River State Park and Forest in the northwest

corner of the state; the Okefenokee Swamp and Osceola Forest in the north, and most of the 27 top quality fresh water springs like Wakulla Springs near Tallahassee.

Miami Area

From Miami, Everglades National Park and the Florida Keys, with unparalleled diving and fishing opportunities, are within easy reach. Closest to Miami is Biscayne National Park, Canal Drive, Homestead, 33090-1369, 305/247-7275. A national park within view of downtown Miami, it is one of Florida's best kept secrets. The waters and islands, like **Elliott** and **Boca Chita Key**, are popular with Miami boaters, but with luck you may be the only one there during the week. The park encompasses South Biscayne Bay waters, the reef off the Upper Keys and some lovely, undeveloped mangrove-fringed islands.

Biscayne Aqua Tours, the Park's concessionaire, 305/247-2400, offer glass

203

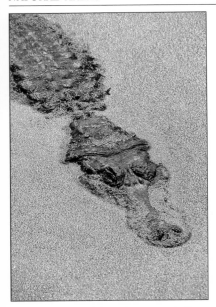

bottom boat sightseeing, snorkeling, scuba, and island tours. The reefs are as beautiful as Pennecamp's which they adjoin and are less crowded on week days.

John Pennecamp Coral Reef State Park, mile marker (MM) 102.5, on Key Largo, 305/451-1202, is only one and a half hour's drive from Miami. The area shelters a large and beautiful segment of the coral reef that defines the Keys.

The park concessionaire, Coral Reef Park Co., 305/451-1621 or toll-free in Florida 800/432-2871, provides access with a large assortment of tours: full and half-day snorkeling, scuba diving, glass bottom boat, rental boats and a fully equipped dive shop. Reservations are necessary. Best conditions in the summer usually prevail in the morning hours before the afternoon breeze picks up.

If it is too windy for the reef, you can rent a canoe and explore the mangrove

Above: Taking a siesta in the swamps.
Right: Father is the best teacher of angling.

channels or a Hobie-cat to sail Largo Sound. The most popular reefs are Grecian Rocks with elkhorn, staghorn, brain coral and Spanish cannons. French Reef has canyons, ledges and caves. Molasses Reef is popular, as is "Christ of the Deep", which is a 4000 pound, 11-foot tall replica of the Genoese "Il Cristo Degli Abissi", a questionable but popular man-made intrusion. Back on shore, you'll find camp sites, beaches, a nature path through the hardwood hammock, and an interpretive center.

Indian Key State Historic Site and **Lignumvitae Key State Botanical Site** lie off-shore, surrounded by turquoise waters south of Islamorada. The Park Service pontoon boat picks up visitors on Indian Key Fill at MM 79, Thursday through Monday for morning and afternoon tours. Reservations are necessary: call 305/664-4815. Indian Key is what early Florida history is all about: Calusa Indians preying on Spanish shipwrecks, first government seat for Dade County, home to Jacob Housman and his high-rolling and hard-playing men who found plenty of work and prosperity salvaging sailing vessels that were driven onto the reefs. His controversial proposal to hunt down the remaining Seminole Indians for removal to the American West, inspired the wrath of the Indian tribe which in 1840 successfully raided and destroyed Housman's outpost.

Today, only foundations, wall fragments and wild-growing sisal remain. You can follow the streets, climb the observation tower and let your imagination wander back in time when the lookout's cry "wreck!" caused a flurry of activity and excitement.

Lignumvitae Key, on the bay side of Indian Key Fill, and rising to 16 feet, is the highest point in the islands. A naturalist's paradise, the fossilized coral rock harbors a healthy tropical hammock, the type that once covered most of the Keys until man's thoughtless intrusion.

Lignumvitae, mastic, ironwood, pigeon plum, gumbo limbo and the three mangroves, red, black, and white, grow here. Among the fauna you will find the Key Largo wood rat, golden orb spider, over 20 different kinds of butterflies, rare tree snails, a host of bird species, and, especially during the rainy season, hordes of mosquitoes. In the small clearing, a typical Keys house of 1919 vintage with cistern and hurricane shelter recalls simpler times.

Boat rentals, too, are easily available at nearby marinas but note that Lignumvitae Key is closed every Tuesday and Wednesday. Bahia-Honda State Recreation Area, MM 37, Big Pine Key, (305/872-2353), has the finest swimming beach in the Keys. Campsites, cabins (high-priced and too close to the road), a marina with launch facilities, plenty of pavilions and cooking grills are available. At the south end of the area is the old Bahia Honda Bridge, where the original road was laid precariously above the railroad trestle. Nature trails along the shore and a tidal lagoon offer insights into the tropical fauna and flora, brought ashore long ago by wind, waves and birds. Rare botanical species include the satin wood tree, spiny catesbaea and dwarf morning glory. The shore and lagoon are favorite fishing grounds for white-crowned pigeon, white heron and roseate spoonbill.

Looe Key National Marine Sanctuary, only 6 miles from land, is accessible by dive boat from either Marathon or Ramrod Key (MM 27). In 1744, the British frigate *HMS Looe* ran aground here. In recent years this rather isolated reef has become enormously popular with snorkelers and divers alike because of its great depth and unsurpassed water clarity. The 115-foot canyon walls are a challenge to experienced scuba divers while the reef crest offers safe snorkeling for novices.

Fort Jefferson National Monument in the **Dry Tortugas** is a favorite spot but

expensive to get to. It combines the historical and natural: located 70 miles west of Key West, it is a 40-minute flight by seaplane, an overnight voyage by boat. Fort Jefferson, on Garden Key, belongs to the seven islands group known as the Dry Tortugas. Ponce de Leon made a landfall here in 1513 and found an abundance of sea turtles, hence the name. Designed to be the largest fort in a line of US Atlantic seacoast defenses, it was never needed as part of an obsolete defense system. It was turned into the infamous "Devil's Island", part of the US prison system. Its most famous prisoner was Dr. Mudd, the physician implicated in President Lincoln's assassination.

Flying in at 500 feet, you might see large sharks cruising the shallows. Your pilot will point out the **Marquesa Islands**, the only Atlantic atoll, and the shoals where many treasure ships went down, among them the *Atocha*, whose riches are on view at **Mel Fisher's Key West Gold Museum**. After an introductory slide show at Fort Jefferson, you

are on your own to explore or snorkel. The parapet affords an incomparable view of the powder magazines, cistern, moat, and surrounding islands.

Overhead, frigate birds with 7-foot wingspan soar, cormorants and royal terns occupy the pilings. Across the channel is **Bush Key** with its nesting colony of sooty terns and brown noddys. In the clear water, blue and grey angelfish, striped sergeant majors, snapper and grouper feed around moat openings, conch and welk crawl over the sandy bottom while urchins hide in the turtle grass.

During spring migration, from March to early May, the fort bustles with activity, not only with birds, but also with bird watchers eager to add a few new species to their lists. The island's isolation and lack of services – you must bring your own water – preserve it for a select few. Environmental groups such as Sierra

Above: You can have interesting encounters along nature reserve paths. Right: Landscape at Ding Darling.

Club and the Audubon Society run late spring boat trips of 2-3 days. Non-members are welcome on a space available basis. Key West Seaplane Service offers half- or full-day, and overnight trips, phone 305/294-6978 for information.

Orlando Area

From Orlando, it is not far to **Ocala National Forest** and the rolling hills and lakes of Central Florida.

A very different habitat is **Merritt Island National Wildlife Refuge** and **Canaveral National Seashore**, 407/867-0667, just north of the Kennedy Space Center. Access is via Route 402, east of Titusville, to a birder's heaven, from fall through spring. Expect to see snipe, avocets, and wintering ducks in the marshes and lagoons. Pick up the map at the visitors center and enjoy a beach picnic with a backdrop of wild dunes. Some beach areas are closed during space shuttle pre- and post-launch periods.

Blue Springs State Park, Orange City 904/775-3663, is situated off I-4 as you drive towards Daytona Beach. If you have never seen a manatee, visit between December and mid-March when a herd of about 60 sea cows gathers here to escape cold waters elsewhere. Plan on an early morning visit to avoid the crowds. There are camp sites, canoe rentals, scuba diving, and trails.

Marjorie Kinnan Rawlings State Historic Site, 904/466-3672, is located 20 miles south of Gainesville, on FL 325, between FL 20 and US 301. Rawlings' "small place of enchantment" tells of a simpler, more authentic life. Fortunately, development has been slow in this little outpost of old Florida where the renowned author wrote *Cross Creek*.

Tampa Area

From Tampa/St. Petersburg outdoors investigations lead to the long beaches

and islands of Florida's West Coast. In spite of a burgeoning population, areas such as **Caladesi Island** and **Cayo Costa** offer prime outdoor recreation in relatively unspoiled natural settings. With its easier access, we favor **Myakka River State Park** and adjacent **Wilderness Preserve**, 813/924-1027, southwest of busy Sarasota-Bradenton, yet a world removed. The Civilian Conservation Corps built the first facilities here in the 1930s. The camp ground tends to get crowded in the winter months, but you can escape to the primitive sites if you can do without civilization's amenities for a while. Hike, canoe, fish, sit, take in the beauty of river, marshes, pine lands, and prairies. Wildlife sightings, especially in winter, are outstanding.

J. N. "Ding" Darling National Wildlife Refuge. Visitors Center and entrance are about 6 miles west of the Causeway on Sanibel Island, 813/472-1100. A 5-mile road winds through the refuge, named after a 1930s journalist, famous for his conservation-minded cartoons that twice won him a Pulitzer prize. Take one of the trails, climb the observation tower or rent a canoe at Tarpon Bay Marina, 813/472-8900. You might find flocks of roseate spoonbills and with luck observe manatees and alligators. Best time for observation is low tide.

Over 250 bird species make this refuge their home or stop over during spring and fall migration. In addition, large numbers of reptiles and amphibians, and 32 mammal species reside here year-round. Additional information on Florida's Natural lands, camping and underwater parks is available from: Department of Natural Resources, Information Office, 3900 Commonwealth Blvd., Room 613, Tallahassee, FL 32399. Free information on camping, hiking and canoeing. Florida Audubon Society, 1101 Audubon Way, Maitland, FL 32751. Specializes in birding and nature trips. Florida Division of Tourism, Tourist Information, Department of Commerce, Tallahassee, FL 32399-2000. Provides free listings of private camp grounds and free maps.

EVERGLADES DAY TRIPS

There may be no other National Park in the United States that is so easily accessible from a large city, and with such a fiercely loyal following. After a first short visit, nature lovers keep coming back again, discovering new and unexpected sights, sounds and vistas. You have a choice of three different day outings, depending on where you are staying.

From Miami, we suggest an all day trip to **Flamingo** by way of the main visitors' entrance, near Florida City. With less time available, a half-day trip to **Shark Valley**, the northern entrance to the park, about 30 miles west of Miami, gives you an introduction to the sawgrass prairie and in winter and spring an almost certain guarantee of plentiful wildlife and bird activity. The trip can be extended to include a visit to the **Miccosukee Indian Village.**

Above: Everglades landscape at dusk.
Right: This snake is taking a sun-bath.

At the Visitors Center stop for an orientation program and pick up guides, maps and tips from the helpful rangers. And do not forget to call for a dinner reservation at the Flamingo Restaurant, a 38-mile drive from the phone to the southernmost point of land in the park.

Along the miles you will encounter biological diversity including pine-lands, hardwood hammocks in a sawgrass prairie, dwarf cypress forests and mangrove coasts. Driving at 50 miles an hour deprives you of what the Everglades offer. Leave your car to experience the broad sweep of sky, the endless sawgrass prairie. Look for alligator hatchlings on a sunny canal bank, an anhinga feeding its young, a hummingbird flitting or a snowy egret delicately lifting its golden slippers. The park service has provided a great many pull-offs, trails and boardwalks.

With only a day to spend, favorite walks include **Royal Palm Hammock**, 4 miles from the Visitors Center. Two trails are worth taking. The **Gumbo Limbo Trail** leads inside a hardwood hammock,

where slightly elevated ground provides ideal conditions for plants such as the gumbo limbo, red maple, live oak and strangler fig. On the **Anhinga Trail** there are a number of these birds swimming snake-like under water or sitting with their wings spread out to speed drying. Alligators, from the big grand-daddy barely moving in the deep water, to babies sunning along the canal bank, make their home here. They have survived for eons without extra feeding. In fact, feeding of all wildlife is prohibited.

The **Pa-hay-okee Overlook**, situated 12 miles into the park, affords a good view of the "River of Grass," as Marjorie Stoneman Douglas, a South Florida writer on the environment, called it. The sights are undramatic, just the play of sky and clouds over the endless prairie. Here it is time to go into slow gear and sit and listen to the quiet solitude of the land.

Mahogany Hammock, at 19 miles, is where you can see what the typical hardwood hammock looked like before loggers destroyed most old growth.

Parautis Pond, at 24.5 miles, named after the rare Parautis palm, is a good spot for a lunch picnic by the lake.

At **West Lake**, 30 miles, fresh and salt water mingle. All three kinds of mangroves and the related buttonwood are represented here. The latter provided the means for making charcoal to the early settlers. It is the mangroves that are the food base for the marine fisheries.

Along most of the boardwalks and trails stand people glued to binoculars and viewing scopes. If you are not familiar with the bird life, most birders will share their discoveries with you. Don't be shy about asking.

At Flamingo, the land meets **Florida Bay**. On calm days, distant islands seem to float above the water and stands of red mangrove provide just the right foreground for a Florida picture. You will find a ranger-staffed visitors' center, viewing scopes, a marina with houseboat, skiff and canoe rentals, motel, restaurant, camp ground, and amphitheater for evening camp-fire programs in the winter.

If you arrive by mid-afternoon and the tide is low, by all means take the tram tour to Snake Bight. It departs from the Visitors Center, although tram and restaurant do not operate in the summer. Florida Bay stretches before you. On a quiet afternoon at low tide, thousands of water birds reflect in the calm few inches of water. Early evening is a good time to dine on the catch of the day at the second floor restaurant overlooking a spectacular bird flat in the bay. White and brown pelicans, cormorants, egrets and herons, large sandpipers and little pips crowd the bar, plus an occasional eagle.

As an alternative, take a sunset cruise into Florida Bay on the concessionaire-operated boat. If you have brought a picnic, drive over to the camp ground and watch the roosting flight of ibis and egret as the sun goes down.

Above: During Spring the Everglades show their true colors. Right: These vultures seem highly interested in today's television program.

Day-travelers to **Shark Valley** learn the Shark River Slough is all fresh water and no self-respecting shark would swim in it. With access from the Tamiami Trail, US 41, the park service has built a 15-mile loop road into the heart of this sawgrass covered, slow-flowing river.

You can rent a bike or take the ranger guided tram which operates year-round. A stop at the southern end of the road lets you climb the observation tower for a birds-eye view of this sea of grass and elevated tree islands known as hammocks. Alligators bask on the banks of a pond or cruise quietly in search of prey. You may surprise a family of white-tail deer along the road, observe Everglade kites – turkey vultures and red-shouldered hawks – or see the limpkin blend with the grass, or the green heron poised to catch his supper. Park rangers will know what you are likely to see that day.

Whatever the season, whatever the time, the Glades are changing but always beautiful. Brilliant, sharp-edged contours and colors characterize the winter days.

Towering clouds are typical of a summer afternoon and gentle shades of mauve, orange and pink color early evening.

Allow 2 hours for the tram ride, 3-4 hours if you decide to bicycle. Bring food and drink, only water is available at the tower. Sit on one of the boardwalk benches and let the quiet surround you.

Miccosukee Indians Today

If you have time on your hands and would like a change of pace, visit the **Miccosukee Indian Village** near the Shark Valley entrance. People living here are descendants of the few hundred Miccosukee Indians who escaped their planned removal to reservations in the American West at the end of the nineteenth-century Indian wars. They were forced to adapt quickly and efficiently to life in this demanding and hostile environment of saw-grass and water, moving into a land whose barest fringes had been populated, at the time of discovery, by the Calusa Indians.

Those inhabitants had been removed to Cuba or had died of imported diseases well before the arrival of the Miccosukee. Don't waste much time watching alligator wrestling and other obvious tourist come-ons. The village is very much a living one with school and tribal council meeting facilities.

Miccosukee traditional life style was irrevocably changed with the advent of drainage and the 1928 opening of the road connecting Florida's east and west coasts. The Miccosukee community is a good place to get a close look at the chickees, which are the open-sided thatch platforms so well-adapted to Florida, where some still prefer to live. Not a single nail is used in their construction.

Miccosukee are famous for colorful jackets and skirts, sewn in attractive, brightly colored patchwork and zigzag patterns. You can try their pumpkin and fry bread in the native restaurant across

the street, which otherwise offers run-of-the-mill American fare. If you must, this would be the place to take an airboat ride. It is a thrill. Less damaging than the popular off-road motor-vehicles, airboat use in the fragile ecosystem of the Everglades is controversial. Nevertheless, the Miccosukee probably offer the best ride, for it includes a stop at one of their settled hammocks in the saw grass prairie. There are two other commercial airboat operators: Everglades Safari and Coopertown Airboats.

On the Naples-Ft. Myers side of the Everglades you may want to drive to the **Gulf Coast Ranger Station** of Everglades National Park, just south of Everglades City on Highway 29. The park's excursion boats take you for an introductory tour of the **Ten Thousand Islands**, the mangrove islands that form the southwestern side of the Everglades. Dolphin, sea turtles, and osprey, fish clutched in their talons, are possible sightings. Here, too, is the start of the almost 100 mile long wilderness waterway.

THEME PARKS

0   100   200 km
0   60   120 miles

THEME PARKS

There is always something new to discover in the wonderland of Florida theme parks. In addition to world renowned Walt Disney World, there are many other appealing attractions. Some are new, others are long time favorites. Often, they are less crowded and less expensive. Travel agents should have the latest information about tour package plans featuring parks of your choice.

Orlando and Disney

Since its opening in 1971, Walt Disney World has become the world's most popular man-made attraction. The **Magic Kingdom**, **EPCOT Center** and new **Disney-MGM Studios Theme Park** are its major areas. At **EPCOT Center's** Future World, new ideas in communications, energy, transportation, land and the imagination are presented.

Its newest pavilion, Wonders of Life, features a ride through the human body.

In EPCOT's World Showcase, 11 nations share cultures in shows, attractions, restaurants and shops. Two more pavilions, the Soviet Union and Switzerland, will be added soon.

Disney-MGM Studios Theme Park is an actual motion picture studio. A guided backstage tour is also offered, along with lively shows and attractions.

Its newest, **Star Tours**, takes guests on a flight simulator ride through outer space. Walt Disney World also includes the **River Country** water park at Fort Wilderness Resort and Campground, and **Discovery Island**, a zoological park. Recent additions include **Pleasure Island** nightclub-dining center near **Disney's Village Marketplace**, and **Typhoon Lagoon**, the world's largest inland surfing park. A fourth theme park will be added during the 1990s, dubbed the "Disney Decade" by the successful company.

Universal Studios Florida, the state's newest entertainment-themed attraction, was opened May 1990, 10 miles southwest of downtown Orlando. A state-of-the-art motion picture and television production facility, it is the largest, most complete studio outside Hollywood.

The park's backlot features entertainment based on popular motion picture and television locations, ranging from Beverly Hills' Rodeo Drive to San Francisco's Fisherman's Wharf. Located at the park entrance is one of the USA's most popular rock 'n roll establishments, The Hard Rock Cafe Universal Studios Florida. Live shows enable visitors to travel *Back to the Future* with Dr. Brown from the popular movie or narrowly escape King Kong as he attacks a New York City aerial tramway. Guests can also tremble in a simulated earthquake, or soar on flying bicycles to E.T.'s planet.

Sea World in Orlando is among Florida's most popular parks. It features a variety of marine animals in themed productions. *The Legend of Shamu*, in Shamu Stadium, stars an entire killer whale family, including its newest addition, Baby Namu, born in 1989. In *New Friends*, Beluga whales and dolphins perform at the Whale and Dolphin Stadium. *Sea Lions of the Silver Screen*, stars otters and walruses.

Guests get close-up views of hundreds of penguins at Penguin Encounter, a large science center which also serves as a living laboratory of polar life.

Multi-media films, a colorful water ski show, Shark Encounter Exhibition, Cap'n Kids' World playground and the "Hawaiian Rhythms" troupe add to the excitement of a Sea World visit. The park also features a nightly Polynesian *luau* dinner show (additional cost). Orlando's **Wet 'n Wild Water Park** has more than a dozen exciting slides, flumes and pools. Visitors experience such challenges as Der Stuka, called the world's fastest water slide; Raging Rapids whitewater thrill ride through torrential rains and waterfalls; the Kamikaze, where brave explorers plunge down a water chute more than six stories above pool level; and

thrilling new Black Hole, an enclosed flume ride with space age effects.

Here, also, visitors discover the giant Bonzai Boggan water roller coaster, as well as such aquatic oddities as Mach 5 and Hydra-Maniac. Other features include wave-pools, a beach, cable-operated knee-board rides, a picnic area, food stands and miniature golf.

Although many successful theme parks can be found in Florida, and particularly in the tall shadow cast by Disney characters around Orlando, not every theme park is a winner. Boardwalks and Baseball closed its doors abruptly in early 1990. Although the theme park shut down, the facility was scheduled to host the Kansas City Royals baseball team. Yet even as Florida's annual baseball theme parks struggle, a Senior Professional Baseball League, consisting of former major leaguers is flourishing.

Cypress Gardens

Bordering Lake Eloise near Winter Haven in Central Florida's famed **Cypress Gardens**, magnificent botanical gardens bloom year round and sightseeing boats wind along waterways bordered by flowers, exotic shrubs and cypress trees. Flower-lined paths also lead through the gardens with over 8000 plant varieties from 75 countries.

Other floral showcases include the All-America Rose Gardens, displaying more than 500 varieties of the nation's official flower. The park's live entertainment features an ice skating revue and a water ski extravaganza showcasing high-powered boat racing and ski jumping. Visitors can also shop and see elaborate model railroads at Southern Crossroads, a replica antebellum town; enjoy panoramic views from a platform atop Kodak's Island in the Sky tower; and tour an animal forest with walk-through aviary, pet zoo, alligator/snake handling demonstrations, and treatment center for injured birds.

Silver Springs

Weeki Wachee

Florida's **Silver Springs**, outside Ocala, is the area's oldest major theme park and site of many Hollywood films, including the original *Tarzan* movies. The popular Glass Bottom Boat Ride floats on crystal clear water where deep springs form the Silver River.

A Jungle Cruise Safari aboard quiet electric boats glides past wildlife preserves inhabited by Barbary sheep, giraffes, zebras, llamas, monkeys and other. Other popular attractions include Cypress Point, an island plaza inhabited by turtles, flamingos and water fowl; a reptile institute, a pet animal zoo, and an antique car collection. Silver Springs Wild Waters includes a huge wave pool, eight flume rides, children's water play area and miniature golf.

Above: What seems so natural and easy needs long and intensive training. Right: Where does the ever present liking for monsters come from?

At **Weeki Wachee Springs**, about 47 miles north of Tampa/St. Petersburg, the park's famed swimming "mermaids" perform behind the glass walls of an underwater theater. The park also features a Birds of Prey display, where injured birds are rehabilitated and returned to natural environments when possible, and a pelican orphanage for injured sea birds.

Trained macaws and cockatoos perform their own show daily and an electric boat cruise explores the Weeki Wachee River for views of native wild life and plants. There's also an Animal Forest pet zoo. The park's adjacent Buccaneer Bay water recreation area includes a beach with river swimming, flume rides, volleyball courts and youngsters' Fantasy Island with mini-slides.

Marineland

On the Atlantic coast south of St. Augustine is **Marineland** of Florida, the world's first marine park. A multi-dimensional film, *Sea Dream*, is presented in the Aquarium Theater. Walkways lead amid semi-tropical jungles, and the Margaret Herrick Shell Museum displays over 6000 rare specimens from around the world. In the park's most popular feature, continuous shows star performing dolphins and over 1000 sea species can be viewed in an aquarium and two huge Oceanarium tanks. Also in St. Augustine, Humboldt penguins are at home in **Whitney Park**, where visitors can also view sealions feeding. Two newer aquariums showcase two unique marine habitats: **Secrets of the Reef** features Pacific fish; **Wonders of the Spring** displays Florida freshwater fish.

Tampa's Busch Gardens

At Tampa's **Busch Gardens**, The Dark Continent, seven distinctly themed sections capture the spirit of Africa with thrill shows and exhibits, shops, restaurants and games.

A new futuristic electric monorail allows visitors to ride through the park's Serengeti Plain in air conditioned comfort, viewing African big game roaming freely across a veldt-like plain. The animals can also be seen from a steam locomotive, sky ride or promenade.

Other areas include Timbuktu, an ancient desert trading center, with its Scorpion looping roller coaster, Sandstorm thrill ride and 1200-seat Das Festhaus dining-entertainment complex with German food, music and dancing.

Morocco is home to the Moroccan Palace Theater, staging the Broadway-style musical review "Kaleidoscope." At Nairobi, baby birds and animals are tended in a nursery and the Nocturnal Mountain's simulated night environment allows visitors to observe species which are active in the dark.

The Congo offers the Congo River Rapids white water raft ride and the ex-

citing Python roller coaster with double spiral. Bird Gardens, the park's oldest segment, displays over 2000 exotic birds; some perform in a trained show and others are at home in natural habitat aviaries. Stanleyville, a bustling African village, includes the Stanley Falls log flume ride and thrill-packed Tanganyika Tidal Wave, a water safari ride through a dense jungle culminating in a 55-foot drop into a lake, thus creating a giant wave that drenches riders.

Other live shows at the park include *Sounds of the '60s*, a musical revue in Morocco's Marrakech Theater, and *Dolphins of the Deep*, performed in Timbuktu's Dolphin Theater.

Adventure Island, a separate water-themed park, is adjacent to Busch Gardens. It features a triple-tube looping water slide; the Rambling Bayou float trip down a lazy river; Tampa Typhoon free fall slide, Gulf Screem speed slide; Barratuba inner tube slide; flume rides and wave, children's swimming and diving pools.

GOLF

0   100km

0   60miles

GOLF AND TENNIS RESORTS

The Sunshine State's benign climate beckons golf and tennis vacationers with some incomparable resort hideaways.

Adding to their appeal, most offer cost effective packages which may include lodging and some meals. Some are self-contained communities, where you might happily spend an entire vacation. Tucked away at **Islamorada** in the Florida Keys is **Cheeca Lodge**. Best known as an anglers' haven, the resort also has a challenging nine-hole executive golf course designed by Jack Nicklaus. There are six lighted all-weather tennis courts on the 27-acre beautifully landscaped site, an ocean beach and fishing pier.

Some of Florida's most famous resorts await on the "American Riviera", the south Atlantic coast. In northwest Miami, **Doral Resort and Country Club** spreads amid palm trees, lakes and softly

Right: First steps into the world of tennis.

rolling hills. Its Blue Course is home of the prestigious Doral Ryder Open PGA Tournament; there are four other championship courses and a par-3 nine-hole beginners' course. Doral's Arthur Ashe Jr. Tennis Club contains 15 clay and composition courts, including stadium seating for 400, and is home of the Rick Day Tennis Academy. Additionally, the resort includes an equestrian center and Olympic-size pool.

Also in the northwest, **Miami Lakes Inn Athletic Club Golf Resort** nestles in an elegant country club community. There is an 18-hole championship golf course, lighted executive course and driving range, nine lighted tennis courts and a racquetball center with glass enclosed championship court. The Athletic Club includes a gymnasium and spa.

At **Palm Beach Gardens**, the **PGA Sheraton Resort** is home of the Professional Golf Association of America and the United States Croquet Association. Site of the PGA Seniors' Championship Tournament, its Champion Course

was recently reopened, following redesign by Jack Nicklaus. The PGA National Golf Academy offers championship golf schools. There are four additional championship courses, 19 clay tennis courts, five croquet courts, a health and fitness center and 26-acre sailing lake.

In neighboring **Fort Lauderdale**, the **Sheraton Bonaventure Resort & Spa** overlooks two championship courses managed by PGA professionals in an exclusive residential community. The resort's spa is one of the nation's largest, and there are 24 all-weather tennis courts, squash and racquetball courts, an equestrian center, indoor roller skating, and bowling.

Another internationally renowned spa and celebrity retreat, **Palm-Aire**, at **Pompano Beach**, has now emerged as a major golf and tennis center. Its owners recently purchased a neighboring golf and racquet club, bringing the complex a total of five 18-hole golf courses and 37 tennis courts. Health and fitness programs are available year round.

At **Boca Raton**, the award-winning **Boca Raton Hotel & Club**, one of America's grand retreats, has two championship 18-hole golf courses on its 200-acre estate. Other amenities: a 29-court tennis center, site of the All American Sports Tennis Academy, fitness center, beach and marina on the Intracoastal.

Another legendary retreat, **The Breakers**, in **Palm Beach**, has undergone a $50-million renovation, with rooms refurbished by interior designer Carleton Varney. Home of the state's oldest 18-hole golf course, a Donald Ross design, it is also the site of the championship Breakers West layout. There are 19 tennis courts, croquet and a fitness center.

The Palm Beach Polo and Country Club is perhaps best known for 7.5 minute-long chukkers and the Piaget World Cup of Polo. After all, Prince Charles has stayed here several times, as have other assorted royalty. And they probably came to take advantage ten polo fields, a clubhouse and equestrian center more than for golf or tennis. The resort is

indeed the international headquarters of polo, but the 54 golf holes are all champinship calibre. One was designed by 1976 US Open Winner Jerry Pate. It is called "The Dunes" and has a Scottish-style. Cypress Course was designed by Pete and B.D. Dye, and there are nine more holes.

Northward, on the "Treasure Coast", a serene, lesser known region, **Indian River Plantation** on **Hutchinson Island** is an idyllic retreat bordered by the Atlantic Ocean and Intracoastal Waterway. There is golfing, on an 18-hole par-61 course with lakeside club house, and tennis on 13 courts, seven lighted. Other amenities include an outdoor spa, private Atlantic beach, deep sea fishing charters and full service marina.

Further up the coast, **Indigo Lakes Resort** is near internationally renowned Daytona Beach Speedway. Its par-72 golf course consistently ranks among Florida's best. The new headquarters resort for the Ladies Professional Golf Association, in 1992 Indigo Lakes will add a new LPGA designed course and resort facility. It also includes ten lighted tennis courts, racquetball courts, an Olympic pool, fitness center-spa and Parcourse Fitness Trail.

One of the USA's largest golf resorts is luxurious **Marriott** at **Sawgrass**, at Ponte Vedra Beach, about 26 miles southeast of Jacksonville. One of two resorts in the world with two Tournament Players Club (TPC) courses, it is also home of the PGA Tour. The resort's five championship 18-hole courses include the TPC at Sawgrass Valley and TPC at Sawgrass Stadium, home of the famous par-3, 121-meter island hole and site of The Players Championship tournament. The tennis center offers ten clay courts; guests also have privileges at the new 11-court Association of Tennis Professionals (ATP), international headquarters of the prestigious organization. Sawgrass also in-

Above: Golf – a game for individualists.
Right: All major hotels do have their own golf-course.

cludes two fitness-health centers; advanced corporate conditioning programs are available through St. Vincent's Wellness Center and the Jacksonville branch of Mayo Clinic.

There's more fine golfing at nearby **Amelia Island Plantation**. Its new Long Point Course challenges with highly elevated fairways and large bodies of water; the other 37 holes mingle island greens with salt marshes and ocean dunes. The Plantation Racquet Park has 23 tennis courts scattered amid live oak trees. All American Sports operates the instructional program. There is also a health-fitness center with racquetball courts and heated indoor lap pool.

The "world's theme park capital", Central Florida, also has fine golf-tennis resorts. At Orlando's 1500-acre **Grand Cypress Resort**, 45 holes of Jack Nicklaus-designed golf include the New Course, inspired by the Old Course at St. Andrews, Scotland. Tennis enthusiasts can polish their game at the 12-court racquet club. There's also a nine-wicket croquet

court and an equestrian center offering English and Western trail rides.

Near **Haines City**, **Grenelefe Resort** on the shores of Lake Marion has three 18-hole championship golf courses. Its 20-court tennis center includes a 1700-set stadium and is featured on the Grand Prix Tennis Circuit. There's a full service marina and staff can organize complete fishing tournaments.

At **Niceville** in the northwest Panhandle, **Bluewater Bay Resort's** 27-hole golf courses are the site of the International Invitational and Florida Cup golf tournaments. Highlights are presentations of the $10,000 Goebel Trophy and the Herman Tissies Memorial "Spirit of the Game" award, honoring the memory of the famed German amateur. Bluewater Bay's active tennis program is on 21 courts with three different surfaces. There is also an Olympic pool and a full service marina.

At nearby **Sandestin** there is more championship golf on 45 holes; 36 more holes are planned. One of the few USA

resorts offering grass courts, Sandestin also has hard and composition tennis courts, making a total of 16. There is a fitness center, full service marina and deep seat fishing.

Marriott's Bay Point Resort at neighboring **Panama City Beach** features golf on two par-72 courses, and there is a 12-court tennis center, site of the Men's Intercollegiate Clay Championship. The Yacht Club is base for the $350,000 July Bay Point Billfish Invitational.

On the southwest Gulf Coast, at **Tarpon Springs**, **Innisbrook** sports and leisure resort offers 63 holes of golf on three recently restored championship courses, meandering amid lakes, woodlands and low hills. Its Tennis and Racquetball Center, home of the Australian Tennis Institute, includes 18 tennis courts and four racquetball courts. There is a separate children's recreation center.

Above: You wear your passion on your head. Right: From Miami to the Caribbean once a week – the Norway.

At **Wesley Chapel** on nearby Tampa Bay, **Saddlebrook Golf and Tennis Resort** has two Arnold Palmer golf courses. Its huge 37-court tennis complex is headquarters of the United States Professional Tennis Association. A "Superpool", as long as a football field, features racing lanes, and there is also a fitness center.

On **Longboat Key**, near Sarasota, luxurious **Longboat Key Club** has an 18-hole golf course in a tropical setting and 27 holes bordering Sarasota Bay. There is an 18-court tennis center along a quiet lagoon and another 20-court complex beside an idyllic inland waterway. Southward, there is tennis on two idyllic hideaway islands.

On serene **Captiva Island**, **South Seas Plantation**, one of the Gulf Coast's top tennis facilities, has 22 courts. There is golf on a nine-hole par-36 course, along with a deep-water yacht basin. On adjacent **Sanibel Island**, world famed for its shelling beaches, **Sundial Beach and Tennis Resort** has seven composition and six clay courts.

CRUISES

Some delightful cruise experiences await voyagers who sail from Florida ports. More cruise ships call the Sunshine State home than any place in the world. Choices may include a one- to four-day cruise to the Bahamas, a week or longer voyage into the Caribbean, a longer sailing to exotic world ports, or a leisurely trip along the Intracoastal Waterway.

Cruise Ports

Over 2.5 million passengers annually pass through Miami, the world's largest cruise port. Its futuristic 12-terminal docking facility on Dodge Island is currently year-round home to 19 cruise ships operated by ten companies. Among them, four of Carnival Cruise Lines' popular "Fun Ships" – **Celebration**, **Holiday**, **Jubilee** and **Fantasy**; Norwegian Cruise Line's magnificent flagship **Norway** (formerly the **France**), **Seaward** and **Sunward II**; and Royal Caribbean Cruise Line's **Nordic Empress**, **Nordic Prince**, **Song of America** and **Sovereign of the Seas**.

Fort Lauderdale's Port Everglades is the nation's second largest cruise ship facility. Altogether 14 lines and 21 vessels now utilize the port, most of them on a seasonal basis. Officials proudly describe it as the "Five Star Port", since so many ships docking there receive high ratings from cruise experts. Among them are such luxurious floating resorts as Cunard Line's **Queen Elizabeth 2**, **Sagafjord** and **Vistafjord**; Holland America Line's **Noordam** and the flagship **Rotterdam**; Costa Cruises' **Costa Riviera**; and Royal Viking Line's elegant **Royal Viking Sun**, **Star** and **Sky**. In 1990, Princess Cruises' stunning new 1562-passenger **Crown Princess** joined the Port Everglades fleet.

Port Canaveral, on the northeast Atlantic "Space Coast", has taken advantage of

a superb deep water submarine harbor to develop a fine passenger port, specializing in imaginative shorter cruises to the neighboring Bahamas.

From Canaveral, Premier Cruise Lines – "official cruise line of Walt Disney World" – offers three- and four-day Bahamas cruises aboard its **Star/Ships Majestic, Atlantic and Oceanic**. A great appeal is that the trips can be combined with a three- or four-day Walt Disney World vacation at no extra cost. Carnival Cruise Lines recently began offering three- and four-day Bahamas cruises from Port Canaveral aboard its comfortable **Carnivale**.

Other Florida cities are also becoming cruise ports. From St. Petersburg, Ocean Quest International has trips aboard its **Ocean Spirit** to popular scuba diving areas: Bay Islands of Roatan and Guanaja, Belize Reef and Cozumel, Mexico. Also from St. Petersburg, Seascape's **Scandinavian Saga** offers daylong sailings into the Gulf of Mexico. And from nearby John's Pass in Madeira

Beach, Europasun Cruises has day voyages aboard the **Europa Sun.**

From neighboring Tampa, Bermuda Star Line's **Veracruz** sails for Cozumel and Playa del Carmen, Mexico. And Holland America Line's **Nieuw Amsterdam** has week-long voyages to Key West, Playa del Carmen, Cozumel, Och Rios, Jamaica, and George Town, Grand Cayman Island.

Palm Beach, the latest Florida city to enter the world of cruising, has three-day trips to Key West, Cancun and Cozumel aboard Crown Cruise Lines' **Crown Del Mar.** In addition, the line's **Viking Princess** offers day cruises to Freeport, on the Bahamas.

Entertainment

Today, more than ever, there's a cruise for every interest. Some companies, no-

Above: On deck of a luxurious cruise liner.
Right: Entertainment and full service included.

tably Holland America Lines, Royal Caribbean Cruise Line, and Norwegian Cruise Line, offer lavish onboard health and fitness programs, along with special diving, snorkeling, golf and tennis programs on various islands.

Cunard Line's **Queen Elizabeth 2**, **Sagafjord** and **Vistafjord** even have floating branches of the famed Gold Door Spa. Costa Cruises recently implemented the SpaCosta program of nutrition and exercise on its **Costa Riviera**, and Carnival Cruise Lines now features spa cuisines on its ships, as well as huge Nautica Spas on its new "SuperLiners," beginning with the **Fantasy**. Many top lines today are vying with each other to stage lavish full-scale live revues, beautifully costumed and choreographed.

Most elaborate are the complete Broadway musicals aboard Norwegian Cruise Line's **Norway** and **Seaward**. Other ships headline big band entertainers, opera, classical music and country and western stars. There are discotheques aboard many ships, adult-oriented mid-

night shows in nightclubs, and late hour dancing in intimate cocktail lounges.

On many vessels, large casinos offer roulette, slot machines, blackjack and other games of chance virtually every moment at sea. The cruise ship staff direct participation in everything from bingo, movies, dancing and exercise classes to poolside mixers and masquerade and cheerful passenger entertainment evenings. Many voyagers, of course, prefer to relax in a deck chair or read a good book.

Booking a Cruise

Most large USA cruise lines have sales agents abroad, and your local travel agent can work with them to book all travel reservations and arrangements before you leave home. Attractively priced package plans will include air transportation as well as pre- or post-cruise stays in popular Florida destinations. Taxicabs, limousines or rental cars are available at major Florida ports, making airport transfers easy. If you have booked a package, you'll find that most lines send representatives to the airport to meet boarding passengers, pick up and transfer luggage, and provide airport to cruise terminal transport, at no additional cost, usually on air conditioned motorcoaches. Your luggage will be delivered directly to staterooms.

Most cruise lines require that you make reservations and purchase tickets through a travel agency. Unless your agent has to incur special expenses (long distance telephone calls, telex or fax messages), you pay nothing extra for this service. The agent's fees come from commissions paid by cruise companies, airlines, tour operators and hotels.

All shipboard meals are included in your ticket cost. You pay extra for shore excursions; wines and cocktails; personal services such as use of the beauty salon or barber shop; medical services; babysitting; and gratuities to cabin, dining room and bar stewards. Deck chairs are complimentary on most ships.

223

FLORIDA SPAS

Travelers seeking pampered treatment and luxurious surroundings in the pursuit of good health need look no farther than Florida's ultra-deluxe health spas.

They provide the perfect environment for starting or sustaining a healthful regimen of exercise and diet, and secondly, they provide more than a modicum of coddling, but within a framework of self-control that falls somewhere short of indulgence.

Many people just want to cut loose on vacation stuff themselves with rich foods, lounge around in the sunshine and generally feel responsible to no or nothing. Yet the popularity and rapid growth of Florida's spas and the industry in general indicate there is a segment of vacationers who prefer a more active and involved approach that luxurious spas are more than happy to provide.

Right: This building boasts being the smallest post office in the world.

It used to be that spa vacations appealed mainly to women, but that is no longer the case, with many spas offering programs for men as well, while some even accommodate children. The common denominator seems to be an interest in relieving stress, minimizing fatigue, looking better, and most importantly feeling better inside your body and about yourself and your outlook on life.

That may be a tall order for a vacation destination, but today's scientific spa programs – created by cardiologists, nutritionists and exercise physiologists – make every effort to see that your needs are taken care of, and in the process provide you with the tools of diet and exercise information to allow you to carry on with the work on your own. You come to a Florida spa to relax, learn to accomplish your goals in a supportive environment and have a wonderful time doing it. This is where you are steamed, saunaed, soaked, herbally wrapped, exercised and fed healthy foods that can, in a short time, make you feel like a new person.

Florida spas cover a range from strict formality to loosely structured, but all have in common an elegant thread designed to offer the best of service and amenities, and to make you feel good about doing good things for your body and your mind. Most are self-sufficient top-class resorts, or connected with large hotels or full service resorts. And the industry trend is toward spa facilities in every top-ranked resort, a sure sign of the popularity of these programs.

From full body massage to world championship boxing workouts, from beauty make-overs to bicycling with your children, Florida's spas offer a variety of special programs and facilities to suit the needs of the most discriminating traveler and health seeker.

Most Florida spas offer one-day spa privileges to non-guests – although resort guests do have priority when space is limited – so you do not have to sign away your entire vacation if you do not want to. In general, all spas provide exercise classes, body massage, facials, herbal wraps and low-calorie haute cuisine.

Beyond these basics, specifics vary, and indeed, all the spas will help individuals work up an exercise and diet regimen suited to personal lifestyles and needs. The facilities are quite spectacular, usually including the latest in high-tech exercise equipment, and all you need do is pack your sweatshirt, shorts and sneakers to partake in the program. Spas do not come cheaply, but then, what is the price of good health?

Sheraton Bonaventure Resort Hotel & Spa, 250 Racquet Club Drive, Fort Lauderdale, 33326, 305/389-3300, or 800/327-8090. Located within one of south Florida's top-ranked resorts, the spa facilities are only part of a 1250-acre complex that offers two golf courses, 23 tennis courts and five pools, as well as facilities for bicycle riding, bowling, horseback riding, fishing and volleyball. Add to this indulgent hotel accommoda-

tion a truly pampering staff and the availability of a low-calorie but expertly prepared spa diet, and you can see why this is one of the most highly regarded spas in the United States.

Women can participate in aerobic exercise sessions, followed by beauty treatments, a traditional spa speciality, while a special independent program has been developed and "specifically geared toward the hard-driving, harried man".

One problem spas like this have dealt with ably is men's vanity. Women have traditionally made up 75% of the spas' clientele. They have long accepted spa programs, but many men who may be sadly out of shape or just in need of some personal attention, are simply too self-conscious to participate.

Instead of lumping the men and ladies together in a potentially embarrassing environment for the professional man who may not want to admit to a lack of coordination or a weakness, the Sheraton Bonaventure Spa offers separate classes. here is no pressure on the men to perform

aerobics with women who may be in better shape, or more familiar with the regimen. Instead, special aerobics and exercise sessions are planned.

In addition, the spa program provides free herbal teas, without coffeine, every morning, along with fresh fruit several times daily. Nutritional guidelines proposed by the American Heart Association, as well as the National Cancer Society, are strictly adhered to, and even macrobiotic or vegetarian diets are available. A free children's activity program is also available, so you can bring the young ones along without having to give up the time you want for yourself.

Palm-Aire Resort & Spa, 2501 Palm-Aire Drive N., Pompano Beach, 33069, 305/ 975-6122 or 800/327-4960. This ultra-deluxe spa specializes in fitness and health programs through exercise and stress reduction. Massage, beauty and

Above: Cheerfulness is not a question of age. Right: Hundreds of thousands retire to Florida .

other personal treatments are available, including several individualized low-calorie diets.

The resort is situated on 1500 landscaped acres, with four swimming pools, 37 tennis courts, three golf courses and a 1/2 mile jogging trail spotted with exercise stations. The haute spa cuisine prides itself on being tailored to individual requirements.

Doral Saturnia International Spa Resort, 8755 NW 36th Street, Miami, 33178, 305/593-6030 or 800/331-7768. Situated next to the 2400 acres that enclose the Doral Hotel and Country Club, and near to the Doral Ocean Beach Resort, spa programs for men and women include options at the other resorts.

For those seeking diversions from the spa routine, these include access to five 18-hole golf courses, one 9-hole executive par-three course, fifteen tennis courts, horseback or bicycle riding, fishing or jogging on a 3-mile track, and a 300-foot beach located at the Ocean Beach Resort.

The spa complex has been designed after the model of the Terme di Saturnia spa in Italy, and the style is Mediterranean lush, with formal gardens and fountains spouting into reflecting pools. Spa programs include beauty makeovers, personal consultation and diet plans, mud therapy, as well as muscle and skin treatments.

Children may not stay at the spa, although children's activities are scheduled at the other Doral properties. Families stay at one of those and while the kids are kept busy, Mom and Dad can slip away for some preservation-minded activities and self indulgence.

Sonesta Sanibel Harbour Resort & Spa, 17260 Harbor Pointe Drive, Fort Myers, 33908, 813/466-2166. With its beachfront location, a dozen tennis courts, a 5500-seat tennis arena, two outdoor pools, condo accommodations and hotel rooms, this 40,000 square foot spa facility is one of the most all-inclusive in the country. It has all the spa programs, and adds a full complement of water activities that many spas do not have.

Safety Harbor Spa & Fitness Center, Safety Harbor, 34965, 813/726-4268 or 800/237-0155. This fitness-oriented spa is possibly the most casual of all the Florida spas, yet perhaps the most serious when it comes to health.

Built around five mineral springs said to have been discovered by Hernando de Soto in the sixteenth century, the spa combines state-of-the-art exercise equipment, technology and instruction with soothing spa treatments. These include a Lancome Institut de Beaute which specializes in skin care, full body massage, herbal wraps, whirlpools and soaking in the healthful mineral waters. Many guests drink the water, too. Different pools have differing concentrations of minerals.

Situated on 35 acres on the west shore of Tampa Bay, the spa includes beauty salon services, a special 900-calorie menu or a la carte dining overseen by a registered dietician, conference facilities, as well as fitness classes in a 100,000 square foot spa and fitness center.

Tennis, golf, biking and walking exercises are recommended by a staff of trained professionals who run 35 exercise classes daily. These include low impact aerobics, strength classes, calisthenics, weight training, aerobic circuit training, beginning and advanced water exercise classes, and a very special new program for men who find the typical spa regimen a tad wimpy boxing training classes and BoxAerobics.

The spa has recently become a professional boxing training camp with top pros in residence, including Olympic gold medalist and world champion Mark Breland, John "The Beast" Mugabi, and Lloyd Honeyghan.

These working professionals actually train at Safety Harbor and participants in

the boxing program are able to work out with these radiantly healthy human specimens, running, skipping rope, hitting the heavy bag or the speed bag in order to tone, strengthen, stretch, slim, increase aerobic capacity, improve coordination and balance and bolster self-confidence. Although many men stay away from other spas, this is one where a macho man can come in complete masculine confidence. In addition, all the typical spa amenities, such as golf, tennis or bike riding are available either on the property or nearby. The spa has seven tennis courts and a driving range on the property, and greens fees at nearby course are included in most spa packages.

There is a Florida spa for everyone, from the ultra-rich who prefer to get their exercise in a rarefied environment of wealth and pampering, to the more democratic approach of a spa that stresses fitness over snob appeal, like Safety Harbor. For every taste or wallet, Florida spas can provide an environment of comfort and ease .

©Zbyszek: "I've got it!!"

©Zbyszek: Conversatio...

HAND-
PAINTED
$20

HAND-
PAINTED
$15

©Zbyszek: A.I. Hand.

©Zbyszek: Until Tomorrow. KF...

HISPANIC INFLUENCE

Miami International Airport is one of the few airports in this country in which airline announcements are sometimes aired first in Spanish. When I first heard them, I was stunned by it – Miami is, after all, still in Florida, which at the last count was still a United State.

But this Spanish first, English second order is not surprising given the pervasive Hispanic influence in the area. In Miami, 900,000 residents of the city's 1.9 million total are Hispanic, with that number growing every day. Small Cuban markets proliferate throughout southeast Florida, and shoppers are commonly spoken to in Spanish. It can be disconcerting to Anglos purchasing a carton of milk or a pack of cigarettes. Bowing to the numbers and therefore the political impact, more Hispanic politicians have

Preceding pages: Artist at Key West. Above: A Hispanic immigrant at work. Right: Exotic friendship.

been elected in recent years. The governor of the state, Bob Martinez, is Hispanic, and so is Miami's mayor, Xavier Suarez.

In one recent, hotly contested Congressional election, a Cuban woman, Ileana Ros-Lehtinen, was elected primarily because of her ethnic base; she felt that the seat should be a Cuban seat. The base in Miami is strong because it is pretty homogeneous; 75% of Greater Miami's Hispanic population are Cuban. As a result, they feel more united and more powerful, although other Hispanics of Central or South American heritage are calling Florida their home, yet without the political base the Cubans have forged in the years since Castro took power. Miami residents hear more Spanish stations on the radio, more Spanish spoken in the street. They note that there has been resistance on the part of some immigrants to learn English.

To some older residents of the area, that is frightening; some are leaving Miami and moving north to Broward and Palm Beach Counties. Some Hispanic immigrants are moving up too. Broward County is quieter, less urban, less political than Miami and some who prefer to be out of the fray would rather live in Broward and drive to their jobs in Miami.

But lately there have been tensions around these groups as well. Census taking in Broward County has come under attack for under-counting the number of Hispanic residents; the Hispanic voters feel they are being undercut politically, that politicians who have seen the Hispanic vote rule in Miami do not want the same thing to happen up north. But others are reminded that 10% of Broward County's 1.3 million residents are now Hispanic, and that number is expected to increase. The Hispanic population in Broward County is not as militant as their compatriots in Greater Miami, but they warn that they represent serious numbers and want to be taken seriously.

IMMIGRANTS

In January, 1989, just before Miami was due to host the football extravaganza of the Super Bowl, riots erupted in a black section of the city. The violent unrest was covered extensively on national television, beaming the exact opposite image that the city wanted to convey.

By the time the two nights of arson, looting and violence were over, one looter had been killed, 385 had been arrested and over $1 million in property damage had resulted. It was not the first time these types of numbers had been tallied. It was the fourth time this type of incident had erupted during the 1980s.

Compared to the other riots, this damage was considered slight. The trigger for this riot, though – the shooting of a black man by a Colombian-born policeman – underscored tensions that have been building for the last 25 years: ethnic hostility between American blacks and more and more Hispanic immigrants moving in waves.

The first wave occurred in 1965, just as the Civil Rights legislation in this country was finally opening opportunities for blacks. Instead of having the field to themselves, though, blacks found themselves in competition with the newly arrived Cubans from Fidel Castro's airlift; 260,000 Cubans arrived in South Florida over the next six years. 125,000 more refugees came in the Mariel boatlift of 1980, a boatlift that was roundly criticized later because Castro had seemingly cleaned out his mental hospitals and jails and sent their occupants to the United States. More recently, Nicaraguan refugees have fled to the area at a rate of 200 a day. Once the Hispanic immigrants come to the area, many dig into the American dream, starting and owning businesses, buying a house.

In contrast, the black residents of the area feel that they have been left behind – their rate of joblessness is higher in con-

trast to that of Hispanics, which is even dropping. Blacks feel that the Hispanic power structure helps its own but does nothing for them.

Adding to the pressure is the police force, criticized from time to time for being prejudiced, out of control, corrupt. The police force is also 43% Hispanic, a fact that only raises the level of animosity between them and the black residents whose neighborhoods they patrol. In the 1989 riot, the black neighborhoods of Liberty City and Overtown, the areas that erupted, got some satisfaction when the police officer was convicted of manslaughter. Mayor Xavier Suarez recommended psychological testing to weed out violence-prone, bigoted police officers. Commissions were named, studies were begun. But until there is equal opportunity for all of the residents of the area, especially for the increasingly resentful blacks, that underlying tension will continue to exist. And one more incident, however accidental or slight, could easily trigger violence again.

RETIREES

The stream of elderly visitors from the frigid north to down south is hardly a new phenomenon; retirees have been moving toward the sunshine for sixty years. The numbers add up: residents 65 and older represented 1 out of 6 in the 1988 census; by the year 2000, that will be 1 out of 5. The repercussions are manyfold: politically, areas with concentrations of retirees and especially the lower three counties Dade, Broward and Palm Beach, have very status quo laws. No new taxes are enacted in these areas, despite municipal need. People on fixed incomes do not want to pay out, especially for services many of them do not need. Municipal ordinances also change when a large block of the elderly are voters: one reason given for the departure of the college students' Spring Break from Fort Lauderdale was the large number of wealthy re-

Above: Jogging on the beach. Right: Watching out for dealers?

tired people in the city. They moved for a life of peace and quiet and did not appreciate the raucous goings-on that happened each year. The ambience of the area also changes when the elderly move in. Entertainment, food stores and restaurants all gear services to over 65 needs; the young in their midst might, justifiably, feel left out. Driving can also get risky; elderly people who have always driven and need to drive to get around are reluctant to surrender their licenses even though many should. With impaired reflexes and judgment, driving can become scary if you are in a car next to theirs. Another aspect of being in an area of elderly retirees was pointed out to me one night at dinner in Broward County. A man at an adjacent table suddenly clutched his chest and slumped over. He was wheeled out on a stretcher. I was dumb-struck at witnessing what looked like certain death. But I was the only one who was alarmed. Sirens or stretchers are commonplace here, where many come to spend their last years – and to die.

DRUGS AND VIOLENCE

The hit TV show *Miami Vice* showed a Miami in which flashy drug dealers lurked behind every palm tree and yacht. To many residents, the show, despite its obscene violence, minimized the reality of Florida's drug scene.

And the way the Coast Guard and Drug Enforcement Administration see it, that is not far wrong. That Miami has been a major drop off point for cocaine and other drugs coming into this country is well known. It is perfectly situated near Central America, South America and Mexico. Since 1982 the federal government has been trying to do something about it, though.

If you drive near Cape Canaveral or near Cudjoe Key in the Florida Keys and see a large balloon tethered to one stationary point, you will see the drug efforts at work. The balloons (the Keys balloon is nicknamed "Fat Albert" by the locals) contain radar devices to help guide Coast Guard and Customs boats sweeping for smugglers.

Smugglers, though, have been using superfast, 80 mph boats, so while the Coast Guard may see them, and catch some, many more easily slip away. Over the years, there have been reports that these efforts have annoyed the drug smugglers to the degree that they have shifted some operations to Texas and California. That may be, but South Florida seems unlikely to lose them for good. Bales of marijuana jettisoned by smugglers continue to wash up on Florida's shores. Enormous ships' holds packed with cocaine cause nary a ripple in the news when intercepted by legal authorities. In their wake are often violent shootouts as drug deals go bad, and the proven untrustworthy are eliminated.

But as menacing as drug violence can be, Florida violence is not always to do with drugs. The state has one of the loosest gun control laws in the country –

there is no waiting period to buy a gun, there is not even a law against carrying a concealed weapon, a de rigueur statute in other places.

A few years ago, after a rash of children getting their hands on their parents' guns and shooting other children, the legislature made it illegal to keep your gun anyplace where children can get it. But that is it. Having the gun is not a problem. And having the law has not cut down on children being shot; since it was enacted, more children have been accidentally gunned down but no one has pressed charges using the law.

Therefore, Florida may not be exactly Dodge City, but it is not a place where one looks to get into a fight with a stranger either, or even to cut-off another car in traffic, which has been known to precipitate gunfire. And watch your head on New Year's Eve. At midnight Floridians shoot guns into the air. The next day's news always contains a report of some poor soul being killed when a bullet crashed into a home.

HURRICANES

Hurricanes in Florida are a fact of life. It is that simple. Every year from June 1 to November 1, squalls will start to develop in the Atlantic, build up steam and head for the mainland.

In 1989, Hurricane Hugo (hurricanes are named in progression by letters of the alphabet, alternating between male and female names) devastated the Caribbean before coming up the coast, threatening Florida and finally coming ashore and flattening Charleston, in South Carolina. While the storm was progressing (with winds of 45 mph, it is rated as a tropical storm, when the winds grow to 70 mph, it is upgraded to a hurricane) the National Hurricane Center in Coral Gables, Florida watched it, tracked it and only hours before it was due on land, told coastal residents where it was going to

Above: A rare natural phenomenon: two tornadoes at the same time. Right: Only in Florida.

go. Even with all the technology, that was all they could do because no one can predict a hurricane's path. If a low pressure area forms, the hurricane gets sucked into it, if a high pressure area forms, it is pushed away. As a result, with the exception of "Hurricane Alley", the section of northwest Florida from the Mississippi River to the Apalachicola River, where hurricanes often do tend to get stuck, there is no section of the state more prone to hurricanes than another. It really is hit and miss. There is one scenario that planners hope does not happen, though – a hurricane coming in from the Keys up to Miami and across the state up to Tampa-St. Pete.

That did happen once with Hurricane Betsy in 1965 when lives were lost and hundreds of millions of dollars in damage resulted. In 1935 a hurricane destroyed the Florida East Coast Railway and devastated the Keys, killing hundreds of residents. In 1960, Hurricane Donna slammed South Florida, causing millions of dollars' worth in damages.

INSECTS

Since Florida is considered a sub-tropical environment, the state gets a considerable number of insects. Mosquitoes are very much in evidence here; lately there have even been two kinds sighted, the typical small, nasty, biting one and a larger one that eats the smaller one.

The smaller one, however, is still in the majority. Beware of them, especially in watery places such as the Florida Keys - keep your windows closed as you drive Highway One.

Another South Florida specialty is the local palmetto, otherwise known as the cockroach – a giant, frightening water bug that flies. These nocturnal creatures love dark hiding places and they also seem drawn to water. They feed on crumbs of food, eat the glue off the back of postage stamps, and generally make an ongoing nuisance of themselves, forcing many residents and virtually all commercial establishments to make liberal use of insecticides.

Some residents make sport of squashing the 2-inch long palmettos, but they make a loud crunch when you flatten one, and the smelly goo that spurts out of them is a most unpleasant substance. If you encounter one of these intimidating insects, said to be related to dinosaurs, better give it a wide berth.

Municipalities also get into the act of insect eradication with mobile or airborne spraying programs, which are primarily aimed at the different mosquito species, to the extent that during the summers, when the bugs are most annoying, the scent of bug spray is nearly as pervasive as the tropical perfumes of foliage and the sea.

So for those with a disinclination to breathe chemical relatives of the now banned DDT, another vacation destination would be in order. Recently, though, the palmetto has been less feared than a new imported bug, the vicious, ever-spreading flying Asian roach. While you are sunning, keep an eye out for what is flying by.

GROWTH AND DEVELOPMENT

Over the last ten years, Florida has become the fourth most populous state, after traditional powerhouses California, New York and Texas. About 900 people a day flood into the state, but the pressures they are placing on existing systems threaten to ruin everyone's good time.

Florida lacks enough housing, roads, schools or jails for new arrivals, keeping contractors busy, building. But some city governments have forced them to stop. A few years ago, a community outside Tampa restricted new construction when the sewer system gave out. The infrastructure was not built to handle this much. Still, it goes on.

Anyone who has to get to work in Fort Lauderdale, Miami or any of the other large cities knows to leave home early – the overloaded roads cannot handle the traffic. And the construction that is trying

Above: A modern skyscraper in Jacksonville. Right: Room enough for a family.

to help is just slowing everything down. The result of all this is that emigres from other cities up north are not sorry that they moved to the state. But they look warily at others moving in.

My sister moved to the suburbs of Miami a few years ago and every time I went to visit, I noticed changes. First, in place of what was essentially marshland, was her new development - street after street of identical homes packaged with a community pool and tennis court and ridiculously cutesy name – "The Hammocks". Months later, as I drove down the previously open expanse of Kendall Drive en route to said Hammocks, I noticed other but similar developments had sprung up one after another. To accommodate the flood of new residents, shopping centers filled in all other open space.

The only holdout was a farm; an expanse of fruit and vegetable fields where you could pick your own for pretty reasonable prices. As the area built up all around it, it began to look either like a refreshing throwback to simpler days, or an endangered species.

A year later when I came down, I realized that the latter was the case – the fields were gone. In their place was a prefab, hideous pink and green shopping center – as if the area needed another. It was inevitable; this is Florida, not the only place that has undergone a massive surge in growth and development but definitely one of the most dramatic. And in many cases, one of the least successful.

In the years between 1980 and 1986, the population grew by 20%. To accommodate these new residents, residential communities like my sister's are being built, as are the many soaring condo units that block out the views enjoyed by residents living in older condo units. Once built, though, these new units do not always earn their keep; some sit unrented or unsold in oversaturated or less desirable areas. Even the supposedly magic touch of tycoon Donald Trump

could not up the vacancy rate of his condo towers in West Palm Beach. Residents of the area chuckled that he had come south to face his first big defeat. In other cases, condos and houses do sell, however the sewer problems near Tampa were by no means unique. The tide of new residents is also clogging schools – there are not enough classrooms to take all of the children. There are not enough roads to handle their parents' cars either; the old highway system was not constructed to handle this many. There are not enough jails in most communities, as Florida cities experience a rise in violent, detainable crime. Helping overwhelmed institutions would require a large infusion of cash – which Florida does not have, due to federal cutbacks and the already heavy demands on its revenues. New taxes have been suggested to raise additional funds – a tax on advertising, a tax on the service industries – but public outcries have voted down new taxes.

One money-making idea that has been floated over the years is the addition of casino gambling in Miami but it could hurt paradoxically, as much as it helps, by causing more overcrowding, congestion on the roads and more behavior that could land people in already crowded jails. One bright spot, it seems, is in the center of the state: the ever-expanding Walt Disney spread near Orlando. It started with Walt Disney World, expanded to Epcot Center, and last year the combined Disney-MGM Studios opened, a production-entertainment complex that occupies 135 acres of the 44 square miles of Disney turf.

Superstar director Steven Spielberg has proclaimed the complex Hollywood's salvation, giving productions a place to go outside crowded, expensive L.A. And the money it brings into the state will provide some salvation for Florida. Still, when something this big moves into town, there are bound to be some complaints. As cars get stuck on the roads near Orlando, residents are bound to grumble that this development has gone just too far.

Nelles Maps ...the maps, that get you going.

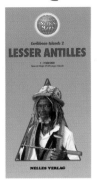

Nelles Map Series:

- Afghanistan
- Australia
- Burma
- Caribbean Islands 1 / Bermuda, Bahamas, Greater Antilles
- Caribbean Islands 2 / Lesser Antilles
- China 1 / North-Eastern China
- China 2 / Northern China
- Crete
- Hawaiian Islands
- Hawaiian Islands 1 / Kauai
- Hawaiian Islands 2 / Honolulu, Oahu
- Hawaiian Islands 3 / Maui, Molokai, Lanai

- Hawaiian Islands 4 / Hawaii
- Himalaya
- Hong Kong
- Indian Subcontinent
- India 1 / Northern India
- India 2 / Western India
- India 3 / Eastern India
- India 4 / Southern India
- India 5 / North-Eastern India
- Indonesia
- Indonesia 1 / Sumatra
- Indonesia 2 / Java + Nusa Tenggara
- Indonesia 3 / Bali
- Indonesia 4 / Kalimantan
- Indonesia 5 / Java + Bali
- Indonesia 6 / Sulawesi
- Indonesia 7 / Irian Jaya + Maluku

- Jakarta
- Japan
- Kenya
- Korea
- Malaysia
- West Malaysia
- Nepal
- New Zealand
- Pakistan
- Philippines
- Singapore
- South East Asia
- Sri Lanka
- Taiwan
- Thailand
- Vietnam, Laos Kampuchea

FLORIDA
©Nelles Verlag GmbH, München 45
 All rights reserved
 ISBN 3-88618-370-X

First Edition 1990
Co-publisher for U.K.:
Robertson McCarta, London
ISBN 1-85365-225-3 (for U.K.)

Publisher:	Günter Nelles	**DTP-Exposure:**	Printshop Schimann, Pfaffenhofen
Chief Editor:	Dr. Heinz Vestner		
Project Editor:	Steve Cohen	**Color**	
Cartography:	Nelles Verlag GmbH, Dipl.Ing. C. Heydeck Dipl.Ing. T. Winter	**Separation:**	Priegnitz, München
		Printed by:	Gorenjski Tisk, Kranj, Yugoslavia

- 01 -

TABLE OF CONTENTS

Traveling in Florida 240

    Accommodation 240
    Airlines 241
    Arriving in Florida 243
    Climate 243
    Clothing 244
    Cruise Directory 245
    Currency and Exchange 245
    Departure 246
    Driving in Florida 246
    Electricity 247
    Festivals and Holidays 247
    Guides 247
    Local Transport 247
    Pari- Mutuel Betting 248
    Postal Services 249
    Shopping 249
    Telephone Service 249
    Tipping 249
    Tourist Information 249

Authors / Photographers 251
Index 252

TRAVELING IN FLORIDA

This section provides additional detailed information about traveling in Florida. It is up-to-date as of publication, but in travel and tourism things change, and perhaps no more dramatically anywhere than in Florida. For further questions consult heading sections for the name, address and phone number of specialized sources for the most currently reliable rate and service information.

Accommodation

Accommodation in Florida runs the gamut from ultra-expensive, ultra-luxurious resort hotels, to remaining old-fashioned motor courts and inexpensive motels, YMCA, YWCA and American Youth Hostels, with every extreme and everything in between well-represented.

Accommodation listed in the travel sections of this book are meant to be among the best in each price range, although there are many more to choose from in most areas of Florida.

A wise travel agent is a good bet for sifting through the voluminous possibilities in accommodation, as well as in planning other trip details such as airline flights or rental cars. Most Florida accommodation has swimming pools and air conditioning, a virtual necessity to be in business in the hot and humid climate throughout the state. Color TVs in all rooms are de rigueur, with Cable-TV an increasingly common free feature. And pay-for-view in-room broadcasts of first-run movies are found mostly in expensive to luxury properties. Many accommodations have in-room service bars, but prices are high for this convenience. For example a Coke may cost $2.00 in your room, or $.50 in a machine yards away down the hall. Where an option is available, view sites overlooking the ocean or a golf course are generally more expensive than similar rooms facing an interior courtyard or a rather boring parking lot.

And most rates are adjusted seasonally, with the highest prices generally in effect from December through April, while the lowest rates are generally charged in the summer, during June, July and August. Buffer seasons sometimes offer bargains, and the savvy traveler realizes that although summers can be extremely hot and humid, there is very little difference in the sublime climate conditions of the high season and those found in May or November, when substantial savings are available. Package prices combining accommodation with air transportation or activity schedules are frequently offered, and for these options you should consult with a travel agent, directly with properties or airlines.

Accommodation for handicapped travelers is increasingly found throughout the state. Check with individual properties for availability.

Many accommodation chains offer centralized reservation systems through toll-free phone numbers that may be called from within the USA or Canada, without charge. The following is a list of these phone numbers for major chains represented in Florida.

Best Western International, 800/528-1234 USA, 800/268/8993 Canada. **Comfort Inns**, 800/228-5150 USA. **Days Inn**, 800/325-2525 USA. **Doubletree**, 800/ 528-0444 USA, except 800/ 325/ 6500 from Arizona only. **Econo Lodges of America**, 800/446-6900 USA and Canada. **Embassy Suites**, 800/362-2779 USA. **Friendship Inns of America**, 800/453-4511 USA, except 800/453-5400 from Utah only. **Hampton Inn**, 800/HAMPTON USA. **Hilton Hotels**, 800/HILTONS USA. **Holiday Inns**, 800/HOLIDAY USA. **Howard Johnson**, 800/654-2000 USA and Canada. **Hyatt Corporation**, 800/228-9000 USA, except 800/228- 9001 from Nebraska only. **La Quinta Motor Inns**, 800/531-5900 USA. **Marriott Hotels**, 800/228-9290 USA. **Preferred Hotels**, 800/323- 7500

USA and Canada. **Quality Inns**, 800/228-5151 USA and Canada. **Radisson Hotels**, 800/228-9822 USA and Canada. **Ramada Inns**, 800/2-RA-MADA USA. **Red Carpet/Scottish Inns**, 800/251-1962 USA. **Red Roof Inns**, 800/848-7878 USA and Canada. **Regal 8 Inn**, 800/851-8888 USA. **Residence Inns by Marriott**, 800/331-3131 USA. **Rodeway Inns International**, 800/228-2000 USA, 800/665-8822 Canada. **Sheraton Hotels & Inns**, 800/325-33535, USA and Canada. **Sonesta Hotels**, 800/343-7170 USA. **Travelodge International/Viscount Hotels**, 800/255-3050 USA and Canada. **Westin Hotels**, 800/228-3000 USA and Canada.

Airlines

A confusing number of airlines serve Florida from within the United States and internationally, and these lines change somewhat as routes are frequently added or dropped. In even more of a constant state of flux than routes are fares. These vary dramatically according to time of year, the particular route you travel, special promotions and package fares.

Airfares from heavy traffic areas such as the northeast US are often competitively priced as airlines fight for the lucrative traffic. Shop around for bargains. Likewise, as international traffic continues to grow, good fares can be found, particularly through connections to the Caribbean, Central and South America, as well as an increasing number of direct flights from European capitals.

For those who prefer to deal with airlines directly, the following is a partial listing of major airlines serving Florida's major airports. Phone numbers for main offices are listed for each one. Many have toll-free numbers which can be dialed from the USA. Dial 1/800-555-1212 for US toll-free information.

Miami International, PO Box 592075, Miami, FL 33159, 305/871-7090; British Airways, 01-759-5511 (London, England); Virgin Atlantic, 293-549-771 (West Sussex, England); UTA, 47.76.41.33 (Puteaux, France); Pan American Airlines, 212/880-1234 (New York, NY); Air Afrique, 32 09 00 (Cote D'Ivoire, West Africa); Iberia, 585-8585 (Madrid, Spain); Olympus Airways, 92921 (Athens, Greece); Trans World Airlines, 914/242-3000 (Mt. Kisco, NY); Transavia Airlines, 020-5187318 (Schipol Centrum, The Netherlands); Gulf Air, 322200 (Manama, Bahrain); LOT-Polish Airlines, 46-04-11 (Warsaw, Poland); Nigeria Airways, 31031 (Lagos, Nigeria); Ghana Airways, 64851 (Accra, Ghana); Continental Airlines, 713/630-5000 (Houston, Texas); Ethiopian Airlines, 52222 (Addis Abababa, Ethiopia); Lufthansa German Airlines, 0221-82 61 (Cologne, West Germany); Air France, 43 23 81 81(Paris, France); Air Algerie, 639234/36 (Algiers, Algeria); Aeromexico, 905/207-6311 (Mexico City); Aviaco, 254 36 00 (Madrid Spain); Royal Jordanian, 22311, (Amman, Jordan); KLM-Royal Dutch Airlines, 020-492227 (Schipol East, The Netherlands); Ladeco, 3955053 (Santiago, Chile); Lan Chile, 578080 (Santiago, Chile); Sabena Belgian World Airways, 02-509-90-60 (Brussels, Belgium); Eastern Airlines, 305/873-2211 (Miami, Florida); Air Paraguay, 95261 (Asuncion, Paraguay); Varig, 212-1820 (Rio de Janeiro, Brazil); Swissair, 812 12 12 (Zurich, Switzerland); American Airlines, 817/963-1234 (Dallas, Texas); Cathay Pacific, H-250011 (Hong Kong); All Nippon Airways, 03/592-3355 (Tokyo, Japan); Japan Air Lines, 03/284-2081 (Tokyo, Japan); Korean Air, 7517-114 (Seoul, Korea); Singapore Airlines, 542-3333 (Singapore); Thai Airways International, 511-0121 (Bangkok, Thailand); China Airlines, 7152626 (Tapei, Taiwan); Viasa, 02/572-9522 (Caracas, Venezuela); Avianca, 2639511 (Bogota, Colombia); Lacsa, 32-35-55 (San Jose, Costa Rica); Varig, 212-1820 (Rio de

Janeiro, Brazil); Yugoslav Airlines, 145-798 (Beograd, Yugoslavia); SAS- Scandinavian Airlines, 08-797-0000 (Stockholm, Sweden); Piedmont Airlines, 919/770-8000 (Winston-Salem, North Carolina); British Midland, 0332-810741 (Derby,England); Air Canada, 514/879-7000 (Montreal, Quebec); Air India, 292728 (Bombay, India); Malev Hungarian Airlines,184-333 (Budapest, Hungary); Aer Lingus, 370011 (Dublin, Ireland); Delta Airlines, 404/765-2600 (Atlanta, Georgia); Air Jamaica, 809/932-3460 (Kingston, Jamaica).

Fort Lauderdale/Hollywood International, 1400 Lee Wagener Blvd., Fort Lauderdale, FL 33315, 305/357-6100: Trans World Airlines, KLM-Royal Dutch Airlines, Delta Airlines, Japan Airlines, Singapore Airlines, Piedmont Airlines, Iberia, Swissair, SAS- Scandinavian Airlines, Continental Airlines, Avianca, Lufthansa German Airlines, Olympic Airways, British Airways, American Airlines, Swissair.

Palm Beach International, International Apt. Building 846, West Palm Beach, FL 33406, 407/471-7400: Delta Airlines, Trans World Airlines, Eastern Airlines, Continental Airlines.

Marathon Airport, 9000 Overseas Highway, Marathon, FL 33050, 305/294-4641: Airways International, 305/887-2794 (Miami Springs, Florida).

Key West Airport, 3491 Roosevelt Blvd., Key West, FL 33040, 305/296-5439: Delta, Piedmont, Eastern Airlines.

Tampa International, PO Box 22287, Tampa, FL 33622, 813/276-3400: Pan American Airlines, British Airways, Piedmont Airlines, Olympic Airways, Gulf-Air, Trans World Airlines, Delta Airlines, American Airlines, United Airlines, Continental Airlines, Northwest Airlines, 612/726-2111 (St. Paul, Minnesota).

Orlando International, One Airport Blvd. Orlando, FL 38287-4399, 407/826-2001: Air UK, 517654 (West Sus-sex,England); KLM-Royal Dutch Airlines, British Airways, Piedmont Airlines, Delta Airlines, Trans-World Airlines, Gulf Air, Olympic Airways, Iberia, Pan American Airlines, Northwest Airlines, Air Europe, 775552 (Surrey, United Kingdom); Lufthansa German Airlines, Avianca, Swissair, United Airlines, Continental Airlines, Sabena Belgian World Airways, Viasa, Aer Lingus, Alitalia, 54441 (Rome, Italy).

Southwest Regional, 16000 Chamberlin Parkway SE, Fort Myers, FL 33913, 813/768-1000: British Airways, Eastern Airlines, Continental Airlines, Northwest Airlines, KLM-Royal Dutch Airlines, Delta Airlines, Trans World Airlines, Iberia, Piedmont Airlines, Lufthansa German Airlines, British Midland, Aerolinias Argentina, Aer Lingus.

Sarasota/Bradenton Airgate Station, PO Box 3004, Sarasota, FL 34278-3004, 813/355-2761: Delta Airlines, Trans World Airlines, Continental Airlines, Eastern Airlines.

Pensacola Regional, PO Box 12910, Pensacola, FL 32521, 904/435- 1746: Delta Airlines, Piedmont Airlines, Continental Airlines.

Tallahassee Regional, 3240 Capital Circle SW, Tallahassee, FL 32304, 904/575-0666:

Pan American Airlines, Delta Airlines, Eastern Airlines.

Jacksonville International, PO Box 18907, Jacksonville, FL 32229, 904/741-2000:

Piedmont Airlines, Trans World Airlines, Pan American Airlines, Delta Airlines, Continental Airlines.

Panama City/Bay County, 3173 Airport Road Panama City, FL 32405, 904/763-6751: Delta Airlines, Eastern Airlines.

Destin/Fort Walton Beach/Eglin Air Base, Okaloosa County Courthouse, Crestview, FL 32536, 904/651-2112: Northwest Airlines, Delta Airlines.

Arriving in Florida

International passengers will need a valid passport and visitor's visa, issued by the US Embassy or consular offices in the country of origin. In order to obtain a visa, visitors will need to produce proof of their intention to return home, such as a plane ticket or other travel documents.

Canadians and British citizens living in Canada, as well as Mexicans' are exempt from visa requirements, so long as their trip originated in the Western Hemisphere. Vaccination certificates may be required for smallpox and cholera from certain countries, so check with the consular officials when requesting a visa.

International visitors to Florida must obtain US Customs clearance on entering the country. Certain specified items noted on the declaration forms given to you on board your plane or ship must be declared. There is no limit to the amount of money that may be brought into Florida, although amounts exceeding US $5000 or the foreign equivalent must be declared. Automobiles may be imported at the time of arrival for personal use without duty. A valid driver's license from approximately 120 countries will be honored in Florida, for up to one year.

Climate

Florida's climate is generally predictable, at least on average. There is very little seasonal change, leaves do not fall off trees in winter and for the most part temperatures can be expected to stay above freezing, even in January, the coldest month. In recent years, however, climatic changes have been pronounced, with winter temperatures falling to freezing as far south as Tampa. These cold spells are generally short-lived, and it would not be uncommon for a cold snap to dissipate in a day or so, with normal temperatures returning promptly.

Although most visitors will pack their swimwear and tennis outfits for a south Florida vacation in winter, recent

temperatures have dropped into the 30-40 degree F range and travelers should probably pack a sweater, too.

Rain is a much more common occurrence than freezing temperatures. Summers provide the most rainfall, on an almost daily basis, and these sometimes violent soakings have the added benefit of cooling things down. At other times of year, rain falls on a more irregular basis, although the farther south you go, the more likely wet weather is.

Average low winter temperatures range from around 40 degrees F in the northern Panhandle to around 65 degrees F in the Florida Keys. Daytime highs, however, can be quite pleasant, averaging 20 degrees F higher than recorded low temperatures.

Average high summer temperatures range from 85 to 90 degrees F. throughout the state, with average lows dropping only about 10 degrees F.

High season pricing has everything to do with Florida's weather, so you can expect to pay more for accommodation during winter in south Florida and during summer in the north Florida Panhandle.

The following listings indicate average low and high temperatures in degrees Fahrenheit in the various regions of Florida, according to records kept by the Florida Department of Commerce. In addition, measurements in inches are provided for average monthly rainfall.

Northwest

Temperature: January-March 44.0 degrees 67.3 degrees, April-June 63.0 degrees 85.7 degrees, July-September 71.0 degrees 89.3 degrees, October-December 48.3 degrees 72.3 degrees.

Monthly rainfall: January-March 4.65 inches, April-June 4.6 inches, July-September 7.28 inches, October-December 3.42 inches.

Northeast

Temperature: January-March 46.6 degrees 68.0 degrees, April-June 63.7

degrees 84.0 degrees, July-September 71.3 degrees 88.7 degrees, October-December 52.7 degrees 72.0 degrees.

Monthly rainfall: January-March 3.56 inches, April-June 4.08 inches, July-September 7.31 inches, October-December 2.57 inches.

Central East

Temperature: January-March 50.0 degrees 71.0 degrees, April-June 64.7 degrees 84.3 degrees, July-September 72.3 degrees 88.7 degrees, October-December 56.3 degrees 75.3 degrees.

Monthly rainfall: January-March 3.17 inches, April-June 4.34 inches, July-September 7.84 inches, October-December 2.48 inches.

Central

Temperature: January-March 52.0 degrees 73.7 degrees, April-June 66.0 degrees 87.3 degrees, July-September 73.3 degrees 91.0 degrees, October-December 58.0 degrees 77.7 degrees.

Monthly rainfall: January-March 2.71 inches, April-June 5.20 inches, July-September 7.80 inches, October-December 2.48 inches.

Central West

Temperature: January-March 52.7 degrees 73.0 degrees, April-June 67.0 degrees 86.7 degrees, July-September 73.7 degrees 89.7 degrees, October-December 57.7 degrees 77.7 degrees.

Monthly rainfall: January-March 2.11 inches, April-June 5.18 inches, July-September 8.56 inches, October-December 2.54 inches.

Southwest

Temperature: January-March 63.7 degrees 77.0 degrees, April-June 72.0 degrees 82.3 degrees, July-September 76.3 degrees 87.3 degrees, October-November 67.3 degrees 79.3 degrees.

Monthly rainfall: January-March 1.69 inches, April-June 3.08 inches, July-September 5.30 inches, October-December 3.25 inches.

Southeast

Temperature: January-March 60.3

degrees 77.7 degrees, April-June 70.7 degrees 85.3 degrees, July-September 75.6 degrees 89.0 degrees, October-December 65.0 degrees 80.7 degrees.

Monthly rainfall: January-March 2.13 inches, April-June 5.82 inches, July-September 7.20 inches, October-December 4.35 inches.

In addition to temperature and rainfall, a Florida visitor is always cognizant of the humidity. It is generally quite high, often equalling or surpassing temperatures in the far south, especially in summer. This tends to make temperatures feel somewhat hotter than readings would indicate. In such places as the Everglades in summer, the combination of heat and humidity can be staggering.

Other weather phenomena to watch out for on a regular seasonal basis are tropical storms, flood conditions, hurricanes, lightning strikes or storms.

Clothing

Clothing styles are more and more casual throughout most of Florida, except for the Palm Beach area, which tends toward the formal. Cool, loose-fitting clothing in natural fibers is recommended – shorts, t-shirts, sandals or sneakers. Swimwear is always acceptable at beach resorts or coastal areas during the day, although not always in the evening. Evenings sometimes call for a sport jackets for men, without a tie; pants or a dress for women. Only the poshest resorts or restaurants will require formal attire.

Light rain gear is probably a good idea, plus an umbrella or waterproof windbreaker, though not entirely necessary. Because of the heat, rainfall can be quite refreshing. Unfortunately, due to the high levels of humidity, once you get wet you may not dry, even when the sun comes out, but remain soggy. No problem if you are in your swimsuit, but some people, particularly the elderly who so love Florida, catch colds darting in and out of air-conditioned structures when wet.

Caps, straw or sun hats are recommended. Sunscreen should be used. A warmer jacket or a sweater is recommended for winter travel in Florida.

Warning: Do not go barefoot in places other than the beach. Florida is largely covered in cement and asphalt that can get very hot in the sun.

Cruise Directory

The following cruise lines are currently serving the Florida ports under which they are listed.

Port of Miami: Admiral Cruise Line, 1220 Biscayne Blvd., Miami 33132, 305/373-7501. Carnival Cruise Line, 5225 NW 87th Ave., Miami 33178, 305/599-2200. Chandris Celebrity-Chandris Fantasy Cruises, 4770 Biscayne Blvd., Miami 33137, 305/ 573-3140; Fax 305/576-9520. Commodore Cruise Line Limited, 1007 N. America Way, Miami 33132, 305/358-2622; Fax 305/371-9980. Dolphin Cruise Line, Inc., 1007 N. America Way, 3rd Floor, Miami, 305/358-2111; Fax 305/358-4807. Norwegian Cruise Line, 95 Merrick Way, Coral Gables, 33134, 305/ 445-0866. Royal Caribbean Cruise Line, 903 S. America Way, Miami 33132, 305/379-2601. SeaEscape Ltd., 1080 Port Blvd, Miami 33132, 305/379-0000; Fax 305/381-8068. Sun Line Cruises, 1 Rockefeller Plaza, Suite 315, New York, NY 10020, 212/397-6400.

Port Everglades: Carnival Cruise Lines. Chandris Celebrity Cruises. Costa Cruises, Inc., World Trade Center, 80 SW 8th St., Miami 33130-3097, 305/358-7325; Fax 305/375-0676. Cunard Line, 555 Fifth Ave., New York, NY 10017, 212/880-7500. Discovery Cruise Line, 1850 Eller Dr., Suite 402, Fort Lauderdale, FL 33316, 305/528-7800; Fax 305/779-3887. Holland America Line, 300 Elliot Ave. W., Seattle, Washington 98119, 206/281-3535; Fax 206/281-7110. Princess Cruises, 10100 Santa Monica Blvd., Los Angeles, CA 90067, 213/553-1666; Fax 213/277-6175. P&O Cruises, Ltd., 77 New Oxford St., London, UX1APP, England, 01/831-1234; Fax 01/831-1280. Royal Viking Cruise Line, 95 Merrick Way, Coral Gables, 33134, 305/447-9660. Seabourn Cruise Line, 55 Francisco St., San Francisco,CA 94133, 415/391-7444. SeaEscape Ltd. Sitmar Cruises, (contact Princess Cruises).

Port Canaveral: Carnival Cruise Lines. Premier Cruise Lines, 400 Challenger Rd., Cape Canaveral, 32920, 407/783-5061. SeaEscape, Ltd.

Palm Beach: Crown Cruise Line, P.O. Box 3000, 2790 N. Federal Highway, Boca Raton, 33431, 407/394-7450.

St. Petersburg: Ocean Quest International, 504/586-8686, or 800/338-3483. SeaEscape Ltd.

Tampa: Bermuda Star Line Cruises, Inc., 1086 Teaneck Rd., Teaneck, New Jersey 07666, 201/837-0400; Fax 201/837-0915. Holland America Cruises. Regency Cruises, Inc., 260 Madison Ave., New York, NY 10016, 800/457-5566; Fax 212/687-2290. Sea Escape Ltd.

Currency and Exchange

Foreign currency is most readily exchanged at the Florida port of entry, or at most major US banks. Some Florida hotels can provide currency exchange services, but possibly at a rate less favorable than a bank.

Despite the prevalence of many sources for exchanging foreign currency, including larger shops and department stores, US dollars travelers checks are probably going to be easier to deal with for the foreign traveler.

Banks are generally open from 9 am to 3 pm Monday to Friday. Some banks will have longer daytime hours one or two days weekly, and many banks stay open from 9 am to noon on Saturday.

Major international credit cards, such as VISA, Mastercard, American Express,

Carte Blanche and Diner's Club are widely used and accepted by most commercial establishments.

Departure

Allow at least 90 minutes for departure formalities, such as ticketing, seat assignment and security checks. Allow longer at Miami International Airport, particularly if traveling during high season or holiday periods. Consult your carrier for any additional departure fees that may be required. Always re-confirm international flights 24 hours prior to departure.

Driving in Florida

Most foreign travelers in Florida are allowed to operate a motor vehicle provided they are holding a valid license issued at home. Residents of certain countries may need to produce an International Driver's permit issued at home. For details and information regarding specific requirements contact Florida Highway Safety and Motor Vehicles Department, Driver Licenses Division, Neil Kirkman Building, Tallahassee, 32399-0575, 904/488-3144.

International travelers should familiarize themselves with certain important Florida driving rules, as follows.

Road Signs and Signals: Red Light: Full Stop. Yellow Light: Warning; signal is changing from green to red. Green Light: Proceed. Green Arrow: Proceed in direction of arrow from appropriate lane. Flashing Red Light: Come to a full stop, then proceed with caution. Flashing Yellow Light: Slow down, then proceed with caution.

Traffic Regulations: Drive to the Right: Motorists must stay to the right of the road. On the highway, the passing lane is to the left. Right Turn on Red: Following a full stop, it is legal to turn right at red, unless otherwise posted. Speed: The national speed limit on highways is 55 miles per hour (88 kilometers per hour). In cities and congested areas, the speed limit is generally between 20-40 miles per hour (32-64 kilometers per hour). On rural highways, the speed limit is 65 miles per hour (104 kilometers per hour). Posted signs on roadways indicate specific speed limits. All limits are strictly enforced.

Accidents: All traffic accidents must be reported to the local police department, County Sheriff's Office, or Florida Highway Patrol.

School Buses: Traffic moving in both directions must stop while a school bus is loading or unloading, except if the bus is stopped on the opposite side of a divided highway.

Emergency Vehicles: All traffic must yield to police vehicles, fire engines, ambulances and all other emergency vehicles which display flashing lights or use audible alarms, or both.

The **Interstate** Highway System provides major north-south and east-west access to Florida. Interstate 95 covers Florida's east coast. Interstate 75 runs down the west coast of the state. Interstate 10 runs from Pensacola eastward to its terminus at I-95 in Jacksonville.

The **Florida Turnpike** is generally less-crowded than the Interstates, probably because there is a toll-charge. It runs north-south out of the Miami area to Wildwood, in central Florida.

Florida toll-roads: Airport Expressway: Downtown Miami to Miami International Airport, 8.8 miles. Bee Line Expressway: Orlando to Cape Canaveral, 53 miles. Dolphin Expressway: Downtown Miami to Palmetto Expressway, 9 miles. Everglades Parkway: Naples to Andytown, 78 miles. Holland East-West Expressway: South Orlando business district, 13.5 miles. Florida Turnpike: Wildwood to Homestead, 318.6 miles. J. Turner Butler Expressway: S.R. 115 to Jacksonville Beach, 9.9 miles. Sawgrass Parkway: Northwest of Fort Lauderdale, 22 miles. South Crosstown Expressway: Tampa, 17.5 miles.

There are many new highways being built all the time in Florida, with newly designed connections springing up constantly. To keep up to date consult a free Florida Official Transportation Map, available from Florida Department of Commerce, Collins Building, Tallahassee, 32399-2000.

Other map sources include most gas stations, which used to give away free maps, but now usually charge $1-$2, or tourism offices, which can generally provide maps for free.

Current gas prices are subject to rapid changes throughout Florida, and depending on whether you choose a self-service station or full-service. Prices for the most expensive fuel have historically not passed high above $1.50 per US gallon.

Electricity

A 110 volt Alternating Current (AC) system operates. Conversion kits are available at appliance stores and at some hotels that cater to a large international clientele.

Festivals and Holidays

The festivals and special events scheduled throughout the year in Florida are too numerous to mention. Suffice it to say that virtually every community that caters to tourists also offers music or film· festivals, art or culinary festivals, as well as cultural festivals galore. For a complete listing of Florida festivals contact Department of Commerce, Division of tourism, 126 W. Van Buren Street, Tallahassee, 33299-2000, 904/487-1462.

The following official public holidays are celebrated in Florida. Local, State and Federal offices, as well as most banks and some businesses are closed.

New Year's Day: January 1. Martin Luther King Jr.'s Birthday: January 15. President's Day: Third Monday in February. Memorial Day: Last Monday in May. Independence Day: July 4. Labor Day: First Monday in September. Columbus

Day: Second Monday in October. Veteran's Day: November 11. Thanksgiving Day: Fourth Thursday in November. Christmas Day: December 25.

In addition to these holidays which are celebrated throughout the state, individual localities may celebrate other dates as well. Religious holidays are celebrated widely in certain areas.

Guides

Foreign language guides are available at most of Florida's major tourist attractions. Advance reservations are sometimes required. Consult with individual attractions or with local tourism officials at the Chamber of Commerce.

Local Transport

Numerous modes of public transportation are offered throughout Florida, including sightseeing trams, Tampa's people-mover and Miami's 21-mile elevated Metrorail system.

Many resorts and hotels offer free airport transportation, and an increasing number will provide free shuttles to nearby attractions or shopping districts.

Taxi service is available for a minimum fixed rate, plus additional mileage charges. Limousine services charge by a fixed rate depending on your destination. Limousines generally charge less than private cabs for trips of the same distance, although you frequently must share a limousine with other passengers, thus possibly reaching your destination by a lengthier and more time-consuming route than in a private cab.

Bus Service: Local bus systems service many Florida cities. Consult with Chambers of Commerce for route maps and schedules. Greyhound/Trailways, Suite 2500, 901 Main St., Dallas, Texas 75202, 214/744-6500; Fax 214/744-6579, serves the following Florida cities for longer distance bus travel.

Greyhound: Avon Park, Boynton Beach, Bradenton, Clearwater, Cocoa,

Daytona Beach, Deland, Delray, Fort Lauderdale, Fort Myers, Fort Pierce, Gainesville, Haines City, Hollywood, Jacksonville, Jupiter, Key West, Kissimmee, Lakeland, Lake Wales, Lake Worth, Marianna, Melbourne, Miami, Naples, North Miami Beach, Orlando, Panama City, Pensacola, Perrine, Plant City, Pompano beach, Port Charlotte, Sanford, Sarasota, St. Augustine, St. Petersburg, Stuart, Tallahassee, Tampa, Titusville, Venice, Vero Beach, West Palm Beach, Winter Haven, Winter Park.

Trailways: Blountstown, Bradenton, Brooksville, Charlotte Harbor, Chiefland, Clearwater, Coral Gables, Daytona Beach, Dunellon, Fort Lauderdale, Fort Myers, Fort Walton Beach, Gainesville, Hollywood, Inverness, Jacksonville, Kissimmee, Lake City, Lakeland, Leesburg, Miami, Orlando, Panama City, Pensacola, Perry, Punta Gorda, Sanford, Sarasota, St. Petersburg, Tallahassee, Tampa, Venice, West Palm Beach, Winter Park.

Railroad Service: AMTRAK, 60 Massachusetts Ave. NE, Washington, DC 20002, 202/906-2002; Fax 202/906-3560, serves the following Florida cities: Clearwater, Deerfield Beach, Deland, Daytona Beach, Delray Beach, Fort Lauderdale, Hollywood, Jacksonville, Kissimmee, Lakeland, Miami, Ocala, Okeechobee, Orlando, Palatka, Sanford, St. Petersburg, Sebring, Tampa, Gainesville, West Palm Beach, Wildwood, Winter Haven.

Rental Cars: It pays to shop around for a Florida rental car. Rates tend to vary widely and special daily, weekly or monthly rates are frequently available, including package rates combining accommodation and car rental.

The following businesses offer rental cars at locations throughout Florida: Alamo Rent-A-Car, PO Box 22776, Fort Lauderdale, 33335, 305/522-0000. Ajax Rent-A-Car, 4121 NW 25th St., Miami 33142, 305/871-5050. Avis Rent A Car, 2330 NW 37th St., Miami 33142,

305/637-4800. Budget Rent-A-Car, 1030 N. Orange Ave., Orlando, 32801, 407/423-4141. Dollar Rent-A-Car, 5012 W.Lemon St., Tampa, 33609, 813/ 276-3772. General Rent-A-Car, 1640 N.W. LeJeune Rd., Miami, 33126, 305/ 871-3573. Hertz Rent-A-Car, 520 N. Semoran Blvd., Orlando, FL 32807, 407/275-6430. Lindo's Rent-A-Car, 1886 US 19 S., Clearwater, 34624, 813/531- 3557. National Rent-A-Car, 2301 N.W. 33rd Ave., Miami, 33142, 305/638-5900. Payless Car Rental, 5510 Gulfport Blvd., St. Petersburg, 33707, 813/381-2758, or 800/PAYLESS. Superior Rent-A-Car, Inc., 4950 Kennedy Blvd., Suite 403, Tampa, 33609, 813/875-0133. Thrifty Car Rental, 2701 N.W. LeJeune Rd., Miami 33142, 305/871-2277. U.S.A. Rent-A-Car System, Inc., 5100 W. Kennedy Blvd., Tampa 33609, 813/286-7048.

Pari-Mutuel Betting
Pari-mutuel betting takes many forms in Florida. Consult with individual sources for seasonal dates.

Greyhound Racing: Biscayne Kennel Club, 320 N.W. 115h St., Miami Shores, 33168, 305/754-3484. Flagler Kennel Club, 401 N.W. 38th Ct., Miami, 33126, 305/649-3000. Hollywood Kennel Club, 831 N. Federal Highway, Hallandale, 33009, 305/758-3647. Palm Beach Kennel Club, 1111 N. Congress Ave., West Palm Beach, 33409, 407/683-2222. Bonita Kennel Club, 28341 Old 41 Rd., Bonita Springs, 33923, 813/992-2411. Daytona Beach Kennel Club, 2201 Volusia Ave., Daytona Beach, 32015, 904/ 252-6484. St. Petersburg Kennel Club, 10490 Gandy Blvd., St. Petersburg, 33702, 813/576-1831. Sarasota Kennel Club, 5400 Bradenton Rd., Sarasota, 33580, 813/355-7744. Tampa Kennel Club, 8300 Nebraska Ave., Tampa, 33674, 813/932-4313. Pensacola Greyhound Track, 951 Dogtrack Rd., Pensacola, 32506, 904/455-8595. Washington

County Kennel Club, Highway 79, Ebro 32437, 904/234- 3943. Jacksonville Kennel Club, 1440 N. McDuff Ave., Jacksonville 32203, 904/646-0001. Orange Park Kennel Club, Highway 17, Jacksonville, 32203, 904/646-0001. Bayard Raceways, US 1 Racetrack Rd., Jacksonville, 32203, 904/646-0001.

Harness Racing: Pompano Park, 1800 S.W. Third St., Pompano Beach, 33061, 305/972-7849.

Jai-Alai: Miami Jai-Alai, 3500 N.W. 37th Ave., Miami, 33142, 305/633-6400. Dania Jai-Alai, 301 East Dania Beach Blvd., Dania, 33004, 305/949-2424. The Fronton, 1415 W. 45th St., West Palm Beach, 33407, 407/842-3274. Florida Jai-Alai, 6405 S. Highway 17-92, Fern Park, 32730, 407/339-6221. Ocala Jai-Alai, State Rd. 318, Orange Lake, 32681, 904/591-2345. Daytona Beach Jai-Alai, 1900 Volusia Ave., Daytona Beach, 32015, 904/255-0222. Fort Pierce Jai-Alai, 1750 S, Kings Highway, Fort Pierce, 34945, 407/464-7500. Melbourne Jai-Alai, 1100 N. Wickham Rd., Melbourne, 32935, 407/259-9800. Tampa Jai-Alai, 5125 S. Dale Mabry, Tampa, 33611, 813/831-1411.

Thoroughbred Racing: Calder Race Course, 21001 N.W. 27th Ave., Miami, 33055, 305/620-2569. Gulfstream Park, 901 S. Federal Highway, Hallandale, 33009, 305-944-1242. Hialeah Park, 102E. 21st Street, Hialeah, 33011, 305/885-8000. Tropical Park, 21001 N.W. 27th Ave., Miami, 33055, 305/625-1131. Tampa Bay Downs, 12505 Racetrack Rd., Oldsmar, 33557, 813/855-4401.

Postal Services
Most post offices are open Monday-Friday, during regular business hours, half-day on Saturday. In addition, postage stamps are sometimes available at super markets, hotels, drug stores, as well as most air, sea and bus terminals. Drop boxes are located at post offices, on city streets, or in hotels. Express overnight delivery services, as well as package delivery are available from the US Post Office, United Parcel Service, Federal Express, and numerous other carriers.

Shopping
Retail trade is the fuel that fires Florida. You can buy anything. Shopping hours are generally 9 am to 9 pm, Monday to Saturday. Sunday hours are generally 9 am to 6 pm.

Telephone Service
Florida has four area codes for different regions of the state. These are 305, 813, 407, 904. Long distance calls with an 800 area code are toll-free.

For long distance calling within one area code, dial 1 + telephone number. For calls outside the area code dial 1 + area code + phone number. For operator assistance dial 0. For collect calls, calls billed to a credit card, calls billed to a third number, or person-to-person calls, dial 0 + telephone number, or if outside the area code, dial 0 + area code + telephone number. For international calls dial 0, or for direct dialing, dial 011 + country code + city code + telephone number. Direct dialing is less expensive than operator assisted calling. Additional discounts on direct dialed calls are available from 5 pm to 11 pm, and even lower rates are in effect from 11 pm to 8 am, as well as all day Saturday and Sunday until 5 pm.

Tipping
Tipping is expected for most, if not all personal services, including airport porters, bellhops, doormen - $.50-$1 per bag; cab drivers - 15%-20% of taxi fare; hotel maids- $1-$2 per day; food servers, barbers and hairdressers - 15%-20% of total bill.

Tourist Information
In addition to the numerous information sources listed throughout this book, the following entities can provide you

with information on current rates, seasonal schedules, facilities and services.

Attractions: Florida Attractions Association, PO. Box 10295, Tallahassee, FL 32302, 904/222-2885.

Boating Registration and Regulations: Department of Natural Resources, Office of Communications, 3900 Commonwealth Blvd., Tallahassee, FL 32399-3000, 904/488-1195.

Camping: Florida Campground Association, 1638 N. Plaza Dr., Tallahassee, FL 32308-5323, 904/487-1462.

Chambers of Commerce: Hundreds of individual chambers dispense free area information. A list of all local Florida chambers is available from Florida Chamber of Commerce, PO Box 5497, Tallahassee, FL 32301.

Diving: Department of Commerce, Division of Tourism, Office of Sports Promotion, Collins Building, Suite 510, Tallahassee, FL 32399-2000, 904/487-1462.

Fishing and Hunting: Game and Freshwater Fish Commission, 620 S.Meridian St., Farris Bryant Building, Tallahassee, FL 32399- 1600, 904/488-1960. Florida imposes the following fees on visitors for freshwater and saltwater fishing - $30 yearly, $15 for seven days. Licenses are available at county tax offices or bait and tackle shops, with an additional service fee of $.50- $1.50 added. The fine for fishing without a license can be $500.

General Information: Department of Commerce, Division of Tourism, 126 W.Van Buren St., Tallahassee, FL 32399-0200, 904/487-1462. Available information includes free domestic or international travel planners, as well as maps.

Golf: Florida State Golf Association, PO Box 21177, Sarasota, FL 34238, 813/921-5695.

Historical Sites: Department of State, Bureau of Historic Preservation, R.A. Gray Building, 500 S. Bronough St., Tallahassee, FL 32399-0250, 904/487-2333.

Hotels and Motels: Florida Hotel/

Motel Association, PO Box 1529, Tallahassee, FL 32302, 904/224-2888.

National Forests: US Forest Service, Suite 4061, 227 N. Bronough St., Tallahassee, FL 32301, 904/681-7265.

Parimutuels: Department of Business Regulations, Parimutuel Wagering Division, 401 N.W. 2nd Ave., Suite N 1026, Miami, FL 33128, 305/377-7015.

Polo: Palm Beach Polo and Country Club, 13198 Forest Hill Boulevard, West Palm Beach, FL 33414, 407/793-1113.

Professional Baseball: Eighteen of the 26 major league teams conduct spring training in Florida cities during February and March. Department of Information, Baseball Commissioner's Office, 350 Park Ave., New York, NY 10022, (212) 371-7800. In addition, a Senior Pro Baseball League comprised of ex-major leaguers over 35 years old plays a 62-game schedule in Florida cities from November-January. SPBA, 2280 One Biscayne Tower, 2 South Biscayne Blvd., Miami, FL 33131, 305/350-7380, or 800/477-7772; Fax 305/374-1005.

Professional Basketball: Miami Heat, Miami Arena, Miami, FL 33136-4102, 305/577-4328. Orlando Magic, PO Box 76, Orlando, FL 32802-0076, 407/896-2442.

Professional Football: Miami Dolphins, Joe Robbie Stadium, 2269 N.W. 199th St., Miami, FL 33056, 305/620-5000. Tampa Bay Buccaneers, 1 Buccaneer Pl., Tampa, FL 33607, 813/879-BUCS.

State Forests: Department of Agriculture and Consumer Services, Division of Forestry, 3125 Conner Blvd., Tallahassee, FL 32399- 1650, 904/488-6727.

State Parks: Department of Natural Resources, Office of Communications, 3900 Commonwealth Blvd., Tallahassee, FL 32399- 3000.

Tennis: Florida Tennis Association, 801 N.E. 167th St., North Miami Beach, FL 33162, 305/652-2866.

AUTHORS

Steve Cohen is a writer and photographer specializing in travel and worldwide adventure. His work appears regularly in more than 150 publications, including *The Los Angeles Times, New York Daily News, New York Times* and magazines as well as numerous publications from around the world. A five-year resident of Florida in the early 1980s, he became expert in the intricacies of Florida travel and tourism. Now based in Colorado, he travels to Florida several times yearly to keep up to date on the continual process of change occurring in the Sunshine State.

Janet and Gordon Groene are a writer and photographer team who have scouted Florida from their home base in DeLand, in their own boat, motorhome, airplane, canoe and hiking boots. Their other books include the best-selling *Cooking on the Go, How to Live Aboard a Boat, Dressing Ship*, and *Living Aboard Your RV*.

Patricia and Edgar Cheatham are a travel writer/photographer team who specialize in cruises, resort travel and Florida. Their work appears frequently in *Delta Sky, Vista USA, Travel-Holiday, Home & Away*, as well as numerous major North American daily newspapers. Their books include guides written for major corporations, including Exxon, Shell, Texaco, Gulf, Amoco and Cunard.

Laurie Werner is an incisive New York based writer who is fascinated by the dichotomy of typical Florida public relations hype and the sometimes less than bright realities found in the Sunshine State. Her work appears in major USA newspapers and magazines including *New York Daily News, Ladies Home Journal* and *USA Weekend*.

Ute and Andrew Vladimir are a Coconut Grove, Florida based travel writing team. In addition to guide book writing, their work appears in many US newspapers and they write a weekly column on travel questions and answers for Florida's *Palm Beach Post*.

Carol and Dan Thalimer are former award-winning travel agency owners who have turned to consulting and travel writing, specializing in the southeastern United States. They write the regular Sunday travel feature for an Atlanta newspaper and are contributing editors of *Georgia Byways*. In addition they write regularly for *Travel Agent Magazine* and *Athens (Georgia) Magazine*.

PHOTOGRAPHERS

Becker, Frank 80, 99, 134, 204
Cohen, Steve 19, 27r., 28, 29, 37, 79, 225, 226, 227, 232
Florida Dept. of Commerce 12/13, 20, 72, 77, 90/91, 92, 106/107, 203, 217
Gaines, James 189
Gleasner, Bill 58/59
Groene, Gordon/Janet Cover 85,128
Grosse, Heinz 103, 209
Hartl, Helene 18, 31, 34, 44, 49, 52, 54, 78, 120, 124, 149,150, 153 l., 178, 181, 183, 188,195, 196, 198, 214, 221, 222, 223 l., 223 r., 235, 237
Kaempf, Bernhard 67, 97, 140, 142, 172, 173
Marks, Walter/Metro Date Country 22, 42, 60/61, 70, 73r.
Newman Associates 139
Skupy, Hans-Horst 1, 2, 10, 14/15, 16, 23, 24, 25, 26, 27 l., 32, 33, 35, 39, 40, 43, 46, 47, 48, 50 l., 50 r., 53, 55, 57, 62, 66, 71, 73 l., 82, 86, 87, 88, 93, 96, 100, 101, 104, 108, 113, 116, 118, 119, 121, 122, 123, 126/127, 132, 135, 137, 138, 141, 143, 146, 152, 153 r., 156, 157, 158, 160/161, 162, 164, 165, 166, 168, 170, 174, 176/177, 186, 190, 192, 193, 194, 197, 200/201, 206, 207, 208, 210, 211, 215, 220, 228/229, 230, 231, 233, 234, 236
Walt Disney Comp. 133, 205, 218, 219, Backcover

A

Alachua County 157
Alligator Alley 101
Amelia Island 28
American Ass. of Retired Ps. 17
American Dream 32
American Revolution 27, 42
Anderson, Loni 52
Anhinga Indian Museum 80
Apalachian Mountains 179
Apalachicola 198, 199
  John Gorrie Museum 198
Art Museums 49
  A. Brest Museum/Univ. of Jackv.
  50
  Bass Museum of Arts/Miami 49
  Cummer Gallery/Jacksonville 49
  Daytona Beach M. of Arts/Scien.
  50
  Fort Lauderdale's Museum 49
  Jacksonville Art Museum 49
  Lowe Art Museum/Coral Gables
  49
  Morse Gallery/Winter Park 50
  Norton Gallery/West Palm
  Beach 49
  Ocala's Appleton Museum 49
  Plant Museum/Univ. of Tampa
  50
  Ringling/Sarasota 49
  Salvador Dali M./St. Petersburg
  50
Art and Craft Festival 47
Audubon Island 195
Audubon, John James 48
Aury, Luis 23

B

Bach Festival 49
Barrancas National Cemetery
  27
Battle of Natural Bridge 28, 38
Battle of New Orleans 31
Battle of Olustee 38
Beecher-Stowe, Harriet 48
Belle Glade
  Lawrence Will Museum 45
Big Pine Key 94
  Coupon Bight State Aquatic Prs.
  94
  National Key Deer Refuge 94
  Watson Hammock 94
Black Culture 42, 44
Boca Chita Key 201
Boca Raton 83
  Boca Raton Resort 86
Bok, Edward 142
Booth, Wilkes 28
Bowlegs, Billy 25, 26
Boynton Beach

  Black Awareness Day 44
Bradenton 17, 21, 124
  Fort DeSoto Nat. Memorial 124
Broward County 77, 78, 81
  Cooper City 78
  Coral Springs 78
  Plantation 78
  Sunrise 78
  Tamarac 78
Bryan, William Jennings 32
Buffett, Jimmy 49
Bush Key 204
Bushnell 24, 38
Buttonwood Canal 103

C

Cabbage Key 48, 122
Caladesi Island 114, 205
Caladesi State Park 113
Caloosahatches River 121
Calusan Artifacts 19
Campbell, Sir Malcolm 34
Canoeing 174, 190
Cape Canaveral 25, 33, 35, 146,
  147, 148, 149, 151
  Shuttle Landing Facility 147
  Vehicle Assembly Building 147
Captiva Island 122
Carambola 55
Castilla San Marcos 21
Cayo Costa State Island 122,
  205
Cedar Key 28, 29
Charles V, King 21
Charles, Prince 51
Chattahoochee River 23
Chayote 55
Chipola River 188
Chrystal River 28
Chumberland Island 170
Churches 46
  Church of Scientology 46
  First Baptist Church 47
  Holy Trinity 47
  Mormon Church 46
  Mount Pisgah Church 46
  Plymouth Congregational
  Church 46
  St. Gabriel's Episcopal Church
  47
  St. Margaret's Church 47
  St. Mary's Church 47
Citrus Industry 64
Civil War 27, 28, 38, 48
Clearwater 109, 117
  Belleview Biltmore 109
  Boatyard Village 115
  Innisbrook Resort 112
  Marine Science Center 115
Clearwater Beach 113
Climate 37

Cocoa Beach 150
Coconut Grove
  Lady of Charity Shrine 46
Coffin's Patch 94
Collier, Baron 32
Confederate Victory 38
Coontie 55
Cooter 55
Coral Gables 32
Cowboys 44
Cowford 168
Crestview 191
Cross Creek 158
Crystal River 19, 21
Cuban Cuisine 52
Cypress Springs 190
Cypress Swamp 45

D

Dade Battlefield 25, 38
Dade County 25, 47
Dade Massacre 24
Dade, Major Francis 24, 38
Dania 77
  Dania Jai-Alai Palace 80
  John U. Lloyd Beach State 79
  Musician's Exchange D.T. Cafe
  80
  Parker Playhouse 80
Davie 78, 80
Daytona 18, 37, 41, 152, 153,
  154, 155
  Bethune-Cookman College 43
  Coney Island South 152
  DeLion Springs 21
  Farmer's Market 154
  Flea Market 154
  Halifax Harbor Marina 153
  Howard University 43
  International Speedway 34
  Marriott 153
  Montreal Royals 44
  Museum of Arts and Sciences 18
  Ocean Center 152
  Peabody Auditorium 153
  Racing 153
  The Boardwalk 152
  The Casements 154
DeFuniak Springs 189, 191
  Chautauqua Day Festival 190
DeLeon Springs 19
Delius Festival 49
Delius, Frederick 49
Depression 33, 66
Destin 198
  Indian Collection 45
Devil's Island 28
Devil's Millhopper 157
Dickinson, Jonathan 21
Dirty Rice 55
Disney World 17, 35, 129, 130,

132, 134, 136, 137, 144, 145, 210
Brown Derby 136
Catastrophe Canyon 135
Chinese Theater 135
Discovery Island 130, 210
Epcot Center 35, 129, 132, 210
Future World 132
Haunted House 132
Indiana Jones Stunt Exhibit 136
Journey into Imagination 132
Living Seas 132
MGM-Disney Studios 129, 135, 210
Magic Kingdom 25, 129, 132, 210
Mickey Mouse Club 135
Pleasure Island 129, 210
Prime Time Cafe 136
River Country 130, 210
Star Tours 210
The Land 132
Tomorrowland 132
Typhoon Lagoon 130, 210
Village Marketplace 210
World Showcase 132
Dolphin 56
Doolittle, James 34
Drake, Sir Francis 21
Dry Tortugas 28, 203
Fort Jefferson Nat. Monument 203
Dunedin 113
Duval County 47

E

East Coast Railroad 30
Eatonville 43
Econfina Creek 190
Edison, Thomas Alva
Thomas Edison Home 51
Ellenton 124
Elliott 201
Empire Mica, Ship 194
Everglades 17, 25, 36, 101, 102, 103, 104, 105, 208
Anhinga Trail 206
Buttonwood Canal 103
Canoeing 103, 104
Coot 103
Day Trips 206, 207, 209
Everglades City 103, 105
Everglades National Park 101
Glades Haven 104
Gulf Coast Ranger Station 209
Gumbo Limbo Trail 206
Mahogany Hammock 206
Pa-hay-okee Overlook 206
Parautis Pond 206
Royal Palm Hammock 206
Shark Valley 45
Snake Bight 102

Ten Thousand Islands 209
West Lake 206
Whitewater Bay 103

F

Falling Waters State Park 189
Fernandina
Bailey House 170
Fairbanks Home 170
Fernandina Beach 23, 46, 50, 169
Florida House 170
Palace Saloon 170
Presbyterian Church 170
St. Peter Parish Church 170
The Swann Building 170
Wiliams House 170
Fisher, Carl 32, 64
Fisher, Mel 21
Flagler Beach 25
Flagler's Railroad 30
Flagler, Henry 29, 30, 46, 63, 64, 83, 84, 93
Flamingo 102, 105, 206, 206
Flan 56
Florida Bay 101, 208
Florida Folk Festival 48
Florida Food 55
Florida Keys 92, 98
Bahia Honda State Recr. Center 94
Biscayne National Park 93
Long Key Viaduct 94
Lower Keys 94
Overseas Highway 92
Seven Mile Bridge 94
Theater of the Sea 93
Upper Keys 93
Fort Ann 25
Fort Armstrong 25
Fort Barrancas 184
Fort Brooke 38
Fort Caroline 21
Fort Casey 25
Fort Chokonikla 25
Fort Clinch State Park 38
Fort DeSoto Park 113
Fort Foster 38
Fort Gatlin 129
Fort Jefferson 28
Fort Lauderdale 25, 37, 45, 77, 78, 79, 80, 81
Bahia Mar Yachting Center 79
Hillsboro Inlet 79
Port Everglades 36
Fort Myers 25, 45, 120, 121, 125
Fort Pickens 26, 184
Fort Pierce 25
Fort Wacahoota 25
Fort Walton 25
Fort Walton Beach 45, 198

Foster, Stephen 172
Fuller, Walter 33

G

Gainesville 156, 157, 158, 159
Fld. Museum of Natural History 157
Island Grove 158
Kanapaha Botanical Gardens 158
Lake A. Wildlife Preserve 158
Living History Farm 158
Marjorie Kinnan R.S. Hist. Site 204
Mayan Palace 157
San Felasco Hammock State Pr. 157
University of Florida 157
Geronimo 26
Gleason, Jackie 66
Godfrey, Arthur 66
Gospel 47
Great White Heron 102
Grey Panthers 17
Grouper 56
Guanaja 113
Guava 56
Gulf Breeze 186
Gulf Coast 187
Gulf Current 193

H

Haldeman, Walter N. 119
Halland, Luther 77
Hallandale 77
Hemingway, Ernest 48
Hillsborough River State Pr. 38
Hispanic Culture 41
Hispanic Influence 228
Hobe Sound 22
Hollywood 78, 80
Holmes Creek 190
Homer, Winslow 48
Homestead 102
Homosassa 25
Horse Country 45
Housman, Jacob 26
Hurricanes 37, 232

I

Ichtucknee Springs St. Park 158
Immigrants 42
Indian History 45
Indian Key Fill 25, 26, 93
Indian Key State Historic St. 93, 202
Lignumvitae Key 203
Lignumvitae Key State Bot. St. 93, 202

Indian Shore 115
Indians
Ais 19
Apalachee 19
Creeks 24
Georgias 24
Jeagas 19
Miccosukees 24, 209
Muskogees 19
Seminoles 24, 25, 26
Tequestas 19
Timucuans 19, 23
Insects 233
Intracoastal Waterway 154
Islamorada 25, 93

J

J.M. Black H. Passion Play 143
Jackson, Andrew 24
Jacksonville 41, 43, 48, 168,
169, 170, 171
Avondale 169
Buccaneer Trail 169
Caroline National Monument
169
Fort Clinch 169
Gator Bowl 37
Jazz Festival 168
Kingsley Plantation 169
Metropolitan Park 168
Pablo Beach 34
Riverside 169
San Marco 169
Jazz Festival 47
Jeanie Festival 48
Jerk Cooking 56
Jicama 56
Johns River 168
Jungle Queen, ship 78
Juno Beach
Marine Science Center 88

K

Kennedy Space Center 35, 147,
148
Canaveral National Seashore
147, 204
Exploration Station 147
Merritt Island 148
Merritt Island Nat. W.lf. Ref.
204
NASA Art Gallery 147
Space Shuttle Exhibits 147
Visitors Facility 147
Key Largo 93
J. Pennecamp C.R. State Park
93, 202
Key West 17, 22, 28, 29, 31, 94,
95
Antonia, Restaurant 96

Audubon House 95
Cafe Marquesa 96
Cafe des Artistes 96
Casa Marina Resort 95
Conch Republic 51
Conch Train 96
Fantasy Fest 51
Fisher's Museum 21
Hemingway House 96
Louie's Backyard 96
Mallory Docks 51
Mallory Pier 96
Mel Fisher's Key West G.
Museum 96, 203
Wrecker Museum 96
Kissimmee 142, 144, 145
Alligatorland 142
Bok Tower Gardens 142
Flying Tigers Warbird Air Mus.
143
Flying Tigers Warbird Museum
25
Gatorland Zoo 142
Kissimmee Cow Camp 38
Lake Kissimmee State Park 44
Reptile World Serpentarium 142
Xanadu 142

L

Labor Day Hurricane 30
Lafayette, Marquis de 27
Lake City 173, 174
O'Leno 174
Osceola National Forest 173,
174, 201
Lake Dora 141
Lake Eloise 211
Lake Okeechobee 101
Lake Wales 38
Lake Worth 83
Lakeland
Southern College 51
Largo 115
Heritage Museum 115
Heritage Park 34
Suncoast Botanical Gardens 116
Lauderdale, Major William 77
Lee County 119
Lee Island Coast 121
Leon County 47
Lincoln, Abraham 28
Live Oak 174, 191
Falmouth Spring 174
Suwannee State Park 174
Long Key 93
State Recreation Area 93
Looe Key 94
Loquat 56
Lower Sugarloaf 94

M

MacDonald, John D. 48
MacGregor, Gregor 23
Madeira Beach 116
John's Pass Village 116
The Southern Belle 116
Madison, James 31
Manatee River 124, 124
Marathon 94
Marianna 188, 191
Florida Caverns State Park 188
Marianna Caverns 188
Marquesa Islands 203
Mayflower 63
McGee 49
McLeod Bethune, Mary 43
Melbourne 150, 151
Merrick, George 64
Merritt Island 147
Miami 23, 33, 44, 49, 63, 64, 73,
74, 201
Artistic Center 63
Bal Harbor 72
Bayside Marketplace 68
Biscayne Bay 64
Carnival 42, 68
Carribean Marketplace 68
Cen Trust Building 66
Center for Fine Arts 67
Christmas Boat Parades 51
Coconut Grove 63, 70
Coral Gables 64, 68
Cultural Facilities 63
Dade County Courthouse 67
Dodge Island 36
Downtown 66
Golden Beach 72
Gusman Center for Performing
67
H.M.S. Bounty 68
Hibiscus Island 71
Historical Mus. of South Fld. 67
Key Biscayne 70
King Mango Strut 51
Latin Cultures 63
Little Haiti 68
Little Havanna 68
Lummus Park 71
Main Public Library 67
Metro-Dade Cultural Center 67
Metromover 67
Metrorail 67
Miami Beach 17, 41, 50
Miami City Ballet 68
Miami Hurricanes 66
Nightlife 72
Ocean Drive 71
Opa-Locka 64
Orange Bowl Parade 51
Palm Island 71
Port of Miami 36

South Beach 63, 71
Southeast Financial Center 67
Star Island 71
Vizcaya 42
Miccosukee Indian Village 206, 209
Milton
Blackwater River State Park 201
Minorcan Easter Cake 41
Miracle Strip 17, 192, 193, 194, 195, 196, 197, 198, 199
Mizner, Addison 32
Moore, James 23
Mosquito 38
Mount Dora 141
Mudd, Dr. Samuel 28

N

Naples 19, 119, 120
Big Cypress National Preserve 119
Corkscrew Swamp Sanctuary 119
Jungle Larry's African Park 120
National Historic District 50
Natural Areas 200, 201, 202, 204, 205
New Smyrna 25, 41
New Year Eve 55
Niceville 191
Nixon, Richard 51
Northern Panhandle 188, 189, 190, 191

O

Ocala 45, 52
Silver Springs 212
Ocean Pound 174
Okefenokee Swamp 201
Okra 56
Oldfield, Barnie 33
Orange City
Blue Springs State Park 204
Orange Groves 18
Orlando 129, 142, 143, 144, 145, 204, 210
Church Street Station 138, 138, 143
Ecola Park 140
Elvis Presley Museum 141
Fire Station No. 3 140
Fun'n Wheels 140
Leu Botanical Gardens 138, 138
Loch Haven Park 140
Mercado 143
Museum of Art 140
Mystery Fun House 140
Ocala National Forest 204
Orange County Hist. Museum 140

Science Center 140
Sea World 137
US Navy Training Center 141
Universal Studios Florida 137, 210
Wet'n Wild Water Park 138, 210
Osceola 25, 174
School's Experimental Center 141
Overseas Highway 30

P

Paddlewheel Queen, Ship 78
Palatka 141
Palm Beach 33, 83, 86, 87, 89
Burt Reynolds Dinner Theater 83
Jupiter Beach 87
Mar-a-Lago 84
Ocean Boulevard 84
Palm Beach Gardens 83
Palm Beach Kennel Club 86
Peanut Island 85
Phil Foster Park 85
Singer Island 85
The Breakers 83
Turtle Watch 88
West Palm Beach Airport 84
Whitehall 84
Worth Avenue 85
Palmdale 119
Cypress Knee Museum 119
Panama City Beach 188, 193, 199
Cavern State Park 194
Coral Reef Theater 196
Eden Mansion 188
Gulf World 196
Marine Institute 194
Miracle Strip Amusement Park 196
Museum of Man and the Sea 197
Ocean Opry Show 197
Ship Wreck Island 196
State Park 188
Wreck Diving 194
Panhandle 37
Paradise Key 101
Payne's Prairie 157
Pensacola 21, 30, 184, 185, 186, 187
Black History Museum 186
Christ Episcopal Church 186
Historic Pensacola Village 185
Julee Cottage 186
Museum of Art 186
Museum of Commerce 185
Museum of Industry 184
Nat. Museum of Naval Aviation 185
Naval Air Station 184

Nort Hill Preservation District 50
Pensacola Bay 184
Pensacola Beach 187
St. Patrick's Day 42
T.T. Wentworth Jr. Fld. Museum 186
Zoo 186
Perrine, Dr. Henry 26
Persimmons 56
Pine Island 122
Pine Island Sound 33
Pinellas County 19
Pirates 23, 30
Plant, Henry 29
Pompano Beach 77, 80
Fisherman's Wharf 79
Population Mix 41
Port Canaveral 150
Premier Cruise Line 36
Port Orange 25
Pre-Columbian Indians 20
Purloo 56

R

Racial Segregation 43
Rainfall 37
Raleigh, Sir Walter 21
Ramroad Key
Looe Key Nat. Marine Sanctuary 94, 203
Rawling, Marjorie Kinnan 48
Real Estate Madness 31
Redneck Riviera 17
Religion 45
Remington, Frederic 45
Retirees 230
Ribault, Jean 21
Rinehart, Mary 48
Ringling, John 33, 51, 123
River of May 168
Roatan 113
Robinson, Jackson 43
Rodeo 45
Royal Palm Hammock 101

S

Saddlebunch Key 94
San Juan Hill 30
Sanford 141
Sanibel Island 122
J.N.D.D. Nat. Wildlife Refuge 122, 205
Sarasota 17, 49, 123, 124, 125, 125
Art Gallery 123
Circus Gallery 123
Jungle Gardens 123
Lionel Train a. Seashell Mus. 123

M. Selby Botanical Gardens 124
Mote Marine Science Center 124
Myakka River State Park 205
Ringling Museum of Art 123
Solo State Theatre 123
University of South Florida 51
Wilderness Preserve 205
Seminole Village 45, 80
Seminole War 23, 23, 24, 25, 26, 38
Shakespeare Festival 49
Shark Valley 105, 206
Shell Island 195
Silver Hair Legislature 17
Snake Bight 102, 103
Snapper 56
Soffkee 56
Sombrero Reef 94
Soto, Hernando de 21
Spanish 21
Spanish American War 32
Spas 222, 223, 224, 225
St. Andrew's State Park 197
St. Augustine 21, 23, 28, 29, 141, 162, 163, 164, 165, 167
Castillo de San Marcos 165
DeMesa-Sanchez House 164
Dr. Peck's House 165
Flagler College 29, 166
Fountain of Youth 21
Fountain of Youth Museum 166
Gallegos House 164
Gomez House 164
Gonzalez de Hita House 164
Gonzalez-Alvarez House 164
Lightner Museum 166
Marineland 166, 212
Oldest Store Museum 165
Ponte Vedra Beach 165
Ribera House 164
Ripley's Believe Museum 166
San Augustin Antiguo 163
Sanchez House 165
Schoolhouse 165
Secrets of the Reef 213
Spanish Quarter 163
Washington Oaks State Gardens 166
Whitney Park 213
Wonders of the Spring 213
Ximenez-Fation House 165
St. Johns River 141, 154
St. Petersburg 33, 109, 116, 117, 205
Great Explorations 112
Haas Museum 112
Historical Museum 116
Museum of Fine Arts 112
Orchard Arbor 116
Planetarium 116
Salvador Dali Museum 112
Sawgrass Lake Park 116

Shuffleboard Hall of Fame 112
St. Petersburg Beach 113
Sunken Gardens 116
Sunshine Skyway Bridge 116
The Lowe House 112
Statehood 27
Suncoast Seabird Sanctuary 114, 115
Sunshine State 37
Surfing 114
Surinam Cherries 56
Suwannee Country 172, 172, 174, 175
Hart Springs Park 174
Manatee Springs State Park 174
Suwannee River 48
Suwannee Springs 173

T

Tallahassee 17, 18, 27, 37, 51, 178, 179, 180, 181, 182, 183
Alfred B. Maclay State Park 180
Apalachicola National Forest 181
Capitol Building 181
Gallie's Hall 180
Golden Eagle Country Club 180
Goodwood Plantation 180
Governor's Club 180
Junior Museum 181
Le Moyne Art Gallery 181
Museum of Florida History 18
New Capitol 179
Old Capitol 179
St. John's Cemetery 181
St. Marks Wildlife Refuge 181
The Columns 180
The Grove 180
Tamiami Trail 101
Tampa 28, 42, 49, 109, 114, 117, 205
Adventure Island 213
Busch Gardens 114, 213
Cigar Industry 30
Gasparilla Days 30
Henry Plant Museum 29
Tampa Bay 21, 32, 109, 110, 111, 112, 113, 114
Weeki Wachee Springs 212
Tarpon Springs 41, 53, 112, 114
Noell's Ark Chimp Farm 114
St. N. Greek Orthodox Church 112
Tarpon, ship 194
Taylor, Zachary 24
Ten Thousand Islands 101
The Grey Ghost, ship 194
The Royal Palm 64
Theme Parks 210, 211, 212, 213
Thurman, Howard Dr. 43
Tin City

Old Marine Market Place 120
Titusville 45, 150, 151
Valiant Air Command Airshow 34
Torreya State Park 189
Trail of Tears 24
Truman, Harry 51
Trump, Donald 51
Turkey Lake Park 141
Turnbull, Dr. Andrew 41
Tuttle, Julia 30, 63

U

Useppa Island 48

V

Vamar, ship 194
Volusia County 41

W

Wakulla Springs 18, 188, 191
Weedon Island I 19
Weedon Island II 19
Wekiva River 141
Wesley, William Henry 189
West Palm Beach 83
Winter Equestrian Festival 45
White Springs 48, 172, 173, 174
S. Foster State Folk Center 172
White, Major Edward 25
Williams, Tennessee 48
Windsurfing 114
Winter Haven 211
Cypress Gardens 138, 211
Winter Park 140
Ch. Hosmer Morse Museum 141
Rollins College 140
Spanish Mediterranean Chapel 140
Walk of Fame 140
Winton, Alexander 34
Wright, Frank Lloyd 51

Y

Ybor City 30, 109, 114
Cigar-Workers House Museum 114
State Museum 114
Yulee, David 27

Z

Zona 78